WIDE ROAD
to the Edge
of the World

世界の果てまで広い道

301 Haiku and One Long Essay:
"A Windswept Spirit"

Afterword "A Circle of Poetic Will"
by Lisa Segal

俳

Jack Grapes

Bombshelter Press
Los Angeles 2017

Second Edition

The first limited edition of *Wide Road* was printed in a run of 100 numbered and signed copies, in a different size and format. This second edition includes new material in the introductory essay. The 301 haiku remain the same.

Some of the haiku written by Jack Grapes
originally appeared in *Cultural Weekly (culturalweekly.com)*
and *The Juice Bar (www.thejuicebar.live)*

Japanese Calligraphy by: Miho Hagino
Cover and Book Design by: Baz Here
Photo of author by Baz Here
Front cover: "The Barrel-Maker of Fujimihara"
by Hokusai Katsushika (1831)

ISBN: 978-1-5393-3613-6
Printed in the United States of America

Dedicated to:

Lisa Segal
for making the suggestion

Josh Grapes
for showing the way

Lori Grapes
for lighting the road

俳

old pond
and a frog-jumps in —
water sound.
-- Matsuo Basho (1644-1694)

俳

autumn evening —
there's joy also
in loneliness.
-- Yosa Buson (1716-1783)

俳

a bath when you're born,
a bath when you die —
inbetween it's all blah blah blah.

-- Kobayashi Issa (1763-1827)

俳

the autumn wind:
for me there are no gods;
there are no Buddhas.

-- Masaoka Shiki (1867-1902)

俳

the samurai doll's face
doesn't know love
either

--Chiyo-Jo (1703-1774)

"A Windswept Spirit"

An Introductory Essay
in 201 Chapters
and 601 Paragraphs

A Windswept Spirit

Making Jelly Sandwiches

I learned to write haiku in fifth grade, the same year I memorized Lincoln's "Gettysburg Address" and the neumonic device for the nine planets: "Mother Very Easily Makes Jelly Sandwiches Under No Protest." Now that Pluto is no longer recognized as a true planet, we can make a perfect 17-syllable haiku with the remaining eight planets:

Mercury, Venus,	[5 syllables]
Earth, Mars, Jupiter, Saturn,	[7 syllables]
Uranus, Neptune	[5 syllables]

Lost Marbles

Except for the fact that haiku required a specific structure — 3 lines, 17 syllables, in a 5-7-5-syllable form — short poems had begun to fascinate me years earlier, when I was just starting first grade at Merrick Elementary School, six blocks from where I lived. I walked those six blocks, past Winn's grocery store on the corner of Freret Street, where I would buy five wax figures filled with sweet syrup for a penny apiece. I enjoyed the walk, searching the ground for lost marbles or a Lincoln penny. School was an anxious experience: I understood little of what was going on, other kids picked on me, and if a line formed, I was always at the end of it. The desks were arranged according to how smart you were, and I was made to sit in the last row by the windows with the other so-called stupid kids, between Jimmy Ciaravella (who became a cardiac surgeon) and Stephen Alcox (who became a state judge). Home was a whirlpool of confusion and tension, my father's drinking and my mother's bouts of screaming, slapping me for the slightest infraction. She called them "pla-vies," a Flemish word meaning a smack in the face.

A Temporary Stay Against Confusion

Robert Frost called poetry a "temporary stay against confusion," and that's what it was for me on that six-block walk to school, dragging my heavy schoolbag behind me. I had learned to read

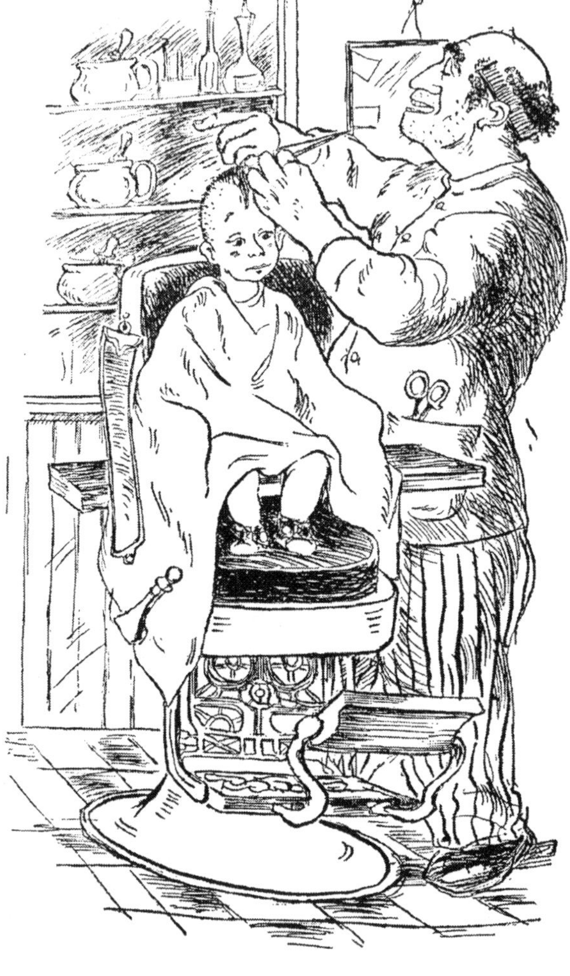

"Lilla boy," said Romani, "none move you head." But little Jimmy kept moving it, so Romani decided to tell him a story.

"How old you, lilla boy?" said Romani.

"I'm four years old," said Jimmy Potts. "I'm gonna be five."

from *Jimmy Potts Gets a Haircut,* 1949

at an early age. The first word I learned to spell was Ritz, from the billboard on Tulane Avenue for Ritz Crackers. Those big letters lit up against the night sky seemed to appear out of nowhere, a constellation of symbols as magical as Orion or the Big Dipper. Books themselves were treasure chests full of specially arranged letters into words and sentences that told a story. I've held onto every book I've ever owned and read, each one a childhood friend that kept me company when my father was out drinking and my mother stormed around the house like a Sherman tank hitting anything that got in her way.

Ignatius Romani Pees in his Pants

The first "chapter" book I read when I was five years old was *Jimmy Potts Gets a Haircut* by George Panetta, illustrated by Reisie Lonette. It took place on the lower-eastside of New York City during the depression and was filled with Jewish, Italian, Irish, German and African-American characters. Even Fiorello LaGuardia, New York's 99th mayor, made an appearance, speaking out on the radio to find the dastardly CAT truck driver who had hit Jimmy, causing Ignatius Romani to pee in his pants. My father grew up on the lower east side, so reading this book made me feel like I was experiencing my father's own childhood, all those stories of boyhood escapes, running from the police after taking a piece of fruit from a neighborhood fruit-stand. In the book was a cast of characters I was sure my father knew. There was Romani the barber and De Wolfe Gottlieb, his helper, "who stood beside his chair like a soldier and wrote poetry that very few people could understand, if any." There was Ignatius Romani, the barber's son, who wrote the word CAT in crayon on Jimmy Potts's shaved head, and Hannah Klien who thought Jimmy got hit by a truck with the word CAT on its front bumper. There was Baby Hippo, the policeman, who couldn't catch anybody he was so fat, and Mr. & Mrs. Finch, Dr. Thorndyke, Patrolman X, Carolo Buti, the Italian crooner who sang in Maloney's Tropical Bar, and Willie Jones, whose father was an undertaker.

> Little Jimmy Potts was going to Romani's barbershop for a hair-cut, and he was walking along Bleecker Street as if it would take him ten years to get there. He stopped to talk to everything, dogs, ants, firepumps, women; once he talked to a horse and be-

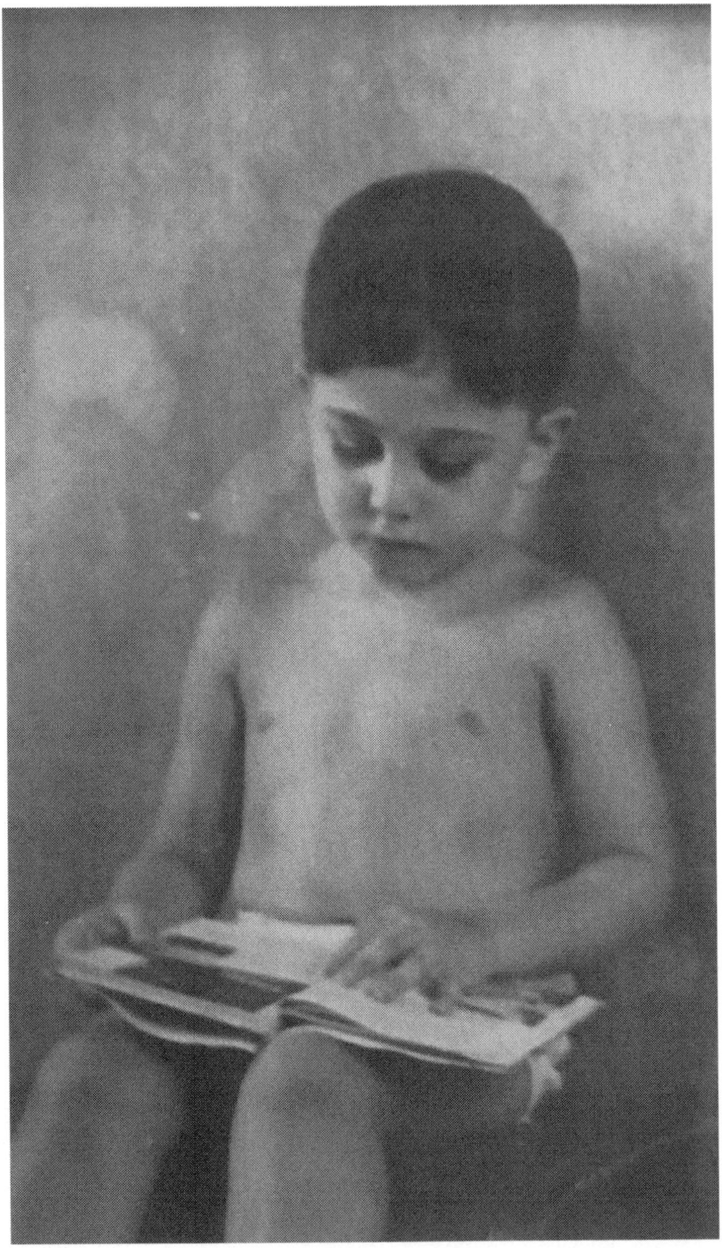

Haiku Poet, 1947

cause the horse answered him, saying yes and no with his head, little Jimmy gave him the note that his mother had given him to give the barber. The horse ate the note.

When Jimmy got to the barbershop, he wanted to go back to the horse and get the note, but somehow he knew he could never get it back.

Jimmy walked in. "I want a haircut," he said.

Romani turned to Gottlieb. "Nuncha hear, Mr Pome Write, lilla boy want haircut."

"I told you," said Gottlieb. "I don't give children haircuts."

"That's good, that's fine," said Romani. "Maybe you like get paid stand up you chair like dope!"

"I want a round haircut," said Jimmy. "My mommy said all around around."

The Purple Cow

But the summer before I turned five, I was going through Book I of a series called *My Book House*, edited by Olive Beaupré Miller. There were thirteen volumes, each one corresponding to a specific grade. Book I was titled "In the Nursery," a compilation of nursery rhymes. It was one of those humid New Orleans afternoons. I could hear the rain pounding on the tin roof of the backyard shed. I couldn't go out to play, so I decided that I would start with the first book and read all the way through to Book 13. I sat on the small bench in the bedroom next to the kitchen, opened the first book and began to read. First was a poem by Robert Louis Stevenson declaiming in rhyme that "the world was so full of a number of things, enough to make us happy as kings." This was followed by patty cake patty cake, this little pig went to market, see-saw Margery Daw, hickory dickory, hey diddle diddle, Mary Mary quite contrary, little Boy Blue, little Tommy Tucker, little Miss Muffett, little Jack Horner, little Robin Redbreast, Wee Willie Winki, old King Cole, old Mother Hubbard, to market to market to buy a fat pig, and little Bo-Peep (which, by the way, goes back to 1364 when Alice Causton – for having given short measure in ale – was condemned to "play bo-peep through a pillory," and the nursery rhyme is also mentioned in Shakespeare's *King Lear*). All pretty standard stuff. But when I came to the picture of a purple cow, I was jolted upright. Underneath the picture was a poem I'd never heard before.

I never saw a purple cow.
I never hope to see one.
But I can tell you anyhow,
I'd rather see than be one.

I was astonished. I felt the body's thrill when touched by language that moves us beyond intellect. The end rhymes were delightful, but the inner rhyme of the last line knocked me out. And beneath the sound was the meaning. The shift from observing to being. What was wrong with a purple cow, I wondered? The cow was a bright purple; it looked nice. So why would it be bothersome to see a purple cow? But in the last line, there's the choice between *seeing* the cow and actually *being* the cow. Somehow, I realized the difference: that if the purple cow was some sort of freak, and seeing it was frightening, then being one would be even worse. At five years old, I'm not sure I understood the larger implications of how we contend with the existential presence of "the other," but somewhere in my gut, I recognized how profound the idea was. I knew that in this nursery rhyme there was a meaning that went far beyond the sound of the rhymes, though it was the sounds – the inner rhyme of "see" and "be" set off by the rhyme of "cow" and "how" and bookended by the repetition of "one" and "one" – that emphasized the difference between seeing and being. In the world of the poem was a harmony missing from the world I lived in. "But I can tell you anyhow, I'd rather see than be . . . one."

A Caged Skylark

In a way, this prepared me in college for Gerard Manley Hopkins' sprung rhythm, based on the accentual verse of nursery rhymes, and on medieval alliterative metres, which permits the juxtaposition of stressed syllables more frequently than does normal English duple or triple metre. Hopkins' aim was to make use of the energies of everyday speech, using rhythms that seemed like free verse based partly on accentual metres. Those same delights I found in "The Purple Cow" were to echo in college when I came across Hopkins' poetry, especially "The Caged Skylark:"

> As a dare-gale skylark scanted in a dull cage,
> Man's mounting spirit in his bone-house,
>   mean house, dwells –
>   That bird beyond the remembering his free fells;
> This in drudgery, day-laboring-out life's age.

At five years old, I wasn't thinking, "Wow, there's Hopkins' sprung rhythm!" But I was already aware of my affinity for sensations in my ear and brain that came from combining meaning and sound.

What I Wanted to be When I Grew Up

That same year I came across the following poem by A. A. Milne from Winnie the Poo:

> Where am I going? I don't quite know.
> What does it matter where people go.
> Down to the valley where the bluebells grow.
> Anywhere, anywhere, I don't know.

Perhaps it would be foolish to believe that at the age of five I was already thinking about what I wanted to be when I "grew up." But I was. When fathers came to school for an open house, most of them were wearing coat and tie. My father didn't wear a coat and tie when he went to work. He wore everyday clothes. He wasn't a doctor or a lawyer, he was a businessman who owned his own store, a place that sold eye glasses. What was I going to wear, what was I going to be, where was I going to go? What did I want to do? I wanted to write poems like "The Purple Cow." When our fifth grade teacher introduced us to haiku, it was a simple step from the sprung rhythms of Gerard Manley Hopkins to the three-line structure of a Japanese haiku.

One Man's Haiku is Another Man's Renga

Haiku is a short form of Japanese poetry "usually" consisting of seventeen syllables (or *on* or *onji*, meaning sound symbol, and *jion*, meaning symbol sound), which are arranged in three lines of five, seven, and five syllables each. The origin of haiku — or at least the origin of the seventeen syllable form of verse — is lost in the cloudy darkness of antiquity, but poems with alternate lines of five and seven syllables were common in the earliest forms of Japanese verse, which first appeared in the 12th century.

It was an elegant pastime in Japan to write short poems. A common parlor game consisted of guests taking turns writing a poem consisting of three verses, with each person adding a verse to the one before it. The resulting poems were called *renga*, literally "linked songs" or "linked verses." A party could go on all night, and the renga might end up having a hundred or more verses.

There's an apocryphal story that one party lasted the entire weekend and produced a renga ten thousand verses long.

You Say Dactyl, I Say Trochaic, You Say Hokku, I Say Haiku Let's Call the Whole Thing Off!

By the 16th century, renga parties were a national fad. The formal structure of alternating five and seven syllable lines was actually a common element of Japanese speech — metrical and syllabic patterns in poetry usually arise out of actual speech, not from an arbitrary invention. For instance, dactylic hexameter was a common speech pattern in ancient Greek (the meter in which the *Odyssey* and *Illiad* were composed). The same is true for iambic pentameter or trochaic tetrameter in English. It was quite natural for the formal pattern of haiku to grow organically out of speech patterns. The three-line verse that started the renga was called a *hokku* (meaning "starting verse"). Eventually, it stood alone, and was called haiku.

The Four Great Classical Haiku Masters

In the 17th century, **Matsuo Basho (1644-1694)** elevated haiku and gave it a new popularity. Today, Basho is internationally renowned, recognized as the greatest master of haiku. His best known work, *Oku-no Hosomichi*, or *Narrow Road into the Interior*, is one of the classic works of Japanese literature. Following Basho were periods of decline and rejuvenation, a pattern that has continued to the present day. The next high point featured **Yosa Buson (1716-1783)**, who is recognized as one of the greatest masters of *haiga*, an art form where painting is combined with haiku. Following Buson by a few decades was **Kobayashi Issa (1763-1827)**, whose miserable childhood, poverty, and devotion to the Pure Land sect of Buddhism were subjects in his poetry. The founder of modern Japanese haiku was **Masaoka Shiki (1867-1902)**, who was chronically ill for a significant part of his life. His disciples were instrumental in spreading haiku throughout the world.

The poet-nun **Chiyo-Jo (1703-1775)** is sometimes mentioned as the "fifth pillar" of classical Japanese haiku. She studied with many of Basho's students, having become popular all over Japan by the age of 17. (The alternative rock band Red House Painters adapted one of her haiku for the chorus of their song "Dragonflies.")

The 3 - Line, 5 - 7 - 5, Seventeen Syllable Form

Since the beginning of the 20th century, many Japanese poets have tested the elasticity of the haiku form, introducing modern images and motifs while straying from the three-line, 17 syllable requirement. But it wasn't until the 1970s that the work of these modern Japanese haiku poets was translated into English, thus influencing the way American poets in the last 50 years have experimented with the haiku form.

Japanese Haiku Translated into English

Japanese haiku was written in one vertical line consisting of seventeen *onji,* which is not the same as an English syllable, because the long vowel in Japanese is pronounced and counted as two syllables. Thus, the seventeen syllable count and the rendering of one Japanese vertical line into three lines of English became standardized as a result of the earliest translations of Japanese haiku into English that appeared in a books published before World War I. That format was maintained in another three books published between the wars in the 1930s. In the decade following World War II, R. H. Blyth and Harold Henderson continued that traditional form in their influential anthologies.

Haiku, edited by R.H. Blythe, 1949-52
An Introduction to Haiku, Harold G. Henderson, 1958

English Translations Pre-world War II

Until the last several decades, most American poets tended to adhere to the three-line, 5-7-5 pattern based on the translations of a few books published in the 1930s: *Haiku Poems Ancient and Modern* by Muyamori Asataro (1932), *The Bamboo Broom* by Harold G. Henderson (1934), which had rhymed translations and included a transliteration of the Japanese and a literal word-for-word English rendering of each poem, and *The Hollow Reed* by Mary J. J. Wrinn (1935).

English Translations Post-World War II

A Pepper Pod by Kenneth Yasuda appeared in 1947 and also included experiments of his own haiku in English. The most influential of all was the 4-volume, *Haiku* (1949-1952) by R. H. Blyth (see page 224). In 1955 *The Anthology of Japanese Literature* compiled and edited by Donald Keene appeared, which included Basho's *Oku-no Hosomichi* (translated by Keene as *The Narrow Road of Oku*) and a section entitled "Conversations with Kyorai," who was a disciple of Basho. This was followed in 1958 with *An Introduction to Haiku* by Harold G. Henderson (which was mostly an update of his 1934 *The Bamboo Broom*), and that was followed by R. H. Blyth's *History of Haiku* (two volumes, 1964). Henderson and Blyth's books set the standard for haiku over the next 25 years, establishing the three-line, 5-7-5 pattern well into the late 70s before translations of modern Japanese poets, who didn't always adhere to that traditional form, began to influence the writing of haiku in English.

American Haiku Makes A Splash

Over the course of the next few decades, dozens of journals and anthologies featuring English language haiku began to appear, along with collections of haiku by individual poets published by various small presses or self-published by the poets themselves. These books were not usually available in bookstores, but had to be ordered through the mail. Perhaps the earliest book of American haiku by an individual poet was a slim volume by William Seltzer, simply titled *Poems*, published by The Rustam Press and Voyages Press in 1958.

In my freshman year of college, I used to frequent the

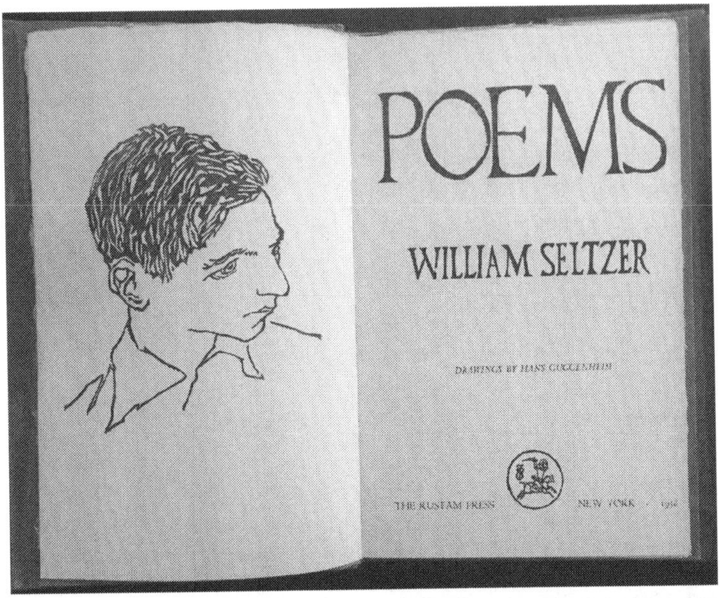

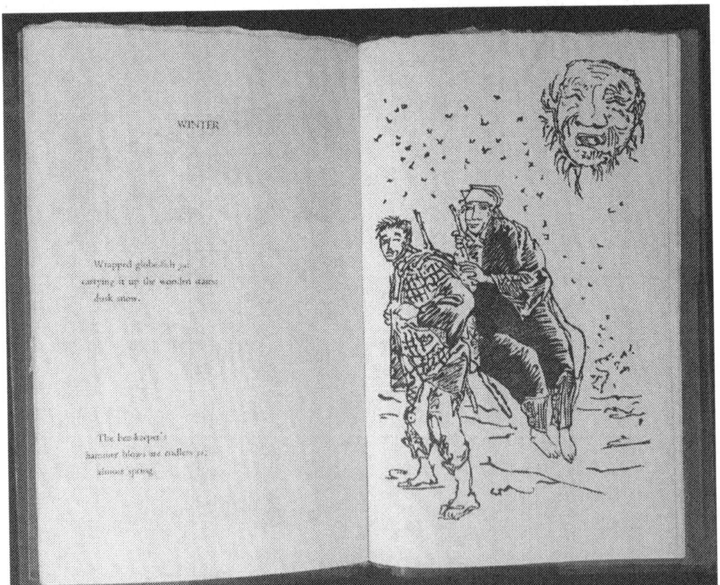

Poems, by William Selzter, with drawings cut in cherry wood by Judith Bishop from designs by Hans Guggenheim, 1958

bookstores and art galleries in the French Quarter, looking for unusual books of poetry. One of the underground literary magazines called *The Outsider* carried ads for chapbooks and other small press publications. I ordered a copy of Seltzer's book. It was a beautifully crafted hard bound book with deckle edged pages and drawings cut in cherry wood by Judith Bishop from designs by Hans Guggenheim. The edition was limited to 100 copies, and mine was copy #38, signed by Seltzer and Guggenhiem. A soft cover edition of 1,000 copies was also published. Most of the poems in the book were throwbacks to the kind of Romantic poems written in the 19th century, with lines like: "But who shall in the sun's last twilight / warm the twisting earth / the shrill peaks of our planet / or the green mellowing valleys?" The last section featured 12 haiku, arranged according to the season, with a preface explaining what haiku was. The haiku featured the standard images of blossoming cherry trees, peonies, cloud-mountains, wild geese, autumn moons, waterbugs, globe-fish, and fog. Still, it was an individual book of haiku by an American poet from Bridgeport, Connecticut, a long way from 17th century Basho. Seltzer even included his *kereji*, or cutting word, in Japanese.

Cherry petal dawn *ya;*
the trees of ten thousand hills
are weightless

From here to there
so many ways
waterbugs *kana*

The silver scissors,
wet
from cutting peonies.

Over hill after hill move
these cloud-mountains *ya;*
horseback journey.

One by one
the wild geese pass behind
a spider's glistening web.

In the autumn fog
walking among the pines,
at the edge of the world.

Along with Seltzer's book, I also sent off for other books of haiku such as Alvaro Cardona-Hine's *The Gathering Wave* (Alan Swallow Press, 1961) and Cor van den Heuval's *sun in skull* (1961) and *the window-washer's pail* (1963), both produced by van den Heuval on his own hand press. Compared to the images and themes common in Japanese haiku, there was

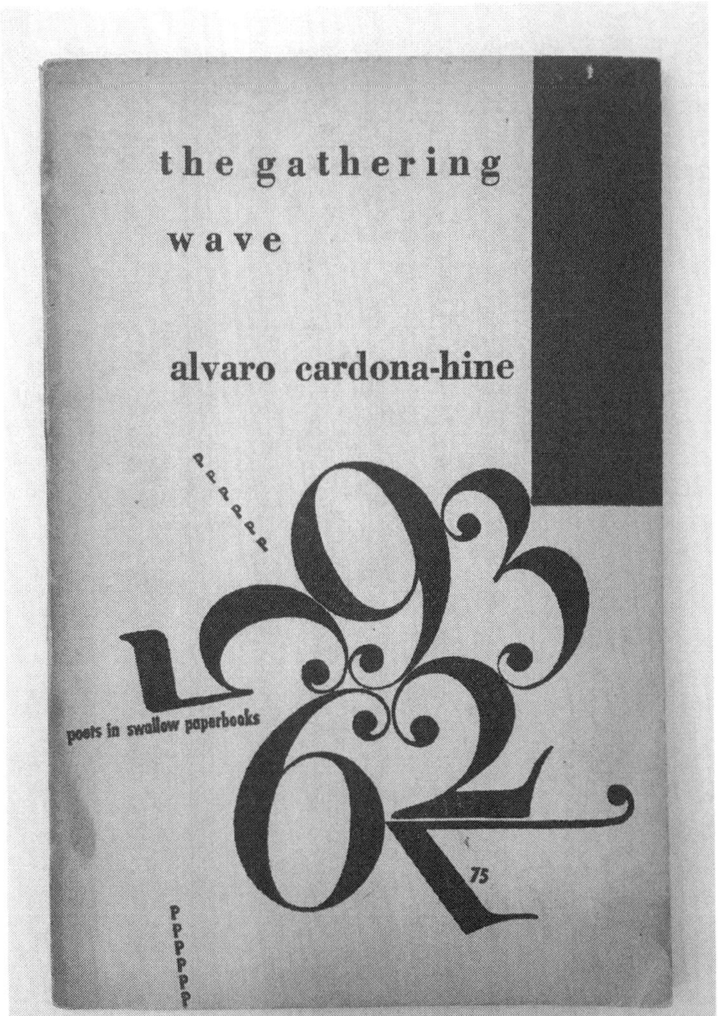

The Gathering Wave, Alvaro Cardona-hine, 1961

something new and striking about van den Heuval's American take on haiku, including poems about baseball.

summer afternoon
the long fly ball to center field
takes its time

after the game
a full moon rises over
the left field fence

in the mirrors on her dress
little pieces of my
self

changing pitchers
the runner on first looks up
at a passing cloud

I also stumbled upon a book of haiku by the Canadian poet Claire Pratt whose shocking images seemed to signal new possibilities for American haiku. Unlike Seltzer's beautifully produced hard-cover book, this was a simple chapbook of 32 pages, 4 inches by 7 inches with color reproductions of three woodcuts in red on the cover. The book was titled *Haiku* with a publication date of 1965. The writing was distinctly contemporary, bold, and emotionally powerful.

Land from sea to sea,
unknowing, sleeping, trying:
waken, weep and bleed.

At the age of four, Pratt contracted polio and subsequently developed osteomyelitis, an inflammatory disease of the bone, which affected her for most of her life. She worked as an editor at various publishing houses before she was forced to retire due to ill health. She often illustrated her haiku with her own graphic art and woodcuts.

Rage, roar, pound, O surf,
upon my bleeding beaches;
wash my body home.

How much of the strength-
giving wind can that pine tree
stand? When is too much?

From the concave throb
of dark, the issue pours in
one tremendous sob.

Wind, blow hot, blow pain,
blow evil, move the still air.
Crack the still white north.

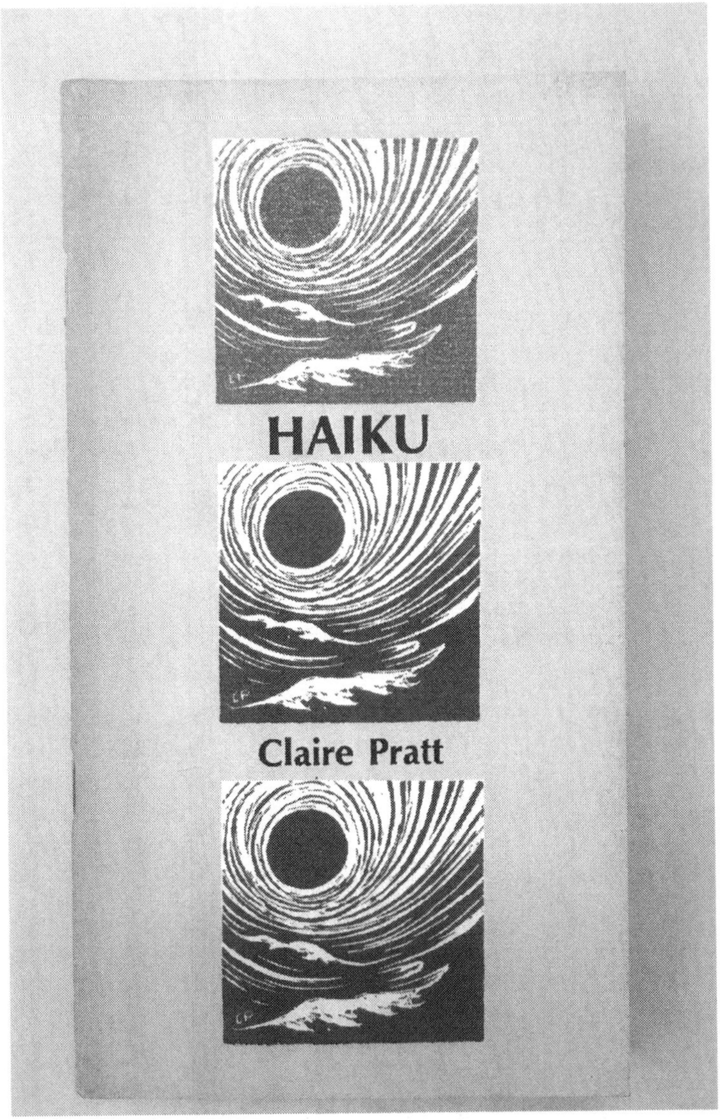

Haiku, Claire Pratt, 1965

A ferris wheel? The rack?
Beyond this bloody cough,
the free and undulating hips.

Lying on this shoal
in helpless mucus, lying
in the absurd: I

For awhile, her haiku was published in various magazines along with her woodcuts, but I'm not aware of any other individual publications of her poetry. In 1971 she published *Silent Ancestors*, a genealogical essay subtitled "The Forebears of E.J. Pratt," a tribute to the descendants of the Pratt family who immigrated to Newfoundland from Yorkshire. Her work was also stimulated by her father's poetry. Many of her Christmas cards featured excerpts from his poems.

Unfortunately, her book did not become well-known, but her book led me to another book of haiku by Robert Spiess, *the heron's legs*, and that led me to O. Southard's *Marsh-grasses* which came out the following year.

There was also a mention in *The Outsider* of a magazine devoted solely to haiku. Edited by James Bull and Don Eulert, published in Plattevile, Wisconsin, *American Haiku* was a charming little magazine that came out twice a year, setting a high standard for the periodicals that would follow. Interest in haiku seemed to be on the rise, and in 1964 Japan Air Lines sponsored a haiku contest conducted by radio stations across the country. They received 41,000 entries, with 85 poems published in a booklet entitled *Haiku '64*, which I assume was distributed on Japan Air Lines' flights. Alan Watts was appointed judge, and selected James W. Hackett (see page 229) the winner for the following haiku:

A bitter morning:
Sparrows sitting together
Without any necks.

In the second issue of *American Haiku* I also came across the following poem by Nick Virgilio, a poet from New Jersey, who won the magazine's haiku contest.

Lily:
  out of the water . . .
    out of itself.

This poem probably has had more influence on the direction taken by Western haiku than any other single haiku (see pages 219, and 270-272.

Even though I was not into writing haiku as such, these publications extended what I'd learned from writing haiku in grammar school, and proved valuable when experimenting with short imagistic poems, though I was soon to move away even from those short poems into more narrative, personal poetry. With James W. Hackett's *The Way of Haiku, An Anthology of Haiku Poetry*, published in 1964, I pretty much closed out my interest in haiku and moved on to those other underground publications that began to publish the new mainstream American poets, which included the New York school, the San Francisco Renaissance, the Black Mountain poets, the Beats, and that loosely defined group of poets associated with the so-called "Confessional School" of poetry (see page 254-255). I lost track of American haiku, which operated under the radar of mainstream American poetry, and I was not to come back to it until I started writing haiku again this past year.

W.H. Auden Makes a Splash

Most poets writing haiku began to modify the traditional form, often writing in one line only, such as this haiku by van den Heuval:

the shadow in the folded napkin

Others stuck to the three-line format without the limitation of seventeen syllables. In 1967, at a cocktail party after a reading in Dubuque, W. H. Auden confessed that he liked to stick to the disciplinary 17-syllables but prefered to manipulate them variously in the three lines. A few of them had been recently published in *The New York Review of Books*, eliciting some complaints from readers that they couldn't be regarded as true haiku, but Auden was unfazed. They were republished in his book *City Without Walls* under the title "Marginalia," and in two other books of his, in which he didn't call them haiku, but referred to them instead as "Shorts."

A dead man,
Who never caused others to die
Seldom rates a statue

He walked like someone
Who's never had to
Open a door for himself.

Some critics pointed out that Auden's haiku were essentially no different from Benjamin Franklin's aphorisms compiled in his *Poor Richard's Almanack*, or Dorothy Parker's quips like "Men never make passes at girls who wear glasses." But this is where the complications arise when it comes to defining haiku in a way that goes beyond the simple mechanics of the 5-7-5-syllabic structure. For poems as brief, if not briefer, than haiku, one could find examples among the poems in the Hellenistic epigrams of *The Greek Anthology*, compiled around 100 BC.

Emily Dickinson Flirts with Haiku

Even Emily Dickinson's gnomic compressions have a haiku-like quality. Trying to differentiate haiku from other kinds of short poems has proved to be complicated, vexing, fraught with semantic difficulties, and in the end, almost impossible. The other sticking point has been the attempts to equate the Japanese concepts of symbol sounds and sound symbols with the English concept of syllables. (The Japanese ideogram has a sound which stands for the pronunciation of the Chinese character, but it also has a sound based on how it's pronounced as the word or idea it's meant to convey.)

American Translations of Haiku Pre-World War I

Emily Dickinson would surely have read Basil Hall Chamberlain's haiku translations in *The Classical Poetry of the Japanese* published in 1880. The first tentative examples of Japanese art and literature were introduced to the Western world as a result of Commodore Perry's initiating a treaty with Japan in 1854, which opened the way for trade and communication. Painters such as Van Gogh and Monet were influenced by what they discovered, and the French Symbolist poets found much in Japanese literature to their liking. Consequently, the Imagist poets of America drew their inspiration from the Symbolists and from the 1911 publication of Chamberlain's other anthology of translations, *Japanese Poetry*, as well as from Yone Noguchi's *The Spirit of Japanese Poetry*, published in 1914. The Imagist poets, among them Ezra Pound, T. E. Hulme, Amy Lowell, H.D. (Hilda Doolittle), John Gould Fletcher, Mina Loy, and Charles Reznikoff modeled their short, imagist poems on these earliest English-language translations of Japanese haiku.

Lafcadio Hearn Comes to New Orleans

Another influential pre-World War I translator of Japanese haiku was Lafcadio Hearn, also known by the Japanese name Koizomi. He wrote many collections of Japanese legends and ghost stories and in 1900 published *Japanese Lyrics*, which included translations of haiku. Hearn lived in New Orleans for 10 years before World War I, and published a vast number of stories, books, and articles that helped create the popular reputation of New Orleans as a place with a distinct culture more akin to that of Europe and the Caribbean than to the rest of North America.

Even though Hearn wrote enthusiastically of the city, he also wrote of the city's decay, "a dead bride crowned with orange flowers." He is little known for his writing about New Orleans, except by local cultural devotees (and those who grew up there, as I did), but more books have been written about Hearn than any other former resident except Louis Armstrong.

When I was introduced to haiku by my 5th grade teacher, most of the translations were by R. H. Blyth or came from those pre-World War II anthologies, but many were by Lafcadio Hearn, whose ghost stories had already been favorites of mine. I discovered his Japanese ghost stories in *Kwaidan, Stories and Studies of Strange Things* (later adapted by Masaki Kobayachi into his 1964 film *Kwaidan*). In college, I came across his translations of French poets and writers, such as Gerard de Nerval, Anatole France, and Guy de Maupassant, not to mention his writings about Louisiana, voodoo and his creole cook books (I still use his recipe for gumbo).

Whether from those earliest 19th century translations of haiku in the traditional 5-7-5, 17-syllable pattern, or from the translations in the 30s, & 40s, especially those of Henderson and Blyth, or from the translations of Japanese haiku published

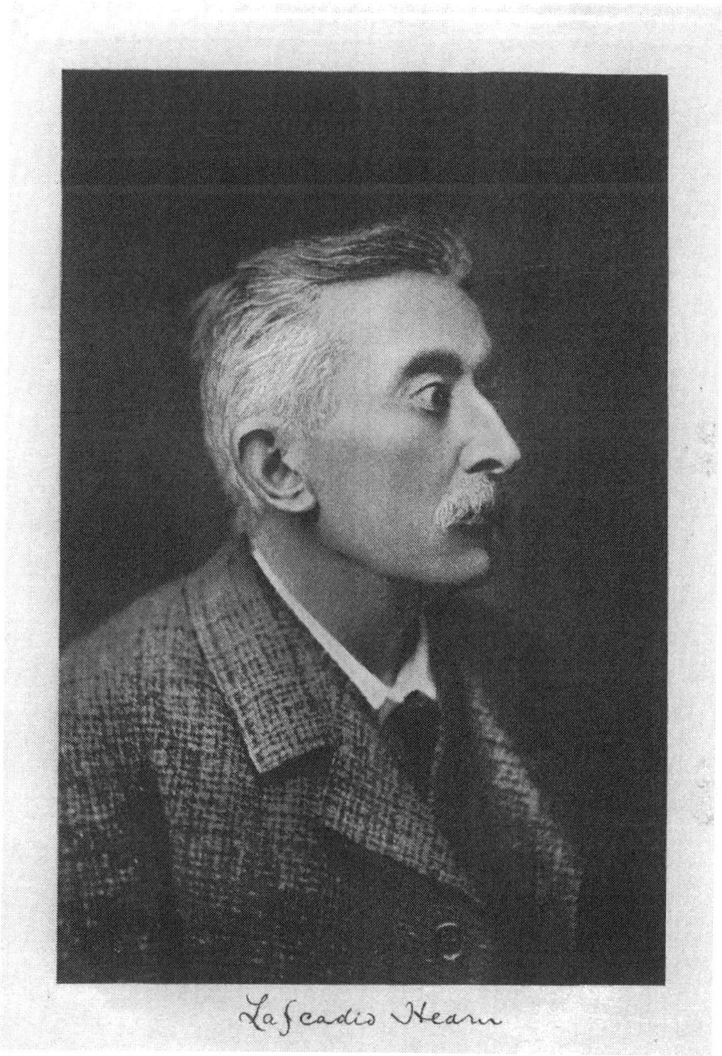

Patrick Lafcadio Hearn, known also by the Japanese name Koizumi Yakumo, was known for his books about Japan, especially *Kwaidan: Stories and Studies of Strange Things*, and his writings about the city of New Orleans.

in the late 50s and early 60s, by the time I entered graduate school in the late 60s, American haiku was finally coming of age.

Today, we've come a long way from the traditional form, and one would be hard pressed to give an exact defintion of what makes a haiku a haiku and what makes a haiku just a very short poem. And when it comes to the breaking of the rules, even Basho wasn't persnickity when it came to getting it right.

Basho Breaks the Rules

Arranging seventeen syllables across three lines of verse in a 5-7-5 syllable pattern is just an exercise in counting — even the great 17th century master Matsuo Basho did not always follow this model. Here's one of his better known haiku in which he uses a 5-5-7 form.

The waters fade	*umi kurete*	(5 syllables)
and the wild ducks' cries	*kamo no koe*	(5 syllables)
are faintly white.	*honoka ni shiroshi*	(7 syllables)

Basho could easily have transposed the lines to make the haiku adhere to the proper form, but he chose not to. He also sent the following haiku to a young pupil. The haiku contains the longest second line in Basho's poetry, with eleven rather than seven syllables:

How reluctantly the bee	*botan shibe*
emerges from the depths	*fukaku wakeizuru hachi no*
of a peony!	*nagori kana*

Basho often experimented with longer or shorter lines. The practice of adding or subtracting a sound unit or two from the established 5-7-5 set, now thought of as "lines," was known as *jiamara*. In one of his most famous poems, Basho added two sound units to the middle line. (For slightly different translations, see pages 103 and 277.)

On a dead branch	*kareeda ni*
a crow settled down	*karasu no tomari keri*
late autumn evening	*aki no kuri*

The second line, *ka-ra-su no to-ma-ri ke-ri*, has nine sound units. In an earlier version of the poem, written on a painting of seven crows with twenty more black birds in the sky, Basho had an extra sound unit, *ya*, in the second line, making for ten sound units. That version also contained the verb *tomari-taru*, in the perfect tense. In the newer version, Basho not only changed it to one crow, but rebelliously put the poem in the past tense, thus breaking another rule, that haiku must be in the present tense, capturing the immediacy of a moment. This verse and Basho's "old pond/frog" poem are his most well-known. Both Basho and his disciple Kyoriku made paintings to accompany this haiku and included only one crow. Basho could have achieved the proper seven-unit count by leaving off the *keri* or cutting word, but he must have considered it important enough to use *jiamari*. It's ironic that this poem has become prized as being quintessentially Basho.

Basho was not the only one of the four masters to break the rules. One of Buson's haiku has a syllable count in the original of 9-8-5, and in the English translation, a count of 11-7-5.

gekko nishi-ni watareba
hana-kege higashi-ni
ayumu kana

As the moon-brilliance westward makes its crossing
so cherry blossoms shadows
eastward slowly go.

Another example by Kawahigashi Hekigado, one of Shiki's primary disciples, has a total of 26 Japanase *onji* or symbol sounds.

konogoro tsuma naki yaoya	(11 syllables)
na wo tsumu negi wo tsumu	(9 syllables)
aruji musume	(6 syllables)

recently wife died, grocer's
stacking greens, stacking onions
husband, daughter

"Even if you have three or four extra syllables," said Basho, "or even five or seven, you needn't worry as long as it *sounds* right. But if even one syllable is stale in your mouth, give it all of your attention."

A Dictionary Definition of Haiku

What defines haiku — other than the traditional 5-7-5 pattern in three lines — is ambiguous, at best. In his introduction to *Haiku in English* (W.W. Norton & Co., 2013), edited by Jim Kacian, Billy Collins admits that haiku is "both easy and impossible to define."

In the 70s, after Harold Henderson co-founded the Haiku Society of America, there was an almost desperate attempt to nail down a definitive definition (see pages 102-103, and 235-236). Anita Virgil wrote to Henderson asking for a "dictionary definition." Professor Henderson, who had been ill with cancer for some time, replied a few days later from his apartment in New York City, expressing dismay that there was really no satisfactory definition in any English dictionaries, even though one would be hard pressed to find a definition in a Japanese dictionary.

Reading their correspondance, as well as the minutes of the countless meetings that took place among the members of the Haiku Society, one can't help but feel the tone of desperation and consternation that if no clear definition existed, poets would be unable to write haiku. As Anita Virgil said in one of her letters, "Form is of great importance in all art . . . . but others such as the majority of teachers in American schools and colleges without this new definition will continue to be hampered." A "comprehensive and correct definition" was needed.

Henderson wrote back that he could find no English dictionaries with a correct definition, but admitted that "it is hard enough to define poetry; a definitive definition of haiku is probably impossible." The haiku was not just a "form," he wrote, "and in Japan the 5-7-5 form is not rigid."

In another letter he went on to assert that he didn't want to make "pronuciamentos." He wrote that "English haiku must be what the poets make them, not just verses that follow 'rules' set down by some authority."

The letters and minutes of their meetings went back and forth for nearly four years. Henderson got a bit fed up with the nitpicking over words and concepts and finally wrote, "If the members cannot agree among themselves on what a haiku is and how it differs from other short poems, perhaps we had better give up the idea of trying to instruct others." Anita Virgil conceded that there would always be "the hazy aura of degree." Gustavel Keyser threw up his hands in exasperation, saying that most haiku appear to be merely "fragments of modern free verse."

Undaunted, Virgil wrote Professor Henderson that she was still "hard at work on the definition business." Later, she quit in frustration, saying that she had to devote her time to her own poetry and to the demands of her family, only to write another letter a month later that she was "happily tackling it again, to my amazement."

Sabi, Wabi, Yugen, Iki, Mujo, Karumi, Mano no Aware

Virgil was willing to accept as part of a definition that haiku were "the most concise distillations of an experience." In some ways, when speaking of form, haiku was much like the sonnet in which many variations evolved from the intial 14th century Italian form. As poets began to stray from the strict 14-line form with standard rhyme scheme, certain variations attained the status of another strict form and rhyme scheme with a name of its own: The Italian Sonnet, the Petrarchan Sonnet (a variation of the Italian), the French Sonnet, the Alexandrian Sonnet (a variation of the French), the English Sonnet, the Elizabethan Sonnet (a variation on the English), the Shakespearean Sonnet (a variation of the Elizabethan), the Spenserian Sonnet (a variation of the Elizabethan), and the Miltonic Sonnet (a variation on the Spenserian).

Aside from the number of lines and the rhyme scheme, what did all those sonnet forms have in common? Well, in the beginning, they all had to do with the torments of sexual love, but over time, the sonnet concerned itself with religion and politics. Thus, if one is willing to dispense with haiku's rigid three-line, 5-7-5 form, one would face a plethora of definitions and charactertistics, most of them vague and so non-restrictive that they could apply to any poem, including the shape-shifting sonnet.

Nevertheless, Japanese poets consider the following characteristics when discussing haiku: *sabi* (a sense of desolation and solitude), *wabi* (a feeling of powerlessness and loneliness, often caused by austere beauty), *yugen* (mysterious profundity or grace), *karumi* (lightness), *iki* (refined style), *mujo* (a sense of impermanence), and *mano no aware* (the pathos of things).

Wabi

The Japanese words *wabi* and *sabi* don't translate easily. *Wabi* originally referred to the loneliness of living in nature, far from society. The *wabi* sense includes melancholy, even misery within austere surroundings. *Wabi* suggested a dispirited, cheerless emotional state, then around the 14th century, the meaning took on a more positive tone. Self-imposed isolation and voluntary poverty came to be seen as opportunities for spiritual richness. For the poetically inclined, such a life fostered an appreciation of everyday life and insights into the beauty of the ordinary and overlooked aspects of nature. Simplicity took on new meaning as the basis for a pure beauty. Whether the object is natural or man-made, *wabi* connotes rustic simplicity, freshness or quietness and an understated elegance. It can also refer to quirks and anomalies arising from the construction of a thing, which add uniqueness and elegance to the object.

Sabi

Don't confuse *sabi* with the American pop singer formerly part of the hip hop band The Bangz. *Sabi* is one of those Japanese words pregnant with implication, and trying to pin it down with a single translation would be futile. *Sabi* is beauty or serenity that comes with age, but it also connotes desolation (*sabireru* means "to become desolate"). Eventually it came to mean something that had aged well, grown rusty (another word pronounced *sabi* means "rust"), or has acquired a patina that made it beautiful. Originally, *sabi* meant "chill" or "withered." Like *wabi*, the meaning shifted in the 14th century and took on a more positive connotation. The following haiku by Matsuo Basho typifies *sabi* in conveying an atmosphere of solitude or loneliness that undercuts — as Japanese poetry usually does — the distinction between subjective and objective:

solitary now—
standing amidst the blossoms
is a cypress tree.

The lush beauty of the blossoms contrasted with the subdued gracefulness of the cypress typifies the poetic mood of *sabi*.

During the last century or two, the meanings of the two words have crossed over so often, that the line separating them has become very blurred indeed. When Japanese today say *wabi*, they may also mean *sabi*, and vice-versa. Often people simply say *wabi-sabi*.

Wabi-Sabi

If you combine *wabi* with *sabi* — finding beauty in things that are not perfect, such as the patina or rust on an aging bronze statue — don't confuse that with *wasabi*, that green spicy stuff you put on sushi.

Though the term *wabi-sabi* is commonly used, linking both ideas, there are differences in their meanings. *Wabi* refers to a way of life, a spiritual path, whereas *sabi* refers to objects, art, and literature. *Wabi* is subjective, inward; *sabi* focuses on the external, the objective.

On March 16, 2009, Marcel Theroux presented "In Search of *Wabi Sabi*" on BBC Four as part of the channel's "Hidden Japan" season of programming. Theroux traveled throughout Japan trying to understand the aesthetic tastes of its people, comically enacting a challenge from the book *Living Wabi Sabi* by Taro Gold to "ask people on a Tokyo street to describe *Wabi Sabi*." Just as Gold predicted, Theroux showed that "they will likely give you a polite shrug and explain that *Wabi Sabi* is simply unexplainable." Most Japanese will claim to understand the feeling of *wabi-sabi* – it is, after all, a central concept of Japanese culture – yet very few can articulate this feeling.

In the Mahayana Buddhist view of the universe, *wabi* and *sabi* may be viewed as positive characteristics, representing liberation from a material world and transcendence to a simpler life. Mahayana philosophy itself, however, warns that genuine understanding cannot be achieved through language, so accepting *wabi-sabi* on nonverbal terms may be fitting. In his book *Practical Wabi Sabi*, Simon Brown notes that *wabi-*

sabi describes a means whereby students can learn to engage in life as it happens, through the senses, rather than be caught up in unnecessary thoughts. In this sense *wabi-sabi* is the material representation of Zen Buddhism.

In one sense *wabi-sabi* is a training. The student learns to see the most basic, natural objects as interesting and beautiful. Fading autumn leaves, for example. One's perception of the world can change so that a chip or crack in a vase appears more interesting and gives the object greater meditative value. Similarly, materials that age, such as wood, paper and fabric, become more interesting as they exhibit changes over time.

Trying to articulate the meaning of the term is often avoided. Associated with Zen Buddhism, the contemplation of emptiness and imperfection is honored as the first step to *satori*, or enlightenment. As is often said of Zen, "Those who know don't say; those who say don't know." Jazz may be a long way from Zen, but when Louis Armstrong was asked to define jazz, he said, "Man, if you gotta ask, you'll never know." While *wabi-sabi* is one of the characteristics of haiku, like haiku itself, *wabi-sabi* defies simple definition. Some Japanese critics feel that ineffability is part of *wabi-sabi*'s specialness.

A good place to start exploring the concept of *wabi-sabi* would be Leonard Koren's *Wabi-Sabi for Artists, Designers, Poets & Philosophers*. An object that exhibits *wabi-sabi*-ness may be tarnished and in disrepair, corroded, even broken or fragmented. The Japanese aesthetic of *wabi-sabi* has long been associated with the tea ceremony, where attention is paid to the rustic hut with its rough mud walls and exposed wood, the imperfect, asymmetrical pottery, and the simplicity of the ceremony. Tea bowls are often deliberately chipped or nicked at the bottom. This "flawed beauty" is one embodiment of *wabi-sabi*, though the term also suggests a spiritual longing. As Richard Powell puts it in his book *Wabi Sabi Simple*, "Nothing lasts, nothing is finished, and nothing is perfect."

The first recorded *wabi-sabi* tea master was Murata Shuko (1423-1502), a Zen monk who opposed the tea ceremony as an elite pastime of the rich. Shuko used intentionally understated, locally produced utensils, tarnished or chipped, and thus began the *wabi-sabi* aesthetic. About a hundred years later, *wabi-sabi* was brought to its apotheosis by Sen no Rikyu (1522-1591), who served in the court of the powerful military ruler Toyotomi

Hideyoshi. Although the late 16th century was a period of almost continuous warfare, it was also a time of great creativity and invention in the arts. Rikyu rejected the slick, perfect Chinese treasures used in the Japanese tea ceremony and brought instead crude, anonymous, Japanese and Korean folkcraft to a simplified ritual. Rikyu compressed the traditional gold-leafed tea-room down to a farmer's hut of rough mud walls, a mere thirty-nine square feet, with nothing more than two tatami mats. But Hideyoshi, a man of peasant origins, was not pleased with Rikyu's taste for the ugly and obscure; he preferred Chinese elegance and refinement. He also grew jealous of Rikyu's acclaim and ordered Rikyu's ritual suicide at the age of seventy. A story is often told of Rikyu's apprenticeship with the famous tea-master Takeno Joo, who asked him to clean Joo's leaf-strewn garden. First he raked until the grounds were spotless. Then, in a gesture pregnant with *wabi-sabi* overtones, he shook a tree trunk, causing a few leaves to fall. *Wabi-sabi* may be clean, but never too clean or sterile.

Haiku's essence of *wabi-sabi* is carried over into poems that are not (strictly speaking, according to the structure 5-7-5, 17-line definition) haiku, but more properly called minimalist poetry that evokes loneliness and transcience, such as Nick Virgilio's haiku:

autumn twilight:
the wreath on the door
lifts in the wind

Modern 20th century poetry emphasized the polished, seamless product, not unlike modernist architecture, which was geometric, slick, light and bright, functional, and exhibited the ideal of perfect materiality. *Wabi-sabi*, in contrast, was ostensibly crude, functionally ambiguous, dark and dim, featuring exposed wood and tarnished materials — beauty coaxed out of ugliness. There is even a *wabi-sabi* in cosmology, which sees the universe as devolving toward or evolving from nothingness (or, perhaps, everythingness — see page 308-310). While the universe destructs, it also constructs. New things emerge out of nothingness. Nothingness itself is not necessarily empty space; it is alive with possibility. In metaphysical terms, *wabi-sabi* suggests that the universe is in constant motion toward or away from potential.

During the 1990s, the concept was borrowed by computer software developers and employed in Agile programming and Wiki to describe acceptance of the state of ongoing imperfection. *Wabi-sabi* was even referenced in a *King of the Hill* episode where Bobby Hill entered a rose growing competition; his sponsors were a smoke shop and showed Bobby that the imperfection of the rose made the rose better.

Yugen

Among generally recondite Japanese aesthetic ideas, *Yugen* may be the most ineffable. The term is first found in Chinese philosophical texts, where it has the meaning of "dark," or "mysterious." Kamo-no Chomei, the author of the well-known *An Account of My Hut* (1212), considered *yugen* to be a primary concern of the poetry of his time. He offers the following as a characterization of *yugen*: "It is like an autumn evening under a colorless expanse of silent sky. Somehow, as if for some reason that we should be able to recall, tears well-up uncontrollably."

A general feature of East-Asian culture favors allusiveness over explicitness and completeness. *Yugen* does not, as has sometimes been supposed, concern itself with some world beyond this one, but rather with the depth of the world we live in, as experienced through cultivated imagination.

Mujo

The idea of *mujo* (impermanence) is perhaps most forcefully expressed in the writings and sayings of the thirteenth-century Zen master Dogen, who is arguably Japan's profoundest philosopher, but here is a fine expression of *mujo* by a later Buddhist priest, Yoshida Kenko, whose *Essays in Idleness* (1332) sparkles with aesthetic insights: "It does not matter how young or strong you may be, the hour of death comes sooner than you expect. It is an extraordinary miracle that you should have escaped to this day; do you suppose you have even the briefest respite in which to relax?"

Mono No Aware

The feeling of *aware*, or gentle melancholy, is triggered by the plaintive calls of birds or other animals, which is why birds, flowers, and insects are so often used in haiku to evoke a sense of life's passing. *Mono no aware* played a role in the world's first novel, Lady Murasaki Shikabu's 11th century *The Tale of Genji*, as well as in the first Japanese anthology of poetry from the 8th century, not to mention the Roman poet Virgil's 1st century BC epic poem, the *Aeneid*, in which Virgil used the term *lacrimae rerum*, "the tears in things," the great sadness at the heart of life, the sad lessons of transcience that nature teaches us. The world of flux that presents itself to our senses, say the Japanese poets, is the only reality: There is no conception of some stable "Platonic" realm above or behind it. The arts in Japan have traditionally reflected this fundamental impermanence — sometimes lamenting but more often celebrating it.

The most frequently cited example of *mono no aware* in contemporary Japan is the traditional love of cherry blossoms. Crowds of people go out every year to view (and picnic under) the cherry trees. The blossoms of the Japanese cherry trees are intrinsically no more beautiful than those of, say, the pear or the apple tree, but they are more highly valued because of their transience, since they begin to fall within a week of their first appearing. It is precisely the evanescence of their beauty that evokes the wistful feeling of *mono no aware* in the viewer.

Translated literally, *mono no aware* means "the pathos of things," or "empathy toward things," or "sensitivity to ephemera," where *mono* means "thing" and *aware*, which was a Heian period expression of measured surprise (similar to "ah" or "oh"), thus translating roughly as "pathos," "poignancy," or "deep feeling." It's not so much a lamentation as a gentle sadness or wistfulness in response to the impermanence of all things, including life itself. The term was actually coined by the Edo period Japanese scholar Motoori Noringa in his literary criticism of *The Tale of the Genji*. Motoori noted that *mono no aware* is the crucial emotion that moves readers.

Storytellers often present the main plot of their novels and stories against a parallel one from the past. For instance, the Japanese director Yasujiro Ozu was well known for creating a sense of mono no aware, frequently ending his films — after a familial and societal paradigm shift, such as a daughter being married off against the backdrop of a swiftly changing Japan — with a character saying, "*Ii tenki desu ne?*" ("Fine weather, isn't it?")

Like Virgil's *lacrimae rerum* and *wabi-sabi*, *mono no aware* is one of those terms without a direct translation into English; their meaning is apprehended through other terms that relate to it, such as *momento mori*, a Latin expression that literally means "remember that you have to die." The expression originated in ancient Rome when a victorious general, returning from battle to the adulations of the crowd, stationed a slave behind him who uttered the words *Respice post te. Hominem te memento* ("Look after you and remember you're just a man."). It was reused during the medieval period in relation to the *ars moriendi*, the art of dying. All things pass, including the self. In Hamlet's graveside speech, he holds the skull he's retrieved from an open grave and taunts it as a symbol of life's fragility.

Hamlet:
There's another skull: why may not that be the skull of a
lawyer? Where be his quiddities now, his quillets,
his cases, his tenures, and his tricks? Why does he
suffer this rude knave now to knock him about the
sconce with a dirty shovel, and will not tell him of
his action of battery? Hum! This fellow might be
in's time a great buyer of land, with his statutes,
his recognizances, his fines, his double vouchers,
his recoveries: is this the fine of his fines, and
the recovery of his recoveries, to have his fine
pate full of fine dirt? Will his vouchers vouch him
no more of his purchases, and double ones too, than
the length and breadth of a pair of indentures? The
very conveyances of his lands will hardly lie in
this box; and must the inheritor himself have no more, ha?

Clown: This same skull,
sir, was Yorick's skull, the king's jester.

Hamlet:
Alas, poor Yorick! I knew him, Horatio: a fellow
of infinite jest, of most excellent fancy: he hath
borne me on his back a thousand times; and now, how
abhorred in my imagination it is! My gorge rims at

it. Here hung those lips that I have kissed I know not how oft. Where be your gibes now? your gambols? your songs? your flashes of merriment, that were wont to set the table on a roar? Not one now, to mock your own grinning? quite chap-fallen?

A hundred and fifty years later Thomas Gray's great poem "Elegy Written in a Country Churchyard," picks up on the same theme, but with a tone more lamenatable than Hamlet's sarcastic one.

The curfew tolls the knell of parting day,
The lowing herd winds slowly o'er the lea,
The ploughman homeward plods his weary way,
And leaves the world to darkness and to me.

Now fades the glimmering landscape on the sight,
And all the air a solemn stillness holds,
Save where the beetle wheels his droning flight,
And drowsy tinklings lull the distant folds:

Beneath those rugged elms, that yew-tree's shade,
Where heaves the turf in many a mouldering heap,
Each in his narrow cell for ever laid,
The rude Forefathers of the hamlet sleep.

Let not Ambition mock their useful toil,
Their homely joys, and destiny obscure;
Nor Grandeur hear with a disdainful smile
The short and simple annals of the Poor.

The boast of heraldry, the pomp of power,
And all that beauty, all that wealth e'er gave,
Awaits alike th' inevitable hour:-
The paths of glory lead but to the grave.

Thomas Gray's poem was translated into Japanese in the 18th century, and was well known by its writers and poets.

Memory plays a big part in the evocation of *mono no aware*, especially with respect to the continuity of the past. Proust's *Remembrance of Things Past* is a good example of this longing for the comfort of memory as a way to assuage the anguish of the passing of time. British novelist Kazuo Ishiguro ends many of his novels without any sense of resolution. There's a note of melancholic resignation when a character realizes that *mono no aware* is a condition of existence, and the realization itself brings comfort and an end to mental anguish.

Iki

It might be simplistic to translate *iki* as "refined style." What, after all, is style? We probably know it when we see it, but otherwise, the idea can be more complex than can be rendered by a simple example or definition. Originally, the idea of *iki* was central to Japanese aesthetic life and derived from forms of erotic relations between men and geisha in the pleasure quarters of the big cities. The French terms *chic*, *coquet*, and *raffiné* share connotations with the term *iki*, but no European word is capable of fully translating the richness of its meanings. It can also imply "brave composure" or "calm under pressure" or simply "stoic resignation," the Buddhist attitude of non-attachment to a world of impermanence.

An interesting study of *iki* was undertaken by Kuki Shuzo (1888–1941) in his book *The Structure of Iki*, arguably the most significant work in Japanese aesthetics in the 20th century. Kuki wrote the first draft in 1926 while living in Paris, toward the end of a seven-year stay in Europe, and published the book shortly after returning to Japan in 1929. It's a phenomenological and hermeneutic study of the phenomenon, in which Kuki mentions the French *esprit* and the German *Sehnsucht* as terms that are similarly untranslatable, for similar reasons of cultural embeddedness. *Iki* can also be exemplified in the attitude toward death on the part of the samurai warrior and his way of living (*bushido*).

Karumi

The last element, *karumi*, or "lightness," (see page 129) would take a separate essay to delineate, but simply put, it can be taken, on the one hand, as frivolous, trivial, or flippant, and on the other, as the opposite of heaviness or pondorous. Some say that in his last days, Basho was trying to shift the style of haiku to one that embraced both the sadness of *sabi* with the lightness of *karumi*, a light touch where profound isolation is rendered with playful stoicism, but even that misses some of the nuance of the Japanese word. Most scholars and poets give the *sabi* element a predominate position in Basho's poetics, but his ultimate poetical value may lie in his use of *karumi*. In his travel journal *Journey of a Weather-Beaten Skeleton*, he wrote:

konoha chiru	leaves of cherry trees
sakura wa	having turned colors
karoshi hinokigasa	are falling on my cypress hat

Karoshi is the adjective form of *karumi*, and it's the first known instance of Basho using the word. But we know from his letters and instructions to his disciples that he was hoping to combine *sabi* with *karumi* in haiku so that haiku as a poetic tradition would not become either too frivolous or too boring. By infusing his haiku with both *sabi* and *karumi*, Basho was opting for a light-hearted approach to the human predicament. There's no reason that even in our most serious art, he seemed to be saying, that we can't have a bit of fun, that this world may be wretched, but haiku can provide comedy rather than tragedy for the too-restrained and too-pessimistic reader.

But even in that regard — attempting to define the abstract essence of haiku — Basho had the last word.

Haikai wa tada fuga nari.	Haiku is nothing
Fuga ni ron wa	but poetry.
Sukoshi mo gasanaku soro.	Poetry needs no theory.

Drops of Poetic Essence

Aside from the formal structure of three lines of 5-7-5 syllables and the characteristics mentioned above, most definitions of haiku hinge on abstract ideas or academic jargon such as "disjunctive tension" or "juxtaposed images" or "the poetics of superposition." Many writers have defined haiku as verse in the form of pithy short poems, epigrams, snapshots, or even telegrams. Zen masters consider haiku to be symbolic of "instant wisdom" — *satori* — or "eternity in tranquility."

Sir George Sansom described them as "little drops of poetic essence." Billy Collins said they should illicit from the reader "a little gasp" or "a moment of dazzling awareness."

In just three lines, haiku can tell a story or paint a picture, leaving it to the reader to locate the "meaning" within the juxtaposed images, images which arise naturally out of the *kokoro* — the heart/mind, as much felt as perceived. The essence of haiku, therefore, is a hidden dualism: two images or ideas juxtaposed in such a way as to provoke an initial response, followed by a deeper understanding. Haiku is not just about the juxtaposition of those images, but a reminder that the stated or implied comparison is about relationships, so that in the idea of the relationship, the reader perceives how all of life is connected, that the universe is one.

A Doll's House

The response to a haiku can be like the response to a Zen koan. It's often a spontaneous moment of joy, truth, insight, even puzzlement, but a Zen-like puzzlement in which the reader apprehends mystery without the need for the mystery to be resolved. When a haiku is too pat, without the tension of the juxtaposed image or idea, it can leave a feeling of *kokai*, which translates roughly as regret or a sense of being let-down. These dualistic elements are often linked by *kiru*, a Japanese term that means "cutting" or "stitching," usually represented by the *kireji*, the "cutting word" which links the two images or ideas. There's also the *kake kotaba*, the "pivot word," which helps create the imaginative leap from one idea to another. It can even be a pause. In English translations, it's often found in the last line or last word, which suggests how the juxtaposed elements are related. In the following translation by Sam Hamill of a poem by Basho, the surprise comes with the image of the doll's house, which can be considered either the cutting word or the pivot word.

> Even this grass hut
> may be transformed
> into a doll's house

Matsuo Basho (1644 - 1694)

Old Pond, Frog Jumps In, Splish Splash, He's Taking a Bath

The cutting word can even come in the first line, a sound-syllable that has no translatable meaning other than the sound. "Wa" and "ya" are frequent cutting words, which in English can be renderedy by "ah" or "oh," for instance. There is a famous cut-syllable, "ya," at the end of the first line of the best known haiku by Basho, perhaps the most famous of all haiku:

Furuike ya	An ancient pond, ah!
Kawazu tobikomu	Suddenly a frog jumps in!
Mizu no oto.	The sound of water.

More has been written about this haiku than any other haiku. It has been translated in more ways than you can imagine, and it has been parodied for hundreds of years. The poor frog has become an iconic haiku character:

The old pond:
A frog jumps into it —
plip/plop
– Lorraine Ellis Harr

Once upon a time there was a frog
Once upon a time there was a pond
Splash!
– Frank Kuenstler

Oh thou unrippled pool of quietness
Upon whose shimmering surface, like the tears
Of olden days, a small batrachian leaps,
The while aquatic sounds assail our ears.
–Lindley Williams Hubbell

My Noble Lord:
The cat just pissed on the Basho translations,
O ancient lake!
– Michael O'Brien

There's a wonderful book by Hiroaki Sato, *One Hundred Frogs*

(Weatherhill, 1983), which provides an in-depth analysis of Basho's "old pond frog" poem, including over one hundred translations, variations, and parodies.

Buddha Gets Smacked with a Broom

Consider this haiku by Billy Collins, a former poet laureate of the United States.

> One more dead calm day—
> I listen to the wind chimes
> I smacked with a broom.

In Collins' haiku, the word "smacked" is unexpected in the context of a calm day. The real "cutting," however, comes with the image of the "broom." Backtracking, we realize that the wind chimes broke the spell of the "dead calm day" because he "smacked" them with the broom handle while sweeping the floor. In Japanese, a haiku master might have simply listed the images to achieve a similar effect:

> calm day,
> wind chimes,
> smack,
> broom.

The Web of Allusion

The history of haiku is filled with poets reworking or paying homage to a haiku that came before them. This web of allusion, so to speak, can be a call-and-response over centuries, using the same image — autumn evening, hazy moon, cherry blossoms, grass hut, old pond, cicadas, crickets, grasshopper, etc. — or reworking the sequence of images to create a new idea, a different perspective. Tradition and the individual talent of the poet are meant to come together to produce a poem that both records the so-called "haiku moment," but responds to an earlier poem resonating with the same image. Basho paid Saigo the compliment of incorporating references to the older poet's work in his own haiku not as an attempt at imitation, but as an act of respect to a former master. Basho's haiku were often invoked by later generations of haiku poets, especially his "Old Pond/Frog" haiku. (I use a translation in the one-line form.)

An old pond: a frog jumps in — the sound of water

Yosa Buson's haiku is an elegant variation, an act of respect to an older master.

In an old pond a frog ages while leaves fall.

Even in his own time, Basho's famous poem was often invoked. In the spring of 1686, Basho and his fellow poets gathered at his house to play the game of matching *hokku* (haiku). Here's a few variations on his frog poem:

Hopping frog — is a cat chasing you, deep in Ono
—Suiya

At daybreak frogs begin saying Buddhist prayers
—Sensetsu

Innocently a frog squats on a floating leaf.
—Senka

When depressed, the toad's voice too — this rainy night.
—Sora

Basho occasionally paraphrased some of the great Chinese poets because his spirit was sympathetic to their esthetic values, and this cross-cultural underpinning made his own poetry richer. This web of allusion, this call-and-response is a significant part of the Japanese poetic tradition. Basho wrote:

A cuckoo fades away
and in its direction,
a single island

Ishigaki Rin, a 20th century modern haiku poet, titles his poem "Island," which calls forth Basho's image:

I live on my island.
In the mirror I look
at myself — a far-off island.

One of my favorite examples of this web of allusion is Collins' poem (mentioned earlier on page 43), which evoked for me a classic haiku by the late 18th century master Kobayashi Isaa:

bamboo soot broom
Buddha's face too
gets a smack
-Issa

one more dead calm day—
I listen to the wind chimes
I smacked with a broom
-Collins

In Issa's poem, the "smack" is the cutting word, whereas in Collins' poem, it's "broom." Both poets use "broom" and "smacked," but each creates a different idea by the position of the cutting word and the object of the smack. Issa smacks Buddha's face; Collins smacks the wind chimes, and both do so with a broom.

Smacking Buddha's face is the more shocking image, the more profound idea. This may not be as extreme as Buddha's adage that "if you meet the Buddha on the road, kill him," but Issa seems to be suggesting that if you're not going to kill the Buddha, at least don't take the Buddha too seriously—even the Buddha needs a smack once in a while. This is not the first time Issa was playful with Buddha.

Buddha on the hill —
from your holy nose indeed
hangs an icicle

Indeed! Part of the comic image involves poor Buddha who cannot swipe away the icicle. And what a lovely touch, in that Issa juxtaposes Buddha's "holy" nose with the preposterous hanging icicle. A pie in the face wouldn't be as funny. Unhappy Issa's ability to poke fun at life as well as himself made his haiku — even those about his dead children, his bitter poverty, and his little insect friends — so memorable. And it's what makes Issa himself more loveable than Basho or Buson.

What I also love about Issa's poem about Buddha getting

smacked with the broom is the word "too." Imagine the poem without that word. Buddha's face gets a smack. Heavy-handed, wouldn't you say? But with the "too," Issa is saying something more, something like: Don't take the world too seriously since everything, including the Buddha, should be taken with a grain of salt—a sentiment with which the Buddha would probably agree. One could take either Issa's or Collins' poem and rhapsodize on its greater meaning, but it's enough to delight in their quotidian essence.

A Zen Thunderclap

The traditional purpose of the haiku is to create deeply-felt meaning by evoking images from nature — birds, flowers, trees, insects, bodies of water, etc. Meaning is apprehended by the psyche and body, not through the intellect. A haiku functions as a kind of Zen snapshot of real life leading to intuitive insight. Scholars and lovers of haiku can spend thousands of words on the contemplation of one haiku — its allegorical meaning, its philosophical or psychological implications — but I love the way haiku, before the intellect takes over, settles on the parched spirit like morning dew. Haiku can exist as bon-bons, or, if the poet has managed to cut deeper and the reader is willing to ruminate on the cut's depth — the effect can be epiphanal, the psyche shaken by a thunderclap. Not bad for a paltry seventeen syllables in three lines.

Basho's Old Pond

Basho's famous haiku — probably the best known haiku in the Japanese language —is deceptively simple. One translation might go:

> Old pond:
> frog jump in
> water sound.

What image could be more mundane? I first read that haiku when I was in fifth grade. The teacher passed around copies she had mimeographed. She was introducing us to this ancient form of Japanese poetry. As a boy, the image resonated for me because it was so familiar — I'd seen frogs hopping along the ground and jumping into one of the many ponds in Audubon Park, a few minutes' walk from my home. But it also excited me — it was a reminder to look around at the world I lived in. It reminded me to *notice* things. The smallest object could be made into a poem: bottlecap on the lawn, plastic whistle on the sidewalk, skate-key tied to a string. Basho's "Old Pond" consisted of an image, an action, and a sound. When I started writing haiku in fifth grade, that seemed an easy formula.

A butterfly,
the sound of the wind,
a leaf fluttering to the ground.

The trick, of course, was to get all that into seventeen syllables in three lines of 5-7-5.

Look! A butterfly.
Sound of wind rustling the trees.
Brown leaves on the ground.

Triumph! So cool! I wrote a haiku. I'm not saying I grasped the finer points of haiku at ten years old, but I got into the habit of seeing the world as Zen snapshots.

A Psychic Thunderclap

Well, actually, they were more like a few seconds of film involving an image, an action, and a sound. The sound or image could come last, "like a psychic thunderclap," the teacher said. She clapped her hands together to emphasize the point. "First, there's the picture of the old pond," she said, "then the frog jumps in – that's the action – then the sound of water." She was silent, allowing us to imagine the ripple on the surface of the pond. Then she smacked her hands together. Bang! We almost jumped out of our desks. "That," she said, "is the psychic thunderclap!" Boy, this was exciting. Better than putting a match to powdered magnesium, watching the flash and puff of smoke, something I did with the chemistry set I'd sent away for. I made lists of ideas that could be worked into haiku – images, sounds, and actions that could elicit that tiny explosion, that pyschic thunderclap.

father in the kitchen,
cup of coffee,
sound of the newspaper crinkling.

Cloudy day,
honk of the horn,
angry bus driver.

Summer evening,
screen door slams,
bird takes flight.

Puddle of milk,
broken glass,
my brother's yelp.

Red sun over Lake Pontchartrain,
motorboat along the shore,
one white cloud.

Then I'd fit them into the three-line, 5-7-5 scheme.

It's a cloudy day
broken by a honking horn—
angry bus driver.

I didn't delve into the meaning of the images, or grope for insight. I didn't even spend much time on the arrangement of the images, whether cloudy day should go last or in the middle, or if brother's yelp should come first, followed by the broken glass, then the puddle of milk. It was the trick of getting those seventeen syllables parsed into three lines that fascinated me, that made writing haiku fun. Who knew from *kireji* or *kake kotaba,* or for that matter, *sabi wabi mujo iki:*

Talking Trees

I wasn't the only one playing the haiku game. My entire class was introduced to haiku in fifth grade. Our teacher had us make booklets of our haiku to display during Open House. I remember that distinctly — our booklets of haiku thumbtacked to the bulletin board as parents marvelled at our creativity.

One day, we were busy writing our haiku on construction paper when the teacher said, "You know, Japan is probably the only country in the world where the family of the head of state is regularly required to write poetry. The poets and monks who wrote haiku sometimes formed writing clubs and gave themselves names, and even today, those who enjoy writing haiku form local clubs, publish their own magazines, and give their clubs names."

Jerry Pinero sat behind me. He was the smallest kid in the class, and his father owned a fruit stand on Carollton Avenue. "What kind of names?" he asked.

"Well," said the teacher, "that depended on who they were. Nishiyama Soin's followers were known as the Danrin School, but they called themselves the 'Talking Trees' because that's what his name meant in Japanese. Basho was part of Soin's group when he was young. Writing haiku was a very popular thing to do, everybody did it. So you could have samurai warriors forming a club, or actors forming a club, or farmers or shopkeepers forming their own haiku clubs. Some groups might be a mixture of samauri and farmers." Then she smiled. "And the best part," she said, "was, the government couldn't tax it or take it away." She laughed at her joke, finding it funnier than we did.

Haiku Clubs

Max Goldman sat in the next row to my right. Max was an instigator, probably the smartest kid in the class. He became a physicist. He and I often exchanged notes during class, usually gossip or funny comments, anything to make the other laugh. Eventually, Max's laughter would get the attention of the teacher who would invariably say: "Alright Max, what's so funny?" And then we'd both start laughing and get a demerit. Five demerits in one day and you had to stay after school. Max leaned over and mouthed the word "club," then raised his eyebrows.

There were a bunch of clubs in school: art clubs, checkers

clubs, baseball card clubs, archery clubs. I belonged to the art club (an art teacher came after school on Thursdays) and the checkers club (my dad taught me a great opening strategy that I use to this day), and the baseball card club (I was a Brooklyn Dodger fan and brought a transistor radio to school so I could secretly listen to the World Series during fifth period History the year they beat the Yankees — the only time Brooklyn won a World Series. Johnny Podres pitched a shutout, and Gil Hodges, my favorite player, knocked in the only two runs scored. I still remember the final out. It was all I could do to keep myself from jumping up and screaming. Duke Snyder, the "Duke of Flatbush" in center, Jackie Robinson at third base, Pee Wee Reese at short, Roy Campanella catching, and Junior Gilliam at second base. I just sat there holding it in until Mr. Hauth shook his head and said, "Alright, Grapes, who won?"). So when Max mouthed the word "club," I got the message and mouthed back to him, "Haiku Club." We thought we'd form one big haiku club, but once we learned about the four great haiku poets, it was inevitable that there would be four haiku clubs, each devoting itself to one of those masters.

Matsuo Basho and "The Frogmen"

By sixth grade we had divided ourselves into clubs of two or three members, with each group touting its own master poet. Jerry Pinero and Max Goldman saw themselves as disciples of the great master and originator of the form, Matsuo Basho, whose poem about his hut becoming a doll's house I loved, along with the one about the frog jumping into the pond. "Old Pond" became the inspiration for their club's nick-name: "The Frogmen."

I liked Basho. He was an ascetic and seeker, but there was also something — what's the word? — dear about him, a gentleness I related to. Though his poems were written centuries before, he was a living presence.

A five-foot thatched hut:
I wouldn't even put it up
but for the falling rain.

I felt I could hear his voice, apologizing for his little hut, but sitting in it all the same, enjoying the sound of the rain on its thatched roof.

A Haiku Clubhouse

Around the corner from where I lived, there was a vacant lot, and a few of us found a pile of empty orange crates stacked behind the local grocery store. We took them apart, slat by slat, then reconstructed them using the same nails and slats to make ourselves a clubhouse. There was a haiku process in that as well. The slats from the orange crates were syllables. A section of several slats were like entire lines. If any slats needed cutting, we used a handsaw I pilfered from the garage where my father built furniture as a hobby. Once all the pieces were laid out, we reassembled them into a clubhouse, slat by slat. On rainy days, after school, we'd buy a few hamburger rolls, a packet of balogna, and a small jar of mayonnaise from Rizzo's grocery store and make ourselves baloney sandwiches. I pretended I was Basho in his thatched hut, trying to write a haiku in the falling rain.

Tokugawa Shogunate Sandwich

I was inclined to join the Frogmen, the Basho club. "Basho was the son of a samurai warror," our teacher said. "When he was eight, he was sent to live in the home of a nobleman, a high-ranking samurai, the lord of a castle in the south of Japan."

"Was he going to be trained to be a samurai?" asked Max.

"No, the times had changed. Thousands of samurai warriors went to war against each other, kind of like our Civil War, except there were hundreds of different states fighting each other. When Japan's civil war was over, Japan became one nation ruled by one shogun."

"What's a shogun?" we asked.

"A shogun," she said, "was a general, but he was also a governor of a region. There were about 300 shoguns in Japan at the time, and each one was fighting the other for more territory. Each shogun commanded hundreds of samurai warriors."

We *oooo*-ed and *aaaah*-ed at this information, imagining the samurai wielding those long swords.

"The shogun who won the civil war was named Tokugawa, he defeated all the other shoguns. He started the Tokugawa Shogunate, which lasted almost 300 years." Again, we *oooo*-ed and *aaaah*-ed, and repeated the word "Tokugawa." There was something delightful about uttering certain Japanese words, words we didn't understand. At first, we just said the word by itself, as if it had some special significance. We could be standing in line for lunch and one of us would say the word with great emotion. "Tokugawa!" Eventually, we started using them in sentences. "Are you eating a Tokugawa Shogunate sandwich for lunch?" or "Ow, I broke my Tokagowa Shogunate!" For weeks, Tokugawa was our favorite word. Tokugawa did this and Tokugawa did that. Still to come was "Hototogisu," "Shirakawa," "Matsushima," and "Oku-no Hosomichi."

World War II

"After years of civil war," the teacher said, "Japan was finally at peace. There wasn't much use for warriors anymore." I had a vague memory of another war, the Second World War, how we had to tear ration stamps from a little booklet and give it to the guy at the gas station who checked the oil and filled the car with gas. In the movies, there were newsreels showing soldiers with bloody bandages on their heads, walking along a road. Planes dropped bombs on cities which went up in flames. Battleships shot enemy planes out of the sky. There was a newsreel showing a big explosion, followed by a big white cloud that looked like an umbrella or a mushroom. Then three men were sitting in chairs, their legs covered with blankets, talking and smiling. My dad said it was the Potsdam Conference with Churchill, Stalin, and President Truman. I asked him what they were doing. "Dividing up the world," he said. But now, that war was over, too.

Basho Trains to be a Samurai

"Why was Basho sent to live somewhere else when he was a little boy?" Jerry asked.

"Basho's father was just a low-ranking samurai, so he wasn't that rich. The best he could do for his son was to send him to be trained in the house of a wealthy landowner. It was like going to boarding school. After the Civil War was over, they began to train samurai in the arts, especially poetry, because it . . . ," then she opened one of the haiku books she had stacked on her desk. It was a thick blue book with gold lettering on the cover that said *Haiku Poems Ancient and Modern.* She turned the pages

Title page of Miyamori Asatarō's *Haiku Poems Ancient and Modern,* published in Japan in 1940 during the height of the Japanese Empire.

carefully so as not to bend them until she came to the page she was looking for, then began to read: "They trained samurai in the arts, especially poetry, because haiku stirs the feelings of the unseen gods and spirits and soothes the heart of the fierce warrior."

In the book was a photograph of Basho's tomb. She passed the book around and we looked at it. There were black Japanese letters carved into the stone. Then she showed us pictures of paintings of cherry blossoms and other flowers and beautiful ladies wearing colorful robes. Another page showed Basho wearing a black robe and a black cap, sitting on the floor. He was skinny and frail with whiskers, and above him, several poems in Japanese letters.

"Look at this," she said, and showed us a page at the begininng of the book. "This is the author's dedication," she said. "His name is Miyamori Asataro, and he dedicates the book to his Imperial Highness, Prince Nobuhito Takamatsu-No-Miya." We were meserized.

"At first," the teacher said, "Basho worked in the kitchen and became the servant for the Lord's son, Todo Yoshitada, who was only two years younger than Basho. But they became good friends. They both loved writing haiku. They even gave themselves special names. Basho was called "Sobo," which was a Japanese form of his given name, Munefusa. Yoshitada's haiku name was 'Sengin,' which means 'wild berries.'

"While they were still teenagers," she continued, "Todo and Basho published a *renga* that had one-hundred haiku verses. But a year after that, Todo died and Basho left the Lord's house. He gave up on the idea of being a samurai because he realized at that point that he wanted to be a poet. Remember, Basho had learned to write haiku when he was only nine years old."

The Poetry Lovers' Society

We couldn't imagine this master poet writing haiku at the same age we were. Eddie Negrotto, the hulking kid who sat in the back row, was more into sports than poetry, but even he got involved. "He was nine years old?" asked Eddie.

"Yes," said our teacher, "A great many poets began writing at that age. Masaoka Shiki was eleven when he composed his first poem in classical Chinese. When he was only thirteen, he and a group of his friends formed a haiku club they called *Doshin*

Ginsha, which means the Poetry Lovers' Society, and they met once a week at each other's homes to read and discuss their haiku. One night, Shiki and his friends climbed the dike by the river on the outskirts of Matsuyama and yelled out their poetry to the stars."

Eddie let out a howl, something between a yodel and a wolf's ulalation. We all laughed, but the teacher's stern look was all it took to quiet us down. "Many of the great haiku poets," she said, "began writing when they were your age." Yelling by the river might be fun, but she was also letting us know that one could discover one's life's destiny even at such an early age.

"What do you want to be when you grow up?" she asked Eddie.

Suddenly, he was being put on the spot. He didn't like that kind of attention. He shrugged and said, "I dunno. A football player."

Fireflies or Lightning Bugs

The teacher nodded. "Good," she said, "it's good to know what you want to be. KuboYorie was about thirteen when she studied with Shiki. Kikusha was about twelve when she started writing haiku, and she was also a painter. Eushima Onitsura was only eight when he wrote his first haiku. When he was a teenager, he studied with several haiku masters." She pulled another book from the stack on her desk, this one was thin with crows and purple ducks on the cover— the crows were flying in one direction, the ducks in the other. "Would you like to hear the poem Onitsura wrote when he was eight?" We nodded and she read aloud from the book:

Although I say,
"Come here! Come here! the fireflies
keep flying away."

"Have you ever tried to catch a firefly?" she asked.

"What's a firefly?" someone asked.

"Oh, I forgot," she laughed, "you call them lightning bugs here."

"Yeah," said Eddie in his gravelly voice, "you can never catch them."

"It's impossible," I said.

"Well," she said, "that's what Onitsura was writing about in his haiku, how when he was eight years old he kept calling out to them, but the fireflies always flew away."

"You mean lightning bug," I said, correcting her.

"Fireflies, lightning bugs, same thing," she said.

Dragonflies or Mosquito Hawks

"There are plenty of fireflies in Japanese poems," the teacher said. "Here's one of my favorites by one of my favorite poets, Chiyo-Jo." She got up and wrote the haiku on the blackboard, then read it aloud.

> The fireflies' light.
> How easily it goes on.
> How easily it goes out again.

"What do you think Chiyo-Jo is saying here?" she asked.

"That's why you can't catch them," said Eddie, "they keep blinking on and off, so you never know where they are."

"That's true," the teacher said, "but Chiyo-Jo is saying something more. What do you think it is?"

Max raised his hand. Most of us just blurted out what we had to say, but Max was always raising his hand. "I think she's saying something about life," he said.

The teacher nodded. "What might that be, Max?"

Max looked around for a few seconds, like he wasn't sure of what to say.

The teacher repeated, "What's Chiyo-Jo saying about life?"

"Well," said Max, "my aunt had a baby last year. But the baby didn't live very long. Just a few days. My mother was upset for a long time. When my aunt came over, they both cried a lot."

"I'm sorry to hear that, Max."

Max gave a little shrug. "It's okay," he said, "she's gonna have another baby soon."

The teacher pointed to the haiku on the board. "What Chiyo-Jo is saying in this haiku is that life is very precious. Like the light of a firefly, it can go on, and then off. You never know."

It was a sobering thought, and we were all quiet for a moment.

"But it doesn't have to be taken literally. One doesn't have to die to have their light go off. Right?"

She let us think about it.

"Like a car can still run," I said, "even if it's lights are out."

"Exactly," she said.

"Like when we're sad?" asked Jerry. We all turned and looked his way. This was a touchy subject. Jerry was probably the saddest kid in class. Sometimes, during lunch, he'd go off by himself and eat his sandwich alone. We all knew what he meant, because sometimes we were sad too about something.

"So, someone's light could go out for awhile," I said.

"Yes," said the teacher. "But don't forget, according to Chiyo-Jo's poem, sometimes it goes back on, too."

We all nodded. We were onto something more than just counting the syllables and the lines. I couldn't articulate it then, but I was becoming dimly aware that poetry could get inside your skin, could say things you didn't want to say outloud, directly.

Then the teacher sat back down and brightened up. "The haiku poets didn't just write about fireflies," she said, "they also wrote about dragonflies, too." She took another book from the stack. This one was a thick, green book, also with gold lettering on the cover that read *The Hollow Reed*. She turned the pages carefully again until she came to the page she was looking for. "Here's a haiku by Natsume Soseki, who was a disciple of Shiki. He died during World War I." (see pages 200-201)

On my shoulder is
it longing for a companion?
A red dragonfly.

"What's a dragonfly?" I asked. I imagined a fly as big as a tree swooping down and carrying me away.

"In the South, you say mosquito hawks," said the teacher. "In some places people say dragonflies. There are many haiku about mosquitos, too. This one's by Shiki."

An autumn mosquito
determined to die
bites me.

Pill Bugs, Doodle Bugs, and Roly-Polies

The teacher said, "People who live in different parts of the country have different names for the same thing. For instance, you know what they call doodle bugs up north?" Everyone shook their heads. "Pill bugs," she exclaimed, as if pulling a rabbit out of a hat.

"Pill bugs!" we yelled. How funny that seemed. "And in some places, they call them 'roly-polies.'"

My mind made room for those dual images: a dragonfly and a mosquito hawk; a firefly and a lightning bug; a doodle bug, a pill bug, a roly-poly. I was beginning to understand the nature of metaphor, without having a word for that concept. It mattered how you named something, what words you used to describe it, because it changed the way you saw it. A lightning bug flashed across the night sky, but a firefly burst into flames. Say dragonfly, and you see a fly as big as a dragon, but call it a mosquito hawk and it swoops down and grabs you as if you were a mosquito. Something else stirred in my brain, nothing I could articulate then, but the notion was implanted nevertheless: Words could evoke auditory, visual, or functional associations. Pill bug was visually descriptive, roly-poly was functional, it rolled along, and doodle-bug was a sound that captured an undefinable essence.

June Bugs, Lady Bugs, and Mary Beetles

"What about a June bug?" I asked.

"When I lived up North," the teacher said, "we called them lady bugs, and sometimes, lady cows."

"Lady cows!" I shouted, slapping my desk with glee.

"Yes, some people called them that. The lady part came from their original name, Notre Dame, which means Our Lady in French. Our Lady refers to Mary, the mother of Jesus. So in Germany, they call lady bugs Mary beetles."

The teacher was expanding the world, expanding our consciousness. And we were talking about bugs!

Death Haiku

"Haiku poets," she continued, "write about grasshoppers and crickets and cicadas."

"What's a cicada?"

"Well," she said, "it's like a cricket, but not quite the same thing. In Japan, the cicada lives most of its life underground in its shell, but with only a few days left to live, it breaks the shell and flies free. They make this shrill noise before they die. Here's a haiku by Murase Shuho, who was a professional Go player known all over the world."

"What's a go player?" I asked.

"Go is a board game played with white and black stones, with very simple rules, but it's more complicated than chess. Shuho introduced the game to Europe about a hundred years ago. He also wrote many wonderful haiku. This one is called his "death haiku."

"A death haiku," I repeated. The word hung in the air. I loved fairy tales about monsters and death. They validated my scary dreams.

"Every haiku poet writes a death haiku," she said. It's called a *jisei*, a poem to life. When you know you're about to die, the *jisei* is a way to celebrate life. So if a poet mentioned the cicada, they were really talking about living most of one's life underground, inside a shell, then flying out at the very end. In this haiku by Shuho, he compares his life to the cicada shell." She read the poem aloud to us, then was quiet for a while.

> Cicada shell:
> little did I know
> it was my life.

"There is the sense," she went on, "that life is a preparation for death. When death comes, life is shed, like the cicada shell, and the spirit is finally free to seek enlightenment. In Japanese haiku, the cicada makes you think of life and death. You know what they call cicadas in Tennessee? Jar flies. In some places they call them tree crickets. In other places, they're called katydids, or long-horned grasshoppers."

Skull Bugs

My mind was swimming with images. Katydid made me think of a girl tap-dancing on a table. A tree cricket was either a bug that lived in a tree, or it could be the tree with long branches that looked like insect legs and made cricket sounds as it walked through your backyard. Best of all was the long-horned grasshopper. I imagined cowboys lassooing a long-horned grasshopper and riding it at a rodeo. "In some places," the teacher continued, "the spittle bug is called a froghopper, but it's really a big beetle. Another beetle is the scarab, but they're also called dung beetles. And you know what a potato bug is?" We nodded our heads, feasting on all the names. "Well, out in California they're called spud bugs. The Navajo Indians called them skull bugs."

"Skull bugs!"

"Yes, but the Franciscan monks thought it referred to Golgatha, the hill on which Christ was crucified. Golgatha means skull hill. So the monks called them Jerusalem crickets." We repeated the names to each other: skull bugs and Jerusalem crickets and dung beetles and froghoppers and spittle bugs! We were getting so worked up, the teacher had to calm us down. "Okay," she said, "here's the last one. The original name for butterfly was flutterby, because it 'fluttered by.' Eventually, they switched the letters and it became a butterfly."

Haiku Nuns

I couldn't wait to write haiku about skull bugs and lady cows. Then the teacher reached for another stack of books on her desk. There were four of them, all the same size. They were small and delicate looking, and she passed them around so we could look through them. "Be careful," she said, "some of the pages are thin as tracing paper, you can see right through them." Each book had the word *Haiku* on the cover. Volume 1 said Winter; Volume 2, Spring; Volume 3, Summer-Autumn; and Volume 4, Autumn Winter (see page 18). I leafed through the book looking for one of the thin pages and found a picture of a boat on the water. The page before it was one of the pages you could see through so that the title lay on top of the picture: *Boat in a Creek, by Kakei, a Chinese painter of the Southern Sung*. On another page, to my delight, there was a painting of grapes, titled *Grapes, by Nikkan, 1127-1279, A Chinese artist of the Sung Dynasty*. All the haiku in the book were arranged according to their subject — poems about dragonflies, wild geese, scarecrows, crickets, birds and beasts. "When writing haiku," said the teacher, "it was traditional to include a word that referred to a season. They called them *kigo* words, so if you mentioned cherry blossoms, it meant spring, and if you mentioned a crow, it was summer. Wild geese meant late fall or winter. That's why these four books of haiku are arranged according to the season of the year."

Each of the four books were written by the same person, R. H. Blyth. "What does R. H. stand for?" I asked.

"Reginald Horace," she said.

This sent us into gales of laughter. We repeated the name several times with an exaggerated English accent. Reginald Horace Blyth. After a few minutes of this, the teacher quieted us down. She took the books back and flipped through them until she came to the page she was looking for.

"Remember we were talking about Onitsura, who wrote his first poem when he was eight?" she asked "Well, here's Chiyo-Jo. She was the younger sister of Mukai Kyorai, one of Basho's ten disciples. Chiyo-Jo started writing haiku when she was only ten. Her poems were even better than her brother's."

Donald Zelanka sat in the back row by the window. Most of us wore khaki pants and sneakers, but he wore pressed slacks and black shoes with tiny holes in the tip, as if he were a businessman on his way to work. We carried our books in a schoolbag. He had a briefcase. Donald was constantly clearing his sinuses with nasal spray, making that sucking sound with his nose. He didn't like being called Don. "My name is Donald," he'd correct us with a smirk, and we'd tease him, "You mean like Donald Duck!"

The teacher continued. "Tagami Kikusha-ni was married at sixteen and had been writing haiku since she was a teenager. Her husband died when she was twenty-four, and in samurai custom, she shaved her head and became a nun." She pursed her lips and drummed her fingers on the desk. "Kaga no Chiyo started writing haiku when she was ten. When she was nineteen, she got married, so she took the name of Chiyo-Jo, to indicate that she was married. When she was only twenty-four, her husband died and the following year her little boy died. After her husband died, she became a nun, too, calling herself Chiyo-Ni."

"Did they all become nuns when their husbands died?" asked Hope Yellen. All the boys in class turned to look at her. As beautiful as Hope was, her placid demeanor made me imagine that she might become a nun one day.

The Year of the Dog
The Year of the Monkey
The Year of the Bird

The teacher flipped through the book, then stopped and read a page to herself. She became thoughtful and spoke so quietly, it seemed she was speaking only to Hope, or to herself. "Whether they were haiku writers or not, women often entered monasteries after their husbands died because they had no other way to make a living. Chigetsu was ten years older than Basho. She married a freight agent, and eventually studied with Basho. She became one of the four most famous poets of her era. She was fifty when her husband died. After that, she became a nun. Her son, Otokuni, also studied with Basho." Then she addressed the whole class again. "Many of the haiku poets were samurai warriors. Learning to write haiku was part of their training, especially after the wars were over. Samurai, like Basho's father, were warriors, but were expected to be cultured as well. Many of them were sent off to learn the art of samurai when they were very young. Would you like to hear the first haiku Basho ever wrote?" The idea of Basho, who was being trained to be a samurai warrior, writing a poem when he was nine years old intrigued us. She then got up and wrote the haiku on the blackboard before reciting it for us.

Oh! It's the friend
of the dog and the monkey!
The year of the bird!

"He was only nine when he wrote that?" I asked.

"Well, maybe he was ten or eleven," she said. "We're not really sure. But it's the first poem of his that we know about. The Japanese gave their years names, such as the year of the dog or the year of the monkey. When Basho was ten years old, it was the year of the bird. Basho was pretty clever. He knew the story of Momotaro, a boy who slew demons with the help of his three friends: a dog, a pheasant, and a monkey."

"I get it!" I said. "The boy who slew those dragons had the help of a dog and a monkey, with the pheasant in-between. That would be Basho, the bird. So the bird comes between the dog and the monkey!"

Making Magic With Words

Basho had made a kind of joke, but he did it in the form of a haiku — that was revelatory to me. A haiku could contain more than images, ideas, sounds. It could contain stories, fairy tales, even jokes. After that, I felt like a scientist in his lab, concocting various compounds using seventeen syllables. So many of my school days were shrouded in family drama, I had trouble paying attention in school, especially after my parents had a fight, fearful that my father would start drinking again or that my mother would be on the warpath when I got home, punishing me for any slight infraction. But these poems distracted me from all that.

I had always liked magic tricks. My father went to New York once and came home with several of them in a box: the one where a red silk handkerchief changed into a blue silk handkerchief, the one where a black ball in a red vase disappeared only to reappear under a pillow on the sofa, and my favorite, where someone picked a card from the deck and I told them to concentrate on the card as I pretended to read their minds. "You're thinking of the king of spades," I'd announce, as if hit by a bolt of lightning. Now, I could make magic with words.

Kaga no Chiyo (1703-1775)

"My favorite haiku poet is Chiyo-Jo," the teacher said, "probably the greatest of the women haiku poets. Remember she wrote the haiku about fireflies."

"Did she know Basho?" asked Hope.

"No, she was born about twenty years after Basho died. For a long time after, she was almost as famous as Basho. When she was sixteen, a haiku master named Kagami Shiki visited her house, and many of the haiku poets from her village came by. They all wrote haiku back and forth. Afterwards, he praised her poems above all the other poets. Her haiku was published in more than a hundred books. She was so famous that the lord of Kaga paid her to make thirteen fans and hanging scrolls with her poems on them, and the lord Kaga gave them as a gift to a visiting diplomat from Korea. Not everyone thought she was a good poet. Some said she didn't write real haiku, just short poems. Shiki's most famous disciple, Takahama Kyoshi, said many bad things about her poetry. He thought they didn't have enough emotion in them. I think many of the people who criticized her poems did so because she was a woman, and others just didn't like them because they were funny or sad, or maybe the emotion that was in them made the critics uncomfortable.

"What did she write about?" I asked.

"Oh, lots of things. When she was just starting to write haiku when she was a little girl, there were no haiku teachers in the small village she lived in, a long way away from the larger towns. Rogembo, a famous writer and teacher of haiku, once happened to visit her village during a poetry pilgrimage. Chiyo-Jo called at his inn and politely applied to him for instruction. Because she was a girl, he assumed she had no talent, so he gave her a very tough assignment. The most common subject, but also the most difficult, was to write a poem about the *hototogisu*."

"What's that?"

"The hototogisu is a cuckoo bird," she said. "When the hototogisu opens its mouth, the inside is bright red, the color of blood. The hototogisu sings all the time, day and night, especially when the moon is bright. It even sings when it's flying. Sometimes, its song is happy, and sometimes its sad, but it's the same song every time: coo-coo-coo. That's why we call it a cuckoo. Some people say that after it has sung its song eight thousand and eight times, it dies. That's why they also call it 'the bird of time,' or 'the messenger of death,' or 'the bird of disappointed love.' After it dies, they say, it flies from this world to the next and back again."

"So what happened when the girl had to write a poem about the . . . . hoto . . . togisu?" I asked.

"Ah," she said. Then she opened one of the desk draws and pulled out a big blue book with gold letters on the cover. It was old and made creaking noises when she opened it. "This book was published many years ago," she said. "It's very special, called Haiku Poems: Ancient and Modern." It was filled with colorful pictures with Japanese writing. She carefully turned the pages until she came to a picture of Chiyo-Jo wearing a beautiful silk robe. She was kneeling on the floor reading a book. The teacher walked around the room and let us look at the picture. "She's only sixteen years old in this painting," said the teacher.

"So what happened with the old teacher?" I asked.

"The famous old poet was quite rude. He walked into the

next room and fell asleep and left Chiyo-Jo alone to work on her haiku. He slept till morning. At dawn, Chiyo-Jo handed him a perfect haiku." The teacher got up and wrote it on the blackboard in Japanese.

hototogisu
hototogisu tote
akeni keri.

"Can you read that?" she asked.

"Hototogisu means the cuckoo bird!" someone shouted out.

"Yes, and *hototogisu tote* means "cuckoo again." The last line is hard to translate, but let's say it means, 'dawn is here,' or 'morning comes.' A better way to translate it would be this way." Then she wrote the haiku in English next to the Japanese and listed the number of syllables as well.

Cuckoo.	*hototogisu*	5 syllables
Cuckoo again.	*hototogisu tote*	7 syllables
Cuckoo up at dawn.	*Akeni keri*	5 syllables

A few of us got it and started laughing. "So," said our teacher, "Chiyo-Jo was saying, in that last line, that the old poet was a cuckoo who slept all night. It has a double meaning. She's writing about the hototogisu and writing about the famous old poet who so rudely dismissed her and fell asleep. The master was humiliated by a child, but he was also struck with admiration and told her that she was already a master of haiku and didn't need an instructor. Just keep writing, he told her."

The teacher wrote several more haiku on the board, all by Chiyo-Jo.

even though
the puddle is temporary,
the frog enjoys it

first snow--
if I write it disappears,
it disappears

I also saw the moon
and so I say goodbye
to this world

The teacher sat back down, opened her poetry book and said, "Her most famous haiku, though, was written after the death of her young son."

"How old was he?" we asked.

"When he died?" she asked. "About your age."

The Dragonfly Hunter

I thought about Martin Shapiro. He was not a good friend, but he lived down the street and sometimes I'd see him at synagogue. A year before his bar-mitzvah, he died of leukemia. I went to his funeral with my parents and there he was, lying in the coffin, his face white and stony. It was the first time I had thought about death that way. You didn't have to be old to die.

The teacher went to the blackboard again and wrote Chiyo's haiku, the one she wrote after her son died. "This haiku," she said, "is titled Boji wo Omo, which means 'Longing for a Departed Child.'"

tombo-tsuri
kyo wa doko made
ittas yara

My son, the dragonfly
hunter, where is he now?
In what fields does he play?

We sat for awhile looking at it on the blackboard. Sometimes in my backyard I'd catch a mosquito hawk, sneaking up on it as it sat on a leaf or the low branch of a tree. Its long wings would go out and up, up and down as it rested there. If you were quiet and careful, with the tips of your fingers, you could grab those long wings when they came together and lift the mosquito hawk right up. Then I'd walk over to another tree, another low branch or leaf, and deposit him there, then watch him fly away. I was a dragonfly hunter, too.

"That's an English translation from the Japanese," she said, "and as you can see, it's not exactly 5-7-5 syllables. Another person who translated the haiku used the phrase, 'my little boy, who ran away.' He said that it was closer to what Chiyo wrote. Why do you think she said that he had run away?"

Chiyo-jo standing beside a well. This woodcut by Utagawa Kuniyoshi illustrates her most famous haiku: she begs for water rather than disturb the vines of a morning glory that became entangled in the bucket by a well.

I thought about it. If I died, would my mother tell someone that I'd run away? I raised my hand. "Maybe," I said, "the mother didn't want to say the word 'died.'"

A Zen Worthy Haiku

Then the teacher brightened the mood. "Remember how Chiyo-Jo proved to the old poet that he had underestimated her? Well, after her husband died, she, too, decided to enter a monastery. The Zen master of the monastery didn't take her seriously, either, especially because she was a poet, and he considered poetry a 'worldly attachment.' So he asked her how a single haiku could be Zen-worthy. In Zen, a thousand meanings can be found in a single thought. So he asked her to write a haiku that could show that." Then our teacher went up to the blackboard again and wrote the verse in Japanese, to show us the 5-7-5 syllable pattern, then the English translation:

tsuki mo mite
ware wa kono yo o
kashiku o kana.

a hundred different gourds
from the mind
of one vine

"The Zen master," she said, "was humbled by the excellence of this haiku and accepted her into his order."

"Did she write haiku when she lived in the monastery?" Hope asked.

"Yes," said the teacher. "One morning, she went to the well to get water, but a morning glory had grown all around the bucket. Chiyo-Jo marveled at how beautiful it looked. She couldn't bring herself to unwind the tendril, so she took her empty bucket and begged her neighbor for water. Afterwards, she wrote a haiku that has been celebrated for centuries." Then the teacher wrote the haiku on the board, first in Japanese, then in English.

asaguo ni	a morning glory clings
tsurube torare-te	round the rope of my well-bucket,
morai mizu	so I beg for water

The teacher sat back down at her desk. "When Basho's friend died," she said, setting the book down, "he left the home of the lord and went to live in a monastery. And then he traveled, taking long hiking trips all over Japan. That's when he wrote many of his poems."

My head swirled with images of camping out and catching fish in the river and cooking them on the campfire. I'd never gone camping, except one time when my parents sent me to a summer camp in Mississippi. The camp was next to a muddy river I hated swimming in because of the jelly-fish. But at night we built campfires and roasted hot-dogs and toasted marshmallows. I imagined doing that and writing haiku in my sleeping bag.

Kobayashi Issa (1763-1827)

The idea of being in the Basho club became quite appealing. But there was one problem. The other two Frogmen, Max and Jerry—well, we weren't great friends. I liked Basho's haiku, but I didn't want to be in their club, I didn't want to be one of the "Frogmen."

I also found myself drawn to the poems of Kobayashi Issa, the humanist whose miserable childhood, poverty, and sad life were evoked in such tender poems. His mother died when he was only two, an age at which he was still nursed at her breast. His grandmother asked neighbors and even passers-by to nurse the child for her. His father re-married, and Issa's cruel stepmother often punished him by withholding food. In his famous autobiography he wrote, "I was beaten 100 times a day, 1,000 times a month, and in the 365 days of the year, there was never one when my eyes were not swollen." The stepmother kept him in old and shabby clothes, even on festival days when all the other children got new clothes. No one would play with him, so he'd sit alone, apart from the others. He claims he wrote this haiku when he was only six and saw a fledgling bird that had just fallen from its nest.

Come with me,
let's play together, swallow
without any mother

Actually, he used the word "sparrow" in the original poem, but a picture Issa later drew to illustrate the poem shows a swallow, so now it's customary to call the bird a swallow. Another poem he wrote while still a young boy was this one:

Once more in vain
the stepchild bird
opens its beak

A Cup of Tea

Issa finally left home at thirteen, right after the death of his grandmother, and joined the hordes of migrant workers streaming into Edo (Tokyo) to provide that city its labor force. He went home for a brief visit, but being poor and unsuccessful, he was again rejected by his stepmother. The next we hear of him, he was twenty-five, mentioned as a member of a haiku club in which he'd adopted the pen name of Issa, or "Cup of Tea." This information was enough for me to romanticize my own emotionally-wrought childhood. When the teacher handed out a mimeographed piece of paper with some of Issa's poems, I spent a long time trying to fathom his haiku about the naughty child:

naughty child
though tethered calling
fireflies

I could imagine being the naughty child, but I wasn't sure what tethered meant, or why he was calling fireflies. Maybe so he could see while hiding in a dark closet. And this one. The idea that someone being drunk could be mentioned in a poem shocked me.

Kobayashi Issa, a pen name meaning cup-of-tea.
Portrait drawn by Muramatsu Shunpo (1772-1858)

in ceremonial robe
he's fallen down drunk —
blossom shade

We lived in what was then called a "shotgun" house: a screened front porch, living room, dining room, kitchen, two small bedrooms with a bathroom between, and a backyard that was no more than a cement slab with a zinc washtub and a small shed. My bed at the back window faced the washtub. How many nights I lay there, watching the rain fill the washtub, listening to it pound the sheet-metal roof of the shed, while from the bedroom on the other side of the bathroom came the voices of my parents, arguing over my father's drinking. When Issa juxtaposed poetic images with something harsh, I knew what he was talking about because I had experienced the same thing.

among the dewdrops
of this dew-drop world—
a quarrel

Going for the Pratfall

I was a cut-up in school, the class clown. Maybe that persona came from the need to cover the child's sorrow, but lo and behold, Issa, the wounded child, was a cut-up too, capable of humor, as well as profundity.

Hey boatman
no peeing on the moon
in the river

pointing
at the fart bug
the laughing buddha

Yes, Issa was the poet for me. He made me laugh, he made me feel less alone, but what I liked best was the way he made fun of the writing of poetry itself.

first winter rain
and all the poets fill
this world with haiku

Afterall, we haiku poets, young as we were, also sat looking out on the gray day, filling our composition books with rain-soaked haiku. That poem by Issa showed that the poet can stumble into a puddle of water, as well as rhapsodize beneath a rain-soaked tree. This idea became fundamental to my own sensibility as a poet: When in doubt, go for the pratfall. I knew that Issa was not only making fun of poetry, but of himself as well. It was my introduction to the idea that poetry was too serious a business to take itself too seriously.

The Hazy Moons of Haiku

And oh, the moon! How the moon inspired us poets! It wasn't unusual for Japanese haiku poets to use the same moon image over and over again in different ways. Here's a few such haiku by different poets, the last three of which use the same image, "the hazy moon."

The moon in the water,
broken and broken again.
Still it is there.
-Choshu

Scooping up the moon
in the wash-basin,
and spilling it.
-Ryuho

The lowing of the cow
in the cow-shed,
under the hazy moon.
-Shiki

Down the river
the sound of a net thrown—
a hazy moon.
-Taigi

Carrying a girl
across the river;
the hazy moon.
-Shiki

On a clear night, with the full moon lighting up my backyard, I wrote haiku with full moons, half-moons, moons obscured by dark clouds, moons seen through moss-covered trees, moons so bright you could read by them, and yes, hazy moons, as well. I was eleven years old, rainclouds and full moons made the poet in me swoon as I rushed to find paper and pencil. When I came across another poem by Onitsura, I couldn't wait to show it to my fellow haiku poets.

Today's moon:
Will there be anyone
not taking up his pen.

I understood, even then, that he was making fun of poets writing poems about the moon. For awhile, our Issa club delighted in writing haiku in which we made fun of ourselves writing about the moon. We also wrote haiku that included jokes and racy slang, and made fun of our teachers, especially Mr. Hauth, our history teacher, who gave out more demerits than anyone. In November, when the harvest moon hung low over the horizon, I wrote this haiku and passed it around to much laughter.

Angry moon, strange moon,
moon like rotten cantelope —
there goes Hauth's big head.

Flowering Thorns

The concept of juxtaposing images wasn't lost on me. This is also a principle of comedy, the switch from one image or idea to another. Haiku and jokes had something in common. Later on, we were to learn that there was a name for haiku that's humorous — *senryu*. Issa's humor is what drew me to his poems, yet I knew there was something deeper at work. Funny or not, there was something sad in them. All those years he spent away, wanting to go home. After his father died, he went home to claim the property due him, but his stepmother and half-brother had changed his father's will.

The place where I was born:
all I come to – all I touch –nothing
but thorn-blossoms.

Thorn-flowers, *bara no hana*, were a common image in haiku, but no one used that image as woefully as Issa. We can compare Issa's poem with one that Buson wrote: Issa's thorn flowers represent his broken heart; Buson's capture a physical image, not a state of mind.

Flowering thorn
how like the roads about the place
where I was born.

I later learned that Issa's misfortunes continued. He took to the road, much like Basho had done. He described himself in this period of his life as: "Rambling to the west, wandering to the east, there is a madman who never stays in one place. In the morning, he eats breakfast in Kazusa; by evening, he finds lodging in Musashi. Helpless as a white wave, apt to vanish like a bubble in froth." When he finally got possession of his home and property (the village mayor decided that the Kobayashi house would be partitioned and that Issa was to get one half of it), he returned home for good and married Kiku, one of the village girls. His happiness is best expressed in this evocative haiku:

Amazing –
in the house I was born,
seeing this moon.

Kiku was half his age, and in ten years bore him five children, all dying from diseases such as smallpox, and, in one case, from accidental suffocation. After the death of one of his sons, Issa wrote this haiku, invoking the *nadeshiki*, the delicate daisy symbolic of virtue.

Why did the daisy
break, oh why
did it break?

A Dew-Drop World

After the death of another child, he invoked the image of the *tsuyu*, the dew drop, which became one of his most inspired images.

A dewdrop fades away:	*tsuyu chiru ya*
This world is dirty, I have	*musai kono yo*
no business being here.	*ni yo nashi to*

Especially devastating was the death of his youngest daughter, a loss he recounted in his journal, *My Spring*. Her death inspired one of his most famous verses:

this world	*tsuyu-no-yo wa*
is a dewdrop world	*tsuyu-no-yo nagara*
yes . . . but	*sari nagara*

The image of the dew drop world was invoked in many of his haiku, especially those written after the death of his beloved wife, Kiku.

Death Poems

Despite his pain, Issa found humor and joy in the smallest of moments, such as the discovery of a snail on his doorstep after a spring rain. Those haiku were silly without being unworthy of serious attention. We could relate to that. As a Buddhist, Issa brimmed with compassion and respect for his fellow beings, even snails and the fly that visited him during his morning meal. He was also a bit off-kilter, giving the world an absurd glance. He called his modest, unkempt home a *kuzu ya*, a "Trash House." He compared a cranky Buddhist to a croaking frog. He made fun of himself when he lost his way, stepping into a pond by mistake during a meditative midnight walk, yet elevated that moment to poke fun at his own sense of self-importance, which tickled me no end.

Scrawny frog, hang tough!
Issa
is here.

But Issa had seen too much in his life, lost too much, grieved too often, to resort to the placid platitudes of a Zen master accepting the world as it is. Under a cloak of calm assurance was a brutal streak.

Writing shit about new snow
for the rich
is not art.

Of all his poems, his "death poem" is one that poses the most interesting problem of translation.

From wash tub to wash tub —	*tarai kara tarai* —
this journey, this life —	*ni utsuru* —
it's all blah, blah, blah.	*chimpunken*

Tarai can be translated as wash tub, wash bowl, or wash basin. Your body is washed at birth and when you die. Between both, life is nothing more than . . . *chimpunkan,* literally "shifting jargon," but idiomatically, it can be translated as foolishness, poppycock, balderdash, fiddlesticks, razzle-dazzle, nonsense, etc. The poem is cynical, but also humorous, *chimpunkan.* I chose to translate that word as "blah blah blah," since he's possibly alluding to all the haiku he'd written, the stuff and nonsense of poetry.

The Bats vs The Frogmen

Basho I revered, but Issa I loved. When I thought of forming an Issa club, Eugene St. Cyr and Oriole MacInroth decided to join up. Like me, they were champions of Issa. But what would we call ourselves? We searched his haiku for possibilities:

in winter wind
the pig giggles
in his sleep.

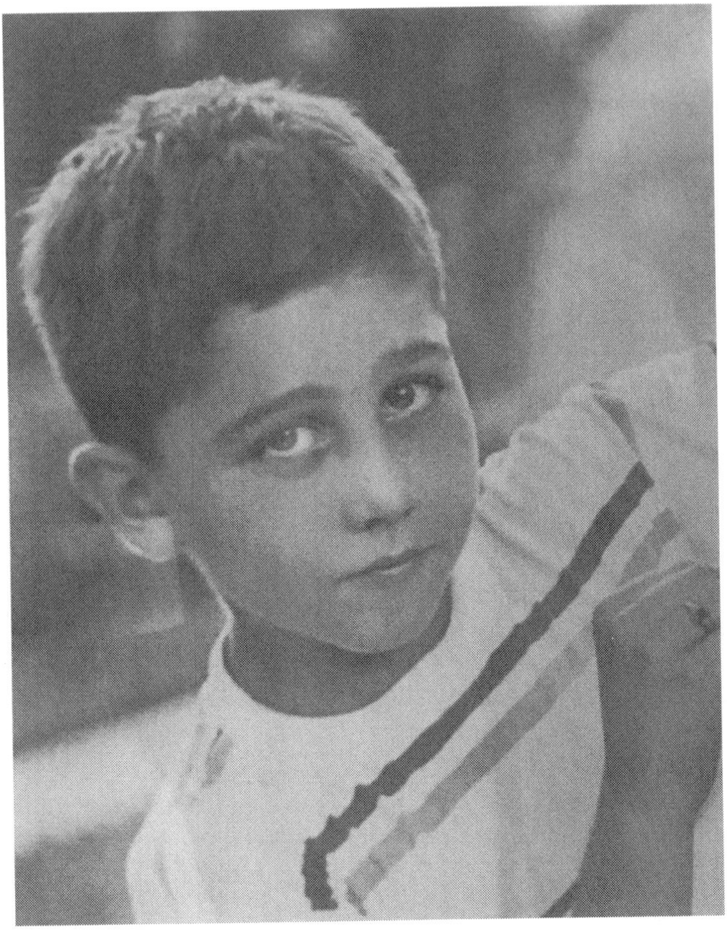

Haiku Poet, 1952

We considered that image for a moment, then Gene said, "I don't want to be a giggling pig." We kept looking:

in winter rain
toward the heart of darkness . . .
honking geese

Oriole got testy: "I'm not a honking goose," she said. So we kept looking, coming across a series of haiku that mentioned birds or insects or animals.

the lucky mouse
crosses then goes back . . .
first ice

on the sleeping dog
gently, a hat . . .
a leaf

on the tip of
Buddha's nose . . .
a fart bug

the stray cat also
picks this inn . . .
bush clover blooming

into the snake's hole
O foolish
mouse

the praying mantis
hangs by one hand . . . .
temple bell

crawling out
the wild dog's hole
a katydid

like people
an upright scarecrow
can't be found

the copycat sparrows
fly along . . .
migrating birds

You Say "Pufferfish," I Say "Mountain Pigeon" Let's Call the Whole Thing Off

None of those possibilities appealed to us. Gene didn't want to be a sleeping dog or praying mantis, and Oriole didn't want to be referred to as an upright scarecrow or a lucky mouse. None of us wanted to be called foolish mice, stray cats, wild dogs, copycat sparrows, migrating birds, or farting bugs. Other haiku mentioned snails, spiders, garden snakes, crooked chrysanthemums, playful mice, hooting owls, jittery deer, woodpeckers, mountain pigeons, autumn butterflies, buzzing dragonflies, tickling crickets, love-making locusts, aristocratic crows, ghost-like foxes, waiting wolves, gargoyles, and monkeys scooping up pufferfish. We couldn't face off with the Frogmen with names like that.

Oriole crossed her arms, petulant. "I'm not a pufferfish," she said. We kept reading, making notes as we went.

"I'm not a mountain pigeon," Oriole said.

"Well, I'm not a tickling cricket," said Gene.

"Well, I'm not a hooting owl," I said.

Gene declared somewhat officiously: "I'm certainly not a love-making locust."

"Eeew," said Oriole.

"Do I look like an aristocratic crow?" I said, doing my best imitation of a crow strutting before the members of Parliament. Gene and Oriole laughed.

"Laughing Buddhas!" I exclaimed. I pointed to one of Issa's haiku with that image:

pointing
at the fart bug . . .
laughing Buddha

Gene and I liked that one, but Oriole wasn't comfortable identifying herself with the Buddha's big belly. Gene and I were both a little — how did the clothing manufacturers put it? — "husky." So the laughing Buddha was fitting, as far as Gene and I were concerned, but Oriole would not be swayed.

"I'm not a laughing Buddha," she said, crossing her arms again.

The Bats

We huddled together during recess, trying to find the right nickname, and in the following haiku (which shows that seventeen Japanese *onji* do not always equal seventeen English syllables), we found it.

Bats flying
in a village without birds
at evening mealtime.

"The Bats!" we all yelled. We would call ourselves "The Bats." With our new nickname, my passion for the Issa club grew. It also helped that I had a crush on Oriole Macinroth. She was a Christian Scientist, and when she fell from the jungle gym and broke her nose during Phys-Ed, she came to school without having seen a doctor. Her nose wasn't the same after that, but that's when I found myself attracted to her. It was her nose, something I can't explain to this day. Maybe it was the imperfection of it that made her approachable, or perhaps it gave her the air of a wounded warrior, but boy, I was glad she was part of our group.

So we sneeringly called ourselves "The Bats," which fit us, not because of the comic book hero Batman, but because we thought of ourselves as being a bit batty, off-the-wall goof-offs, "class clowns." I was surely the chief class clown, but Oriole and Gene came in a close second. By seventh grade we were feeling our hormonal oats, and one way to release those oats was to blurt under our breaths in a Japanese-sounding grunt the name of our haiku leader, Issa.

So during a lesson in Louisiana history, when Mr. Hauth was showing us a picture of one of the explorers planting a flag in the ground and naming the city Baton Rouge — French for "red stick" — Max and Jerry would blurt out "Basho," making it sound like a cough, so they wouldn't get a demerit from Mr. Hauth. "Cough Basho!" Seconds later, Eugene or I or Oriole would do the same with Issa, except Issa worked better as a muffled sneeze. "Cough Basho! Sneeze Issa!" When I think back on it, I marvel that our teachers were able to teach; that we were, despite the clowning around, able to learn.

Masoaka Shiki (1867-1902)

But that wasn't the end of it. There were two more masters — Shiki and Buson — and two delinquent kids who, for one reason or another, loved haiku. Like Shiki, they were the troublemakers, in jeans and tee-shirts with rolled-up sleeves, and so counted themselves as disciples of the most modern of the masters, Masoaka Shiki, the rebel and rabble rouser, the tough guy who stood up to everyone.

Shiki was the poet for Eddie Negrotto, a football player who, by high school, had grown tall and muscular. In college, he was to play for Auburn. I'm sure his ears perked up when he heard that Shiki was often credited with introducting baseball to Japan. Eddie was the first of the bunch to bring whiskey to school in a small TIPS bottle, which had originally held some kind of breath freshener, like Binaca or Listerine.

One day in sixth period, sitting in the library, Eddie passed around the TIPS bottle and we each had a few sips, imagining that we were drunker than we were. Pardon the pun, but we were less drunk than we thought and more "tipsy" than we realized. Eddie and Donald challenged us to a haiku contest. Eddie's haiku had an occasional "bad" word, like fart, or dick, or cigarette butt, and even though he was an unabashed anti-semite who later would call me kike and jew-boy when we played football in high school, I admired his courage to write poetry that wasn't "poetic" or old fashioned. Masoaka Shiki also played baseball in high-school, and perhaps that's why Eddie liked him, but his club-mate, Donald Zelanka, liked him for other reasons.

Donald was a sickly kid, always missing school for asthma attacks or bouts of the flu. Shiki was a prolific writer (a laughable understatement since he is said to have written 25,000 haiku, 4,000 in one year). He was a trouble-maker who got himself banned from public speaking as an adolescent. He was also chronically ill for a significant part of his life, eventually dying of spinal tuberculosis when he was only thirty-four years old. Perhaps Donald had a presentiment of his own death in his early thirties and related to Shiki's "sickbed" poems. In his late-teens, Shiki began coughing up blood, which explains why he adopted the pen-name Shiki from the Japanese word *hototogisu.* (It's a Japanese conceit that the cuckoo coughs up blood as it sings.) Shiki wrote many poems about cuckoos.

A temple in the hills:
the snoring from a noon siesta –
and a cuckoo's trills.

the moon begins to rise
behind the grasses; a wind stirs them;
and a cuckoo cries.

To ears
stuffed by sermons –
a cuckoo.

The Cuckoos

Thus, in response to the Basho club calling themselves "The Frogmen," and our calling ourselves "The Bats," Eddie and Donald called their Shiki club "The Cuckoos." Somewhat fitting, since I found out much later that Shiki started a new school of haiku when he was the editor of the *Nippon*, a newspaper in Tokyo. Shiki believed that the culture of the past was obsolete and it was time to reinvigorate the haiku. His group experimented with new forms, shocking the traditionalists, who called them "The Cuckoo School."

Shiki disliked the stereotypical haiku writers of the 19th Century who were known by the deprecatory term *tsukinami*, meaning "monthly," after the monthly or twice-monthly haikai gatherings that took place at the end of the 18th century, and eventually the term came to mean "trite" and "hackneyed." Eddie and Donald saw themselves as trouble-makers, getting into fights in the schoolyard, playing pranks, and even criticizing school policy to the teachers' faces. They loved to write scatalogical haiku and often used current slang for familiar body parts. They picked the perfect haiku poet under whose

Masaoka Shiki (1867-1902)
He played baseball as a teenager
and was inducted in the Japanese Baseball Hall of Fame in 2002.

banner they would march. The Cuckoos and the Bats tried to outdo each other, whether it was pulling pranks in class, or arguing over how to write haiku. The class came across a Shiki poem which could well have been written with our haiku clubs in mind:

> on how to sing
> the frog school and the cuckoo school
> are arguing

Perhaps Shiki meant that haiku to be a metaphor for all the haiku poets forming different schools. He wanted to give haiku new energy. He eventually became a war correspondent for the newspaper, covering the Sino-Japanese War, and when he returned home, he advocated the use of everyday speech in poetry instead of the refined diction of classical Japanese. Don't just imitate Basho, he said — there were thousands of haiku poets of the Edo period producing lifeless imitations of Basho's works or compositions devoid of serious intent.

Haiku was a short, economic form, but it wasn't simplistic. Rather, Shiki argued, it is the very brevity of haiku that constitutes its strength and makes it capable of expression impossible in other forms. Modern diction and contemporary sensibility could still be used in the 5-7-5 sound pattern; even the use of a seasonal reference, the *kigo*, could be effective (though, like many of the classical haiku writers, Shiki departed, at times, from that pattern). Like Ezra Pound in America, Shiki wanted poets of his day to "make it new," without giving up haiku's classical, traditional requirements.

The Birds of Haiku

When haiku rose to popularity in 16th Century Japan, it was being written only in the monasteries, or by "court" poets, those educated courtiers or rarified *mikados*. A century later, the writing of haiku spread among the general population, but the treatises elucidating correct form and rules continued to be followed. Mention of autumn moons, spring flowers, and other seasonal references (*kigo*) were mandatory. Harmless puns were common, as well as countless literary allusions and subtle variations on those literary allusions. Birds were recurring characters: a crow, the cuckoo, that strutting sparrow, the swallow, the nightingale, the bush warbler, the reed-thrush, the seagull, the woodpecker, the heron, the skylark, the kingfisher, water fowls, hawks, wrens, wild-geese, even the falcon and the dove-tailed whatchamacallit.

Over and over
the she-crow's voice
crying in the dark.
-Issa

Buson's bush warbler starred in at least fifty of his haiku:

This year's first bush warbler
so out of practice
it sounded like a mistake.

There were many poems about pheasants. This one by Basho has a most unexpected *kerij*.

The voice of the pheasant;
How I longed
for my dead parents.

Woodpeckers and hawks made frequent appearances:

Now that the eyes of the hawks
are darkened in the dusk,
the quails are chirping.
-Basho

In the far depths of the forest,
the woodpecker
and the sound of the axe.
-Buson

The woodpecker
keeps on in the same place:
Day is closing.
-Issa

Issa must have written hundreds of haiku featuring those small song-birds with their spotted brown-gray plumage.

The wren
earns his living
noiselessly.

The wren is chirruping
but it grows dusk
just the same.

Look! This lonely grave
with the wren
that is always here.

Wild geese appear in many haiku. Their northern migration begins in early spring, thus showing a complete un-Japanese disregard for the blooming of the cherry blossoms. Matsungaga Teitoku's haiku chastised the wretched wild goose who would prefer pudding rather than praise.

dumplings before cherries,
he says, and back he goes,
the wild goose.

As it was in the 17th century, so it was in the 20th, where the reference to the wild goose elicites another comparison in the following anonymous haiku:

undergraduates,
by and large shabby:
wild geese flying off.

Any important event in life may stir the haiku poet, but above all it is nature that has been the chief inspirer. The Japanese in general have this notion that man is not only part of nature but that the two are one. Much of Japan is still mountainous, wild, unsettleable. The unmelted snow in spring, the cherry-blossoms, summer fireflies or morning glories, autumn's harvest moon, its red maples leaves and the first chill winds, the hailstorms and withered fields of winter — all these have been the inspiration of Japanese haiku, and they can still be found today, however startlingly readjusted. Trees were also customary. Buson mentions plum trees and weeping willows in dozens of poems:

These two plum trees
I love the way
one blooms early and one late.

I was going to hammer
the post sticking up
but there was the weeping willow.

The Flowers of Haiku

If a poet mentioned a particular flower in one haiku, he or she probably mentioned it in a hundred: wild roses, lilies, morning glories, birdweed blossoms, irises, miscanthus, forsythia blossoms, cockscombs, honey locust blossoms, wisteria, cherry blossoms, weeping willows, plum blossoms, poppies, sponge gourd blossoms, bushclover, pear blossoms, chrysanthemums, asters, buckwheat, wild azaleas, narcissus, violets, safflowers, mallow flowers, hollyhocks, smart weed, duck weed, knotweed, knotgrass, flowers-of-the-hour, mustard flowers, pampas grass, peonies, and goldenrod (sometimes translated as "harlot flower," "lady lily," "maiden flower," or occasionally, "old woman's meal," since the word for goldenrod is *ominaeshi*, and *omina* can mean "old woman"), and rape-flowers (from rapeseed, known as oilseed rape, often consumed as a vegetable, deriving its name from the Latin for turnip, *rapa* or *rapum*). For each poet, a particular flower was mentioned so often, it became a character associated with that poet. Buson wrote about twenty haiku on the subject of peonies.

The Fruits and Vegetables of Haiku

The same was true for fruits and vegetables. I tried counting the number of times a poet made reference to a specific fruit or vegetable, and ran out of patience. Of fruits, there were: apples, oranges, pears, tangerines, melons, persimmons, and bananas;

of vegetables: pumpkins, eggplants, green onions, red peppers, radishes, and mushrooms. I came across this one by Shiki:

a red apple
a green apple
on top of the table

One day, Shiki decided to go through his haiku box to sort some of the poems, and ended up writing this haiku:

I catalogued
three thousand haiku
on two persimmons

If ever there was a case of a particular fruit being associated with a poet, it was persimmons with Shiki. He preferred the older Japanese variety, which was quite astringent. His doctor limited him to three a day — persimmons, that is, not haiku. His most famous "persimmon haiku" references the Horyu Temple, the oldest wooden building in the world, venerated since it was built in the seventh century. It contains wonderful, old wall paintings and sculptures. But it's difficult for someone who isn't from Japan to understand the significance of Shiki's juxtaposition of Horyu-ji and the bitter persimmon.

Persimmons: as I chew,
a temple bell begins to boom
from Horyu-ji.

So much is suggested; so little is specified. Shiki juxtaposes taste and hearing. The taste of that astringent fruit sends a shudder through the body, while the boom of the Buddhist temple bell reverberates in the chest. The immediacy of the persimmon, the faraway sound of the bell, both call out to Shiki. This is an example of how haiku's brevity can suggest expansive associations.

Snakes, Snails, Spiders and Ants

There is a fine line between cliché and the tried-and-true image. It was mandatory that traditional haiku reference seasons and birds, so long as there was variation in how the subject was handled. If the poet didn't name the season, he mentioned an image associated with that season. In Western poetry, we might consider these recurring images redundant or cliché, but in haiku, with syllables at a premium, the images were a kind of short-hand for complex experiences understood by the readers of Japanese haiku: wild geese, spring grass, yellow roses, rice-planting, harvest moon, morning snow, willow branches, barley leaves, plum blossoms, the rains of May, November mist, tree frogs, shadows of the pines, groves of bamboos, sleeping skylarks. Among the deutzia blossoms and lily flowers were fleas, flies, mosquitoes, ants, and even the ubiquitous arachnid.

> Don't worry, spiders,
> I keep house
> casually.
> -Issa

And snails and snakes! Don't get me started. Snails and snakes are frequent protagonists in haiku.

> A snail,
> one horn short, one long—
> What troubles him?
> -Buson

> Under the evening moon
> the snail
> is stripped to the waist
> -Issa

> The snake slid away,
> but the eyes that stared at me
> remained in the grass.
> -Kyoshi

> little snail, no different
> asleep
> awake
> -Issa

The snake fleeing away,
the mountain is silent.
This lily flower!
-Shiki

An Old Hermit Named Dave

Basho and Issa helped transform haiku into a powerful literary form that ceased to belong only to Japanese nobility. Within a century, however, writing haiku once again became a quaint pastime practiced by exalted shoguns and ruling warriors. Like many such forms of the European Renaissance (at that time, Japan was experiencing its own late Medieval Period), haiku from this time was little more than a display of refined wit. Eventually it became a national fad, called *haikai*, from two words meaning "sportive" and "pleasantry." Haikai became a popular literary sport or social activity among the common people, merchants and farmers reacting to the formality of earlier eras by writing in the diction of natural speech. Sometimes the poems were comic, verging on the scatalogical, not unlike limericks that operate as dirty jokes—"There once was a hermit named Dave . . . ," etc.

It was Buson who rescued it from a trivial pursuit to an art form worthy of serious attention, but over the course of the next century, the writing of haiku once again became mannered and quaint, and by the end of the 19th century, it was no longer taken seriously by the poets of the day. Once again, it needed rescue, and this time it came in the person of Shiki, who elevated the form to artistry, but a form that could also contain political satire and modern diction, even the coarse language of the street and the stance of the anti-establishment rebel.

In our sixth grade class, the Cuckoos, taking their cue from Shiki, became our resident rabble rousers and anti-formalists, writing haiku that would have landed them in hot water were the teacher to read them. Shiki had been a critic of Basho, which irritated the Frogmen no end. We took our haiku seriously, even as we goofed around with it. During history class, while Jerry and Max were coughing up Basho, and Eugene, Oriole and I were sneezing Issa, Donald and Eddie would get the hiccups, and at the end of each hiccup there'd be a squeaky, high-pitched "Shiki!" Thus, our musical performance: Cough! Basho!

Sneeze! Issa! Hiccup! Shiki!

Sketching From Life

Eventually, I drifted away from Issa and moved toward Shiki's haiku, shifting my club membership as I did so, probably because of this poem, which made me think of my father:

> Sounds of snoring—
> a plate and a sake bottle
> set outside the mosquito net.

Like the world of the Japanese intellectual at that time, Shiki was influenced by Western culture. He favored the painterly style of Buson and was particularly interested in the European concept of *plein-air* painting, which he adapted to create a style of haiku as a kind of nature sketch in words, an approach called *shasei*, literally "sketching from life."

Yosa Buson (1716-1783)

Buson was the fourth of the great masters of haiku poetry. A century after Basho, he led a movement he called "Back to Basho," following in the footsteps of his idol by traveling through the wilds of northern Houshu, which had been the inspiration for Basho's famous travel diary *The Narrow Road into the Interior* (*Oku-no-Hosomichi*). Buson popularized his views by publishing his haiku and essays in newspapers, often illustrating them with artwork. He's recognized as one of the greatest masters of *haiga* (an art form in which painting is combined with haiku or haikai prose). His affection for painting can be seen in the visual emphasis of his haiku based on his painterly style as an artist.

> In nooks and corners
> Cold remains:
> Flowers of the plum.

> Tethered horse;
> snow
> in both stirrups.

Yosa Buson (1716-1784) was known in his day primarily as a painter.
Drawing by Matsumura Goshun.

Is that the sound of tears
shed by geese on lakes in China?
A haze veils the spring moon.

There's Always Hope

The club of Buson had but one member, Hope Yellen. Oh my god, Hope Yellen. By seventh grade, Hope carried herself with the grace of a goddess. Most of the boys in the class had a crush on her, but Hope's head was in the clouds and she barely noticed us. We flattered her, teased her, even ignored her, but nothing worked. She barely gave us the time of day. Hope floated through our pre-adolescent lives like a creature from another planet.

One day, Eddie passed around a haiku written on a scrap of paper, the last line of which was the double-entendred, five-syllabled prayer, "But there's always Hope." I have no idea why she liked Buson, but when it came to the haiku clubs, Hope played her part. Whenever we'd go into our haiku symphony (especially when a substitute teacher had to endure us for a day), it would begin with the initial cough of Basho, then the sneeze of Issa, followed by the hiccups of Shiki, all melodically resolved by Hope's beautifully drawn out soprano.

(cough) Basho!
(sneeze) Issa!
(hiccup) Shiki!
Buuuuuuu Sonnnnnnnn.

But there was one more tweak to our symphonic haiku quartet—rock & roll. After Basho, Issa, and Shiki, all of us would chime in with a line from that 1954 recording by The Cheers, "Bazooom! I Need Your Lovin.'" Buson had morphed into Bazoooom!

A Weeping Willow

Intially, Hope was a member of our Shiki club, and it was Shiki who led her to Buson. Shiki was the poet who modernized Japan's two forms of traditional verse, the haiku and the tanka. Buson had fallen out of favor, and after his death his work was overshadowed by the popularity of Basho. That all changed with Shiki's treatise *Haiku Poet Buson* in 1897, in which he analyzed Buson's work from the viewpoint of modern realism, declaring that Buson was "equal to, or even surpassed Basho." At the time, Japan was in the process of transforming itself into a modern nation, and haiku seemed like a relic of the past. Shiki took Buson as his inspiration in establishing and leading a reform movement that successfully revived haiku as a viable poetic form for the 20th century.

As Buson had led a movement to return to the aesthetics of Basho, Shiki led a movement three centuries later to return to the aesthetics of Buson. Like Basho, Buson often provided prefatory comments to his haiku, and even invented a form called *haishi* in which he blended Chinese and Japanese verse styles. Some say haishi are the forerunners of Japanese modern poetry, a hundred years ahead of its time.

Shiki's work as a war correspondent took him to China. When he returned he started a new school of haiku known as the "Nihon School." Later, he started a magazine called *Hototogishu* (The *Cuckoo*), which became the most influential haiku publication in Japan.

Hope liked Shiki's haiku, but like Shiki, she was her own person, even in sixth grade. She liked to paint, and perhaps that was her attraction to Buson— he was also a painter. In any case, she announced one day that she was forming her own Buson club, and that she would be its only member. She called herself "The Weeping Willow," from a poem by Buson:

Now that the plum blossoms
have fallen
the weeping willow is all by itself.

Hope had also read Buson's account of a Chinese legend in which a man was given the elixir of life, only to have his wife steal it and drink it. This turned her into a supernatural being, and she flew away and became the spirit of the moon. "I'm the spirit of the moon," Hope told us one afternoon as we were waiting for art club to start. She then unfolded a copy of Buson's haiku:

Is there woman here somewhere
who would steal the elixir of life
in the hazy spring moonlight?

Japanese Haiku, Peter Pauper Press, Mount Vernon, New York, 1955
Two-Hundred Twenty Examples of Seventeen-Syllable Poems

Thinking back on it, I realize that we knew very little about Hope. We idolized her for the way she glided through the halls, neither overly confident nor unduly insecure. I can't imagine her as a real person, as a seventy-year old now, for instance. She was and remains mythic in my mind. Was Hope a weeping willow, was she a spirit of the moon? Did she marry, have kids, teach them to write haiku? Does she remember me today, as I remember her? I doubt it. Hope was a luminous being to the boys. Her light left us in the dark. My guess is that we were shadowy figures to her, fellow travelers through childhood stumbling together onto something remarkable — haiku — which linked us in spirit, if not in flesh.

Peter Pauper Books

We kept the clubs going even into junior high school — Basho's Frogmen, Issa's Bats, Shiki's Cuckoos, and Buson's Weeping Willow. On the last day of 7th grade, our haiku teacher gave us all a present: a small book of haiku titled *Japanese Haiku.* She called them Peter Pauper books. "That's because even a pauper could afford them," she said. They were slightly bigger than a deck of cards and fit neatly into your hand. No more than 60 pages, they contained 220 haiku by Basho, Buson, Issa, Shiki, Sokan, Kikaku, and others. Each haiku was illustrated with a different Japanese ideogram. So many of the haiku delighted me, especially those with comic images:

this snowy morning
that crow I hate so much
But he's beautiful!
–Basho

"Yes, come in! I cried
But at the windy
snow-hung gate
knocking still went on
– Kyorai

windy winter rain —
my silly big umbrella
tries walking backward
– Shisei-Jo

Cold first winter rain —
poor monkey,
you too could use
a little woven cape
– Basho

Heartbreak Hotel

Eventually, though, each of us found ourselves focused on other pursuits: sports, the opposite sex, and the rock & roll of Elvis

Presley.

Well, since my baby left me,
Well, I found a new place to dwell,
Well, it's down at the end of lonely street
At Heartbreak Hotel.

Whether it was the fault of Elvis Presley or adolescent hormones, our haiku clubs slowly dissolved and I drifted away from the writing of haiku. No more coughing, no more sneezing, no more hiccups, no more buzoooom.

I can't speak for Hope. She moved away that year, and Eddie, Donald, Jerry, and Oriole became involved in other pursuits. I was the only one who continued to write, who thought of himself as a writer, though not as a writer of haiku. I felt the limitations of such a short form. Writing haiku required restraint, like chiseling symbols into blocks of stone, compared to the stories that enthralled me — science fiction novels and murder mysteries: Robert Heinlein's *Time for the Stars*; Erle Stanley Gardner's *The Case of the Demur Defendant,* featuring Perry Mason and his lovely secretary Della Street; Isaac Asimov's *Foundation Trilogy*; and Agatha Christie's detective novels. All were full of imaginative plots and characters with snappy dialogue. There were no plots in haiku, and no room to tell a story. I didn't like being hog-tied by three lines and seventeen syllables. Could there anything shorter than haiku? Well, actually, there was.

Short Poems vs Haiku

In 1968, the Haiku Society of America spent two years and used some 20,000 words in exchanges among its members before reaching an official definition for haiku (see pages 32-33). *A Haiku Path* was finally published in 1994, which documented the process by which they arrived at a final definition: "They're the world's shortest poems, usually consisting of seventeen syllables arranged in a sequence of 5-7-5." The English poet James Kirkup supplied an example:

Haiku should be just
small stones dropping down a well
with a small splash.

Imagism

Haiku are among the world's shortest poems, but are they the shortest? The Imagists wrote two- or three-line poems inspired by Ezra Pound (see pages 214-219). He declared in 1914 that modern poetry should be written clearly with precise visual images in the "language of speech," without "excess verbiage" or "muddy abstractions" characteristic of Georgian Romanticism. When Hilda Doolittle, who went by H.D., sent Pound a short poem that fulfilled this criteria, he forwarded it to *Poetry* magazine in Chicago and wrote after her name, "*Imagiste.*" Thus, Imagism was born—short poems that focused on the accurate presentation of a subject— no commentary, no philosophy, no interpretation, just the image (see page 215). Pound had been translating Chinese and Japanese poems and came across Basho's first masterpiece, written in 1682, about the same year his disciples planted a banana tree in his back yard. (The word for banana plant in Japanese is *basho.*) This haiku, usually accompanied by a painting of a crow on the branch of a dead tree, established Basho's style. It also established haiku as a serious art form. At that time, Basho was a member of the Danrin school of poetics led by Nishiyama Soin (1605-1682). Those poets usually wrote haiku as part of a drinking party. It was more of a parlor game then an attempt to write serious poetry. Basho's poem became the Japanese form most influential on the English language poets, inspiring Imagism. (For a different translation, see pages 30 and 277.)

On a leafless bough
a crow has perched —
autumn dusk.

Imagist poems were often shorter than haiku, and weren't bound by syllabic rules. The most famous Imagist poem is the one that Pound himself wrote in 1914, inspired by Basho's poem, titled "In a Station at the Metro."

Ezra Pound photographed in 1913 by Alvin Langdon Coburn. Pound's contribution to modern poetry was "Imagism," a movement dervied from classical Chinese and Japanese poetry.

The apparition of these faces in the crowd,
Petals on a wet, black bough.

Inspired by Pound's example, Amy Lowell wrote several "imagist" poems that have a haiku feel about them, though written in two lines.

Over the shop where silk is sold
Still the dragon kites are flying.

While the poem has the objective quality of an imagist poem, or a Buson-like "snapshot," a Japanese reader would supply the missing commentary in that the poem refers to the Year of the Dragon, it's New Year's Day. Lowell, as Pound had done in his two-line poem, supplies a title, which is equivalent to a third line, or a sort of commentary. She titled it "Poem." How are we to take that? Did she mean it was just a poem, or that the suggestion of the purely descriptive image that the dragon kites are still flying over the shop where silk is sold says something about the nature of poetry itself? Another two-line poem by Lowell (without a title) goes beyond mere objective description in that the world "constantly" supplies both action and commentary.

Outside a gate on the floor of the empty palanquin
The plum-petals constantly increase.

Pound was rather critical of Lowell's imagist poems; he dubbed her efforts as "Amygism." But Pound, especially in his essay on "Vorticism" — another short lived movement he founded — applied his own mistaken idea of the haiku principle of juxtaposition, which he called "superposition." The haiku poets presented two images that were (or could be) unrelated, letting the reader supply the connection or meaning. Haiku did not contain metaphor or simile, they were meant (at least in the hands of Buson or Shiki) as pictures only, snapshots of a moment. In Pound's translation of the following Japanese haiku, he adds the phrase "are like," thus linking the two images as metaphorical, something the Japanese poet would never do.

The footsteps of the cat upon the snow
(are like) plum blossoms.

By adding the simile, Pound weakens the possibility of a more profound insight. The two images can be connected or not, and the reader is left to consider the larger meaning of those two separate images. By linking them, Pound narrows the meaning, restricts further elaboration in the mind of the reader. Despite Pound's misunderstanding of the haiku concept of juxtaposition, he was to use his technique of superposition throughout the *Cantos* where one action (or image, or comment) follows another, such as the image of the Italian merchant totalling his receipts and bills at the end of the day superimposed over the image of a bright, full moon rising over the rooftops of Lucca.

More Haiku-Like Short Poems

Wallace Stevens' masterful, signature piece, "13 Ways of Looking at a Blackbird" is a series of thirteen haiku derivations also inspired by Basho's poem about the crow perched on a branch (see pages 30, 103, and 277). The poem was published in 1917, and many consider it the first haiku sequence written in English. Here are three of the thirteen:

Among twenty snowy mountains,
The only moving thing
Was the eye of the blackbird

I was of three minds,
Like a tree
In which there are three blackbirds.

When the blackbird flew out of sight,
It marked the edge
Of one of the many circles.

Carl Sandburg wrote a nifty short poem titled "Fog" in which "fog comes on little cat feet," and William Carlos Williams wrote many short poems, including the sixteen-word "The Red Wheelbarrow."

So much depends upon
a red wheel barrow
glazed with rain water
beside the white chickens.

But so much depends on how one breaks the lines, if one is trying to point out it's haiku-like sensibility. Consider this version:

So much depends
upon

a red wheel
barrow

glazed with rain
water

beside the white
chickens.

If the first line is removed, we find ourselves with the simplicity of a haiku without commentary by the poet, in which the two images of the wheelbarrow and the white chickens speak for themselves.

a red wheel barrow
glazed with rain water
beside the white chickens.

But it's the first line that makes this poem more than a haiku, and more profound. It's the "so much depends" that changes the way we experience that wheelbarrow. So much depends upon it. The crop, the farm, the life, the lives — all come down to that red wheelbarrow. Another Williams poem is "Prelude to Winter," also containing sixteen words.

The moth under the eaves
with wings like
the bark of a tree, lies
symmetrically still.

Jack Kerouac also tried his hand at short haiku-like poems:

*

Missing a kick at
the icebox door.
It closed anyway.

*

In my medicine cabinet,
the winter fly has
died of old age.

Romantic poets of the 19th century tossed out a few short, memorable poems.

*

Ivy serpentine
with its dark buds and leaves,
wandering astray.
(William Wordsworth)

*

The frozen wind crept
on above,
the freezing stream below.
(Percy Shelley)

*

As a dare-gale skylark scanted
in a dull cageman's mounting spirit
in his bone-house.
(Gerard Manley Hopkins)

*

The innocent moon
that does nothing
but shine
(F. Thompson)

*

By the sea,
under the yellow
and sagging moon.
(Whitman)

The Couplet

And then there's the couplet, a short form that goes back to Greek and Latin poetry, such as this one by Catullus (84-54 B.C.):

The fleet-foot girl was a golden apple
that loosed the girdle tied too long.

Many couplets were more pithy than profound, like this oft-quoted one by Dorothy Parker:

Men never make passes
at girls who wear glasses.

Basil Hall Chamberlain was translating Japanese haiku in the 1880s, and he decided that the nearest equivalents in English for the Japanese haiku, which was written as one vertical line, was the English epigram, so he translated haiku into couplets, instead of three lines. Harold Stewart's *A Net of Fireflies* (Charles E. Tuttle Co., 1960), which has gone into 100 printings, featured both color paintings and haiku, which he translated into rhyming couplets. Stewart wrote long metaphysical narrative poems in a neo-classical or Augustan style combined with Eastern subject matter. He once described himself as a "conservative anarchist." Here's the one by Tomoda Sogyo which provided Stewart with the title for his book.

What a delicious game it is to set
Fireflies loose in bed beneath the net.

Another translation of a haiku by Yamagushi Sodo who was a friend of Basho:

yado no haru / nani mo naki koso / nani mo are

In my ten-foot bamboo hut this spring,
There is nothing. There is everything.

Malcolm de Chazal (1902-1981) Mauritian writer, painter and visionary, known for his *Sens Plastique,* a work consisting of several thousand gnomic aphorisms and pensées.

Lafcadio Hearn published his translations in 1898, an anthology of 320 haiku written over a span of five centuries, and following the Japanese vertical line, he transposed his into one horizontal line, as he did with the famous Basho frog poem:

> Old pond — frogs jumping in — sound of water.

These haiku almost read like aphorisms, and aren't some aphorisms poems of a sort? "A penny saved is a penny earned," and "If wishes were horses, beggars could ride."

The Gnomic Verses of Malcolm de Chazal

Malcolm de Chazal (1902–1981) was a Mauritian writer, painter, and visionary, known especially for his *Sens-Plastique* (1948), a work consisting of several thousand aphorisms and pensées, visionary statements that are haiku-like in their ineffableness. He was born and raised on the island nation of Mauritius in the Indian Ocean and groomed to take over his family's large plantation, which is why he went to Louisiana State University to study agriculture and engineering. While at LSU, he discovered poetry. When he returned to Mauritius, he decided to dedicate himself to poetry. He spent the rest of his life in a hotel room, writing his short, aphoristic verses and lunching alone, much to the distress of his family. When I was a graduate student at Tulane, I met a poet who was attending LSU who had discovered de Chazal's work. I was struck by the thousands of gnomic aphorisms, which read like one- or two-line haiku:

> We know the halls of the eye like welcome visitors
> but we live in our mouth.
>
> Shifting in reverse while making love can kill you.
>
> Monkeys are superior to men in this:
> when a monkey looks into a mirror, he sees a monkey.
>
> Women make us poets, children make us philosophers.
>
> Art is nature speeded up and God slowed down

The idealist walks on tiptoe, the materialist on his heels.

Sayonara to Haiku

Haiku can test one's patience if one yearns for elaboration. A single image can suggest paragraphs, but a paragraph can make an image indelible. The restriction of form may be liberating, but may also function as a strait jacket, depending on one's literary intention, or even on one's personality. By the time I was in seventh grade, I was chomping at the bit, hungry for expansive self-expression, that Whitmanesque urge to "sound my barbaric yawp over the roofs of the world." I was done with haiku. Sayonara to haiku. I began to write short stories instead, each one longer than the last. Finally, in eighth grade, I decided to tackle the novel.

Death on the Nile* meets *The Big Sleep

I typed my first novel on an Royal typewriter that my father bought me when I was twelve-years old the summer I announced that I was going to be a writer. Before that, I had printed my stories in black composition notebooks. Once I got the typewriter, I taught myself "touch typing," using the *Ruth Benry Touch Typing Method*. It was a twelve-week course, but by the sixth week I grew tired of the lazy brown fox jumping over the something-or-other and began typing grisly detective novels like the ones I had started reading: Agatha Christie's classic who-dunnits featuring the Belgium detective Hercule Poirot, *Murder on the Orient Express*, *Death on the Nile*, as well as her classic novels *And Then There Were None* and *The Murder of Roger Ackroyd*; Raymond Chandler's novels featuring hard-boiled detective Philip Marlowe in *The Big Sleep*, *The Long Goodbye* and *Farewell, My Lovely;* Dashielle Hammett's books featuring another hard-boiled operative, Sam Spade in *The Maltese Falcon*, *Red Harvest*, *The Thin Man*, *The Continental Op*, and *The Dain Curse*; and James M. Cain's pulpy and sordid stories such as *The Postman Always Rings Twice*, *Double Indemnity*, *The Magician's Wife*, and *The Root of His Evil*.

I joined the Walter J. Black Mystery Book Club and finished each book the day it arrived at my door: books by Ellery Queen, Brett Halliday, Kenneth Fearing, Ngaio Marsh, Rex Stout, George Harmon Coxe (featuring that master sleuth Jack "Flashgun" Casey), Nicholas Blake (featuring master

Royal Typewriter, 1955 with first page of *The Living Corpse*

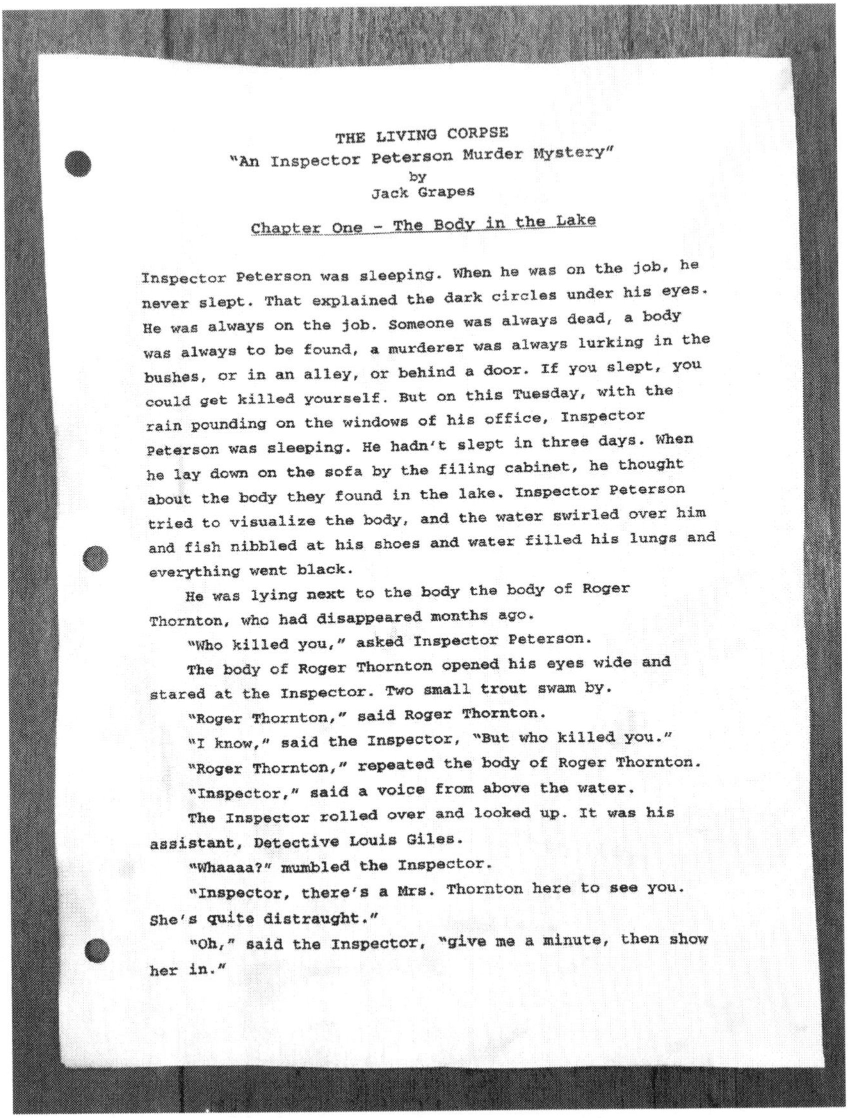

THE LIVING CORPSE
"An Inspector Peterson Murder Mystery"
by
Jack Grapes

Chapter One - The Body in the Lake

Inspector Peterson was sleeping. When he was on the job, he never slept. That explained the dark circles under his eyes. He was always on the job. Someone was always dead, a body was always to be found, a murderer was always lurking in the bushes, or in an alley, or behind a door. If you slept, you could get killed yourself. But on this Tuesday, with the rain pounding on the windows of his office, Inspector Peterson was sleeping. He hadn't slept in three days. When he lay down on the sofa by the filing cabinet, he thought about the body they found in the lake. Inspector Peterson tried to visualize the body, and the water swirled over him and fish nibbled at his shoes and water filled his lungs and everything went black.

He was lying next to the body the body of Roger Thornton, who had disappeared months ago.

"Who killed you," asked Inspector Peterson.

The body of Roger Thornton opened his eyes wide and stared at the Inspector. Two small trout swam by.

"Roger Thornton," said Roger Thornton.

"I know," said the Inspector, "But who killed you."

"Roger Thornton," repeated the body of Roger Thornton.

"Inspector," said a voice from above the water.

The Inspector rolled over and looked up. It was his assistant, Detective Louis Giles.

"Whaaaa?" mumbled the Inspector.

"Inspector, there's a Mrs. Thornton here to see you. She's quite distraught."

"Oh," said the Inspector, "give me a minute, then show her in."

Page one of *The Living Corpse*, 1955, typed on my Royal typewriter.
note the uncorrected typo of "the body"

sleuth Nigel Strangeways), Helen McCloy (a castle, a deserted village, and murder in the Scottish Highlands!), Roy Vickers, and Mabel Seeley, to name a few.

Inspector Peterson and the Living Corpse

My own novels featured a Bulldog Drummond-type detective named Inspector Peterson. Bulldog Drummond was a British fictional character, created by H. C. McNeile but published under his pen name, Sapper. As the cover of the first of these novels proclaimed, Bulldog was a "detective, patriot, hero, and a gentleman!" His arch nemesis was Carl Peterson. Even though I fashioned my detective after Bulldog Drummond, I thought it clever that I named *my* protagonist after Bulldog's nemesis. When I finished typing them, I bound each novel in one of those clasp folders and hand-titled the cover as an "Inspector Peterson Murder Mystery."

The first novel I wrote was titled *The Living Corpse*, typed double-spaced on onion skin paper with two carbons. I managed to produce 68 pages before Inspector Peterson gathered the suspects in the library or the billiard room and pointed to the old chauffeur. "There's your murderer," he said. Then he ripped off the chauffeur's fake beard, mustache, and wig, revealing the supposed victim, who had staged his own murder so his wife could collect the insurance money and they both could retire to a mountain chalet in Switzerland. Thus, "the living corpse"—a clever switcheroo designed to impress the likes of Dame Agatha.

By tenth grade, I'd written half a dozen Inspector Peterson mysteries in which each plot twist was twistier than the last. The final Inspector Peterson mystery was titled *Murder in the Kitchen* and totalled 250 pages. I discovered that one way to add more pages was to write lots of dialogue. The more dialogue the better. The dialogue could be short, quippy questions, followed by rim-shot answers, not unlike the last line of a haiku. All that practice writing haiku came in handy when it came to pithy dialogue.

"Can I be honest?" said the femme fatale.
"Don't strain yourself," answered Inspector Peterson.

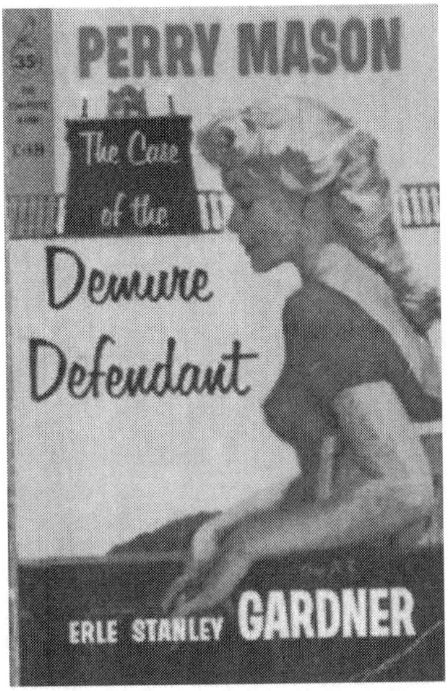

Creator of the Perry Mason detective series, Erle Stanley Gardner's books sold for 25 cents and 35 cents in the 1950's. Gardner published detective novels under many pseudonyms such as A.A. Fair, Kyle Corning, Les Tillray, Robert Parr and Carlton Kendrake.

"Mind if I smoke?" asked the killer.
"I don't care if you burn," said Inspector Peterson.

"Are those your knees," asked Inspector Peterson of the blond playboy in tennis shorts, "or are you just smuggling walnuts?"

The Case of the Moth-Eaten Mink

I've often thought about what I learned from reading those books in my early teens. After struggling in school to read Melville and Dickens, I felt as if I'd come up for air with the straight-forward sentences found in those mystery novels, especially Erle Stanley Gardner's Perry Mason series. I devoured each one, and was drawn to the titles for their poetic, post-haiku ring: *The Case of the Musical Cow*, *The Case of the Moth-Eaten Mink*, *The Case of the Sleepwalker's Niece*, *The Case of the Long-Legged Models*, *The Case of the Counterfeit Eye*, *The Case of the Stuttering Bishop*, and *The Case of the Final Fade-Out*.

I read at least fifty of the Perry Mason novels and realized at one point that there was no description of Perry Mason anywhere in the books, yet I had a picture of him in my mind. Why? The dialogue, his actions, his demeanor, his turn of mind — all contributed to the picture I had of him in my mind. I was reading like a writer, even at thirteen, paying attention to the sentences, the style, the dialogue, and how plot was handled. Though a long way from haiku, these stories demonstrated how a small detail could convey the sense and sensibility of a character or situation. Something else about those Perry Mason mysteries: Critic Russell B. Nye called Gardner's novels "as formal as Japanese Noh drama."

Murder Mystery Haiku

The titles of those mystery novels seemed haiku-like to me. Just for the fun of it, I've created five haiku in the 5-7-5 syllabic pattern, using only the titles of those books, three different authors for each haiku.

the maltese falcon,
the case of the musical cow —
dain curse: red harvest.

farewell, my lovely,
the postman always rings twice,
and then there were none.

death on the nile,
the case of the moth-eaten mink—
the root of his evil

the magician's wife,
the sleepwalker's niece —
the living corpse

murder up my sleeve
thin man, big sleep, continental op—
the final fade-out

What I loved about those detective novels was that, at their best, they combined the haiku sensibility of simplicity and relatable images with the intriguing narratives I loved. However, when I came upon James. M. Cain's preface to *Double Indemnity*, I knew that I had found an important key to what made writing effective.

> I make no conscious effort to be tough, or hard-boiled, or grim, or any of the things I am usually called. I merely try to write as the character would write, and I never forget that the average man, from the fields, the streets, the bars, the offices, and even the gutters of his country, has acquired a vividness of speech that goes beyond anything I could invent, and that if I stick to this heritage, this logos of the American countryside, I shall attain a maximum of effectiveness with very little effort.

The Train of Fate

After my first attempt at a typed novel of 68 pages, I tried to write a 100 page novel. Each novel after that was an attempt to write more pages than the previous one. The only way I could do that was to pad the book with the characters' thoughts, since there was only so much dialogue, action or narrative I could come up with. Often, in moments of great drama, I had characters thinking about how new shoes hurt one's feet or why lying in bed on a Saturday morning with nothing to do was so sweet.

Finally, in my junior year, I came across a copy of Ayn Rand's novel *Atlas Shrugged* in my father's den. I'm not sure why I decided to read such a hefty book, well over a thousand pages. What I remember is the paper — silky smooth and creamy. I liked the way it felt to turn the pages. It was a far cry from mystery novels. *Atlas Shrugged* had chapter headings like "Non-Contradiction," "Either-Or," and "A is A," the latter being an entire section devoted to Aristotle. This sent me scurrying to my father's set of *The Great Books of the Western World*, where I discovered Kierkegaard's *Either/Or*, Plato's *Republic*, and Socrates's dialogues, not to mention a few other books in my father's library, Marx's *Communist Manifesto*, Lenin's *State and Revolution*, and Mao Zedong's *On Contradiction*.

When I chanced upon Aristotle's *Metaphysics*, a trap door opened in my brain. His essay began with "All men by nature desire to know," and went on to discuss the difference between "the man of experience" and "the man of art," who doesn't just strive to produce something, but strives to acquire knowledge for its own sake. Nevermind that after a few pages I could barely understand what he was talking about — first causes, efficient causes, final causes, and the transcendental attributes of being. (I took solace years later when I read that the Arabian philosopher Avincenna said that he'd read the *Metaphysics* of Aristotle forty times without understanding any of it.)

What mattered was that I had fallen down a rabbit hole into another world, reading complex narrative and ideas, and began to imagine writing something more challenging than murder mysteries. The first sentence of *Atlas Shrugged* — "Who is John Galt?" — became as indelible to me as *Moby Dick*'s opening sentence — "Call me Ishamel." I filled a notebook with possible first sentences to novels I might write someday. Again,

Becky Finkelstein, the siren song of poetry

the essence of haiku with its juxtaposition of images came to my aid. I probably wrote hundreds of "first" sentences in that notebook, which I carried with me to school, making entries in the middle of class when something popped into my head.

> Summerville wasn't a ghost-town,
> but ghosts ran city hall.
>
> Before the incident with the X-ACTO knife,
> Walter used to have ten fingers.
>
> "Wait here," said Mrs. D'Andrea, removing her gloves.
>
> Open or closed, he hated doors.
>
> Just before the brakes failed,
> Winston remembered he'd forgotten to change his will.
>
> I woke up one morning in a strange room,
> in a strange bed,
> a strange woman lying next to me.
>
> Cracked mirrors, carpets smelling of urine,
> tattered drapes covering the windows.
>
> The dog sat before the closed door,
> waiting for it to open.

When I finished reading *Atlas Shrugged*, I decided to write something less formulaic than the mystery novels I'd been writing. I came up with a three-hundred page novel I titled *The Train of Fate*, but I'd reached my limit — three-hundred pages was all I could muster. I was tired of onion skin and carbon paper and all that plotting. I had written twelve novels by the time I graduated high-school, and enough was enough. I was also involved in sports and extra-curricular activities. And I was dating Becky Finkelstein. That's another story. There was just no time for novels the size of *War and Peace*. So I decided to pare down, write short stories instead. Eventually, the short stories got shorter. By the time I got to college, I was writing vignettes, and even shorter pieces that today would be called micro- or flash- or sudden-fiction.

The Siren Song of Poetry

You'd think at that point there was nowhere to go but up, but no, there was something shorter than short short stories and vignettes: There was poetry. Not haiku, mind you, but poetry similar in size to the poems I was introduced to in college, especially those poems by "academic" poets collected in the basic college textbook, Oscar Williams' *Little Treasury of Modern Poetry*. There was T. S. Eliot, Ezra Pound, Hilda Doolittle, Marianne Moore, Yeats, Frost, Wallace Stevens, Robinson Jeffers, e.e. cummings, and W.H. Auden. There were poets whose work required tortuous exegesis: John Crowe Ransom, Allen Tate, Robert Lowell, Jean Garrigue, William Empson, Elizabeth Bishop, Vernon Watkins, Hart Crane, Muriel Rukeyser, Dylan Thomas, John Berryman, Anne Ridler, Stephen Spender, and Delmore Schwartz.

It wasn't long before the beat poets and the new wave of non-academic poets, many associated with bohemian Greenwich Village, broke upon the scene, and I was devouring poems by Allen Ginsberg, Leroy Jones, Diane DiPrima, Lawrence Ferlinghetti, Gregory Corso, Denise Levertov, May Swenson, Frank O'Hara, Robert Creeley, William Carlos Williams, John Ashbery, Sylvia Plath, Jack Spicer, Larry Eigner, Cid Corman, Lew Welch, Ann Sexton, and Charles Olson. I was a long way from the novels and stories I'd written in high school, and even further from those pithy haiku.

Then, after college and two years of MFA training in Theatre, I put the novels and short stories in a box and moved to California to pursue an acting career. Heartbreak Hotel became Hotel California. Today, those stories and novels are in my attic somewhere, along with those awful college poems I wrote in imitation of my idols.

Falling Asleep in the Rain

After half a dozen novels, dozens of short stories, and prose vignettes, I turned again to writing poems, and I've been writing poems ever since. The question then became (and remains) how to marry my desire to produce work that combines the vision of a novel to my love of poetry's shorter form. I still read haiku for pleasure now and then, but couldn't help feeling there was something easy about it.

Modern poetry seemed to have a more complex structure — it involved story, as well as image and emotional revelation. Haiku was for kids in school, or adults playing games with words; I saw it as a way to avoid the exploration of emotional conflict. Even now, I can't believe I've embarked once again on the writing of haiku. Maybe I'm tiring out as a poet, maybe I'm just an old fart throwing bocce balls in a park or an old boatman pissing on the moon in a river. Maybe that's why my original title for this book was *Falling Asleep in the Rain*, an apologetic image of laziness, of wasting one's time.

Meat and Potatoes or Cucumber Sandwiches

Poetry is irrelevant enough, but haiku? As it happened, however, a few months ago I mentioned in one of my classes that I was thinking of making my next book even smaller than my last one *All the Sad Angels*. Lisa Segal, a wonderful writer and sculptor, raised her hand and said, "Why don't you just write haiku?"

The idea struck me as preposterous. I was sure she was making a joke. But a week later, I found myself in a conversation with Belinda Griffin, a friend who was thinking of having a "renga gathering," and she asked me to attend. Traditionally, in such a gathering, guests write a collaborative *renga*, a linked poem in several stanzas, often comic, adding to the standard 5-7-5 haiku form a couplet composed of seven syllables to create a stanza of 5-7-5-7-7 syllables, called tanka. These linked stanzas can run on for pages.

The idea of a linked poem intrigued me. I didn't have to confine myself to that classic haiku pattern of three lines and seventeen syllables. I could write a series of linked tanka, go for a shorter form and still allow myself room to kick down a door or two. After all, I'm a meat and potatoes man, I don't sit well at high tea, eating sandwiches made with cucumber and cream cheese on white triangles of bread. But something was nudging me. My son Josh was already working on a book of adaptations of traditional haiku. He called his haiku form "centipedes." His poetry was masterful, and I could see that there was power in that condensed form. The wheels in my head began to turn.

City Lights Pocket Poets Series: *Howl,* 1955; *Kaddish,* 1956; *Kora in Hell,* 1957; and *The Love Poems of Kenneth Patchen,* 1960

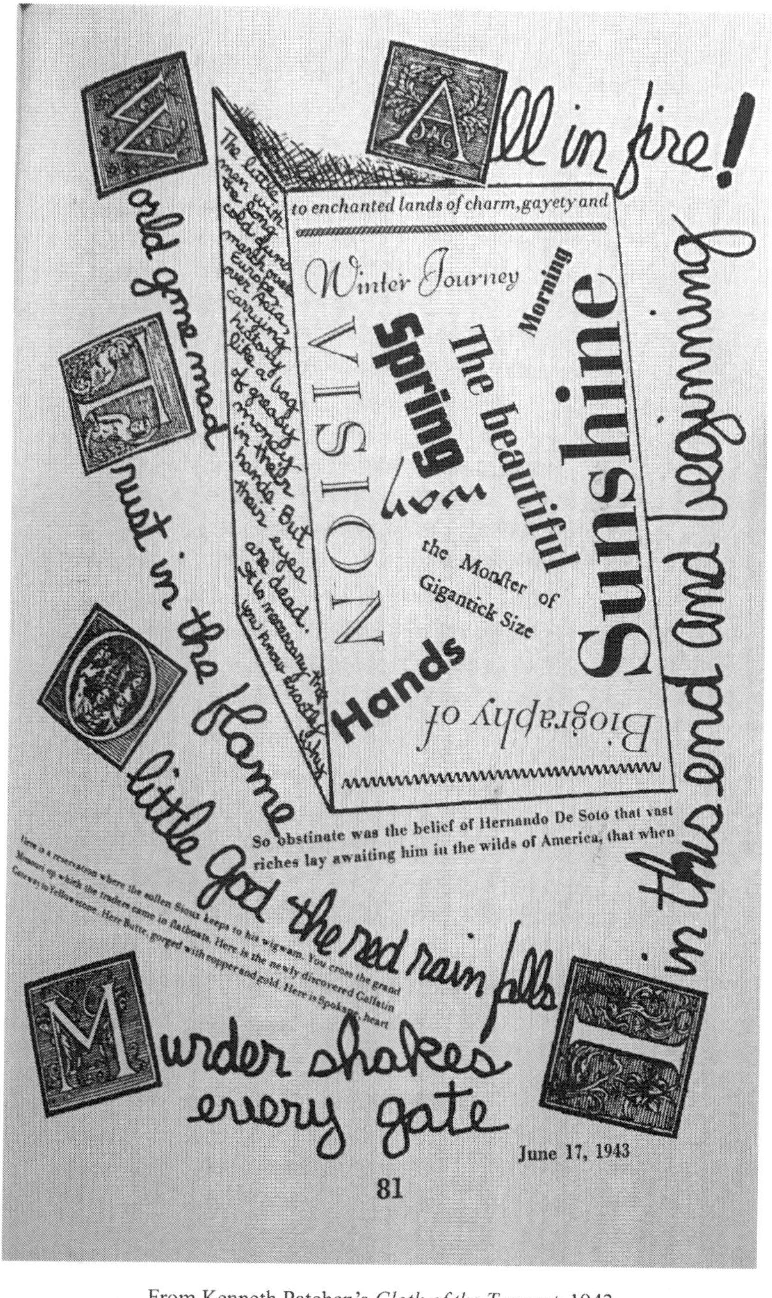

From Kenneth Patchen's *Cloth of the Tempest,* 1943

Pocket Poems

Then, on the first day of one of my classes, Jim Sloyan handed me a copy of *52 Views: The Haibun Variations* by Jim Natal. The *haibun* was a form that Basho had used in writing *Narrow Road into the Interior*, a form that combined short prose passages with a closing haiku at the end of each prose passage. All around me were indications that I did not have to confine myself to that shortest of forms, but could go for something fuller and still make my little book.

I know it's silly to imagine the size of a book first and then fill it with appropriate text, but that's the way it is sometimes with the creative process. You see an empty wall and paint a mural, not because you want to paint a mural, but because you want to paint a wall. And I wanted my next book to be a little book no bigger than the palm of your hand, something you could stuff in your pocket or purse or in the glove compartment of your car, the way I used to carry around the pocket-sized books published by City Lights Pocket Poets, inspired by the French poetry series *Poètes d'aujourd-hui*. Lawrence Ferlinghetti launched his innovative series in 1955 as an alternative press to the academic institutional presses that held sway at the time. I didn't imagine that my little book would end up being the size of a brick (the intial run of 100 copies was indeed brick-like, but I had to reformat this edition into a more conventional size so it could be distributed through Amazon...)

I still remember reaching into my coat pocket for *Lunch Poems* by Frank O'Hara or *Howl* by Allen Ginsberg, as well as many other books in that series he published (and still publishes all these years later): *Kora in Hell* by William Carlos Williams, *Gasoline* by Gregory Corso, *Pictures of the Gone World* by Lawrence Ferlinghetti, *Love Poems* by Kenneth Patchen, *Poem from Jail* by Ed Sanders, *Red Cats* by Anselm Hollow, and *The Chinese Written Character as a Medium for Poetry* by Ernest Fenollosa.

I also remembered those attractively designed little books published by the Peter Pauper Press. As my teacher had quoted, the books were sold at "prices even a pauper could afford." It reminded me of that Erasmus quote, "When I have a little money, I buy books; if I have any money left, I buy food and clothes."

In 1928, after studying with famed book and type designer

Peter Pauper Press books at $1 a piece, “prices even a pauper could afford.”

Frederic W. Goudy, 22-year-old Peter Beilensen set up a small press in the basement of his father's home in Larchmont, New York, and designed and printed nearly 700 editions before his death in 1962. From the 1930s through the 1950s, Peter Pauper Press produced handsome, finely bound letterpress volumes of prose and poetry, including Beilensen's translations of Japanese haiku. He adhered to the 17-syllable count, but broke the poems into four lines, the middle two indented, and all in small capitals, which suggested a bolder reading than the original Japanese, which used no capitals at all.

While those palm-sized pocket books by City Lights were part of my college years identifying with beat poetry, those little Peter Pauper books were part of my childhood, learning to write haiku. Among the hundreds of Peter Pauper books were four that focused on haiku: *Japanese Haiku* (1955), the one my teacher gave us in 6th grade, and the other three that I purchased myself for one dollar — *The Four Seasons* (1958), *Cherry Blossoms* (1960), and *Haiku Harvest* (1962).

I thought back to my experience in fifth grade, when I was allowed to sit on the floor after lunch next to the bookcase in the far corner of the classroom and do whatever I wanted. I could memorize "The Gettysburgh Address," read about the planets in our solar system, or write haiku until the bell rang. And, of course, I thought back to the haiku clubs that were a central part of my identity in those formative years.

Mrs. Aime and Basho

The fifth grade teacher who let me sit on the floor and write was Mrs. Aime, Vita B. Aime, the teacher who had introduced us all to haiku. It's too complicated a story to tell here, but she was my teacher in fourth and fifth grades, then in junior high and high school, she taught me English and Spanish in every grade, except for tenth grade English taught by Mrs. Troescher. When we graduated in June of 1960, it felt as if Mrs Aime graduated with us.

Mrs. Aime was a stickler for grammar and syntax, but she also encouraged us to write truly about visible things and to bring in a personal point of view. And isn't that what Basho had done in his own time, transforming the haiku tradition from something mannered and comic to a style centered in human consciousness? I'm sure that was why she favored Basho over all the other haiku poets. When she talked about Basho, she was telling us about herself, her appreciation for the present moment, her passion for knowledge, her insistence that talent not be wasted. She taught us about the poets and writers she loved with a passion. Being part Greek and part Italian, she recited Homer and Dante in their original languages.

Her interest in literary traditions inspired us. Poets were influenced by other poets, she said, and each poet carried some part of the past into the future. These traditions, whether referenced, carried forward, or reacted against, became a great dialogue among writers and readers throughout the centuries. She told us that Basho was influenced by the literary tradition of Chinese poets like Tu Fu and Li-Po, and the priestly tradition of the Zen monk Iio Sogi (1421-1502), considered the greatest master of renga, whose poem below links the two countries in a shared history.

does not China also
lie beneath this self same sky
bound in misery

Mrs. Aime shared this haiku by Sogi, written toward the end of his life. It's a *jisei*, or "death poem."

everything that was
has vanished from my aged heart
leaving not a trace

Basho's Death-Bed Haiku

Basho had Sogi's poem in mind when he dictated his last haiku from his death bed to sixty disciples. During his final illness, he discussed Zen, poetry, and his new idea, a philosophical essence for haiku he called *karumi*, or lightness (see page 42). The aim was to write with detachment and ease, and to take a step back from the folly of this life. He felt the writer of haiku should be a bystander, and an invisible one at that. The poet should focus merely on the objective reality of nature, letting the reader infer the emotion from the direct presentation of the image. (This later became the touchstone of Ezra Pound's Imagism and William Carlos Williams' Objectivism, as exemplified by their poems

"In the Station at the Metro" and "The Red Wheelbarrow," respectively. See pages 105, 106-107, and 240) To be without feelings or emotions was how he thought the poet could cope with the depressing fragility of life.

Basho's efforts to infuse haiku with *karumi* was not met with total acceptance by his disciples. He tried once more to explain his technique of lightness. "The style I have in mind," he said, "is a light one in form and in the method of linking verses, one that gives the impression of looking at a shallow river with a sandy bed." For many, this was at odds with his disciples' efforts to produce a more rigorous, serious haiku, an approach they had gotten from Basho himself. They resisted this new turn. Some thought about starting their own groups, while retaining the direction of Basho's previous instruction, that all things be mutually communicable and that a person can become one with other creations of nature. Basho became impatient with the battles between egos among his disciples and stopped seeing some of them altogether. He closed the gate to his hut and fastened it shut "with a morning glory," as he wrote in one haiku. He explained to one of his disciples, "If someone comes to see me, I have to waste my words in vain. If I leave my house to visit others, I waste their time in vain. Following the example of Sonkei and Togoro, I have decided to live in complete isolation with a firmly closed door. My solitude shall be my company, and my poverty my wealth. Already a man of fifty, I should be able to maintain this self-imposed discipline."

His experiment in artificial solitude lasted a little more than a month, but he didn't give up his idea of "lightness" as a spiritual attitude informing the poet's point of view. Many of Basho's later poems exhibit this lightness of tone, a counter-move to the self-centered tone and ponderous themes of many haiku written by his disciples. Take this one haiku by Basho, for instance, in which he parodies a poem written in admiration of Confucius by the Chinese poet Mu Fu (1051-1107), which goes: "Confucius, Confucius, ah great Confucius." Basho wrote the following haiku on spring — how many haiku on spring he must have read (and written himself)!

ah spring spring
how great is spring
and so on

Issa incorporated this lightness into many of his haiku, even when writing about something dark and tragic, as in his poem about life being nothing more than a bath when you're born and a bath when you die, and in between, it's nothing but *chimpunken*, "blah blah blah."

A few weeks before his death, Basho wrote the following haiku, expressing both an awareness of his approaching death, as well as the *sabi*, the loneliness he felt realizing his attempts to persuade his followers to infuse their haiku with the lightness of *karumi* was falling on deaf ears.

kono michi ya / yuku hito nashi ni / aki no kure

this road
that no one goes on
autumn's departure

One way Basho had tried all his life to side-step unhappiness was to go on a journey, so he decided to make one last trek. He gave his house away to family, and left, despite his ill health, for the southern shores of Lake Biwa, accompanied once more with his former taveling companion, Sora. But Basho's condition deteriorated. He became depressed. At a dinner in his honor, he ate some mushrooms and became ill. He spent his last days confined to a bed at the home of a physician and poetry student.

When it became evident that he was dying, his longtime friend Kyorai asked Basho to give them a "*jisei*" — the sum of his philosophy. Basho refused. "Tell anyone who asks," he said, "that all of my everyday poems are my *jisei*."

In other words, all the poems he'd written, starting with "Old Pond," were written as if they were death poems. The next morning, however, he called his disciples to his bedside, saying that during the night he had dreamed, and that on waking a poem had come to him. Then he recited the following haiku (I offer here five different translations):

tabi ni yande
yume wa kare no o
kake meguru

ill on a journey
dreams in a withered field
wander aimlessly
(trans. Jane Reichold)

Sick on my journey,
only my dreams will wander
these desolate moors
(trans. Sam Hamill)

fallen sick on a trip
dreams run wildly
through my head
(trans. Dallas Finn)

on a journey, ill,
and over fields all withered,
dreams go wandering still
(trans. Harold Henderson)

falling sick on a journey
my dreams go wandering
over a field of dried grass
(trans. Anon)

"That poem," Basho said, "was composed during my illness, but it is *not* my death verse; but it cannot be said that it is *not* my death verse." Basho was aware that at this point, so close to death, he should be focusing his mind on prayers rather than poetry, but he continued to mentally review his work, even in his last hours, even after he had composed what could, or could not, be considered his death poem. After he wearily recited it, he said, "This is the last of my obsession!" Then he closed his eyes. But a few hours later, when he awoke, he dictated a "revision" of a haiku he had composed earlier that year. The last two lines had been bothering him. He felt that they basically repeated each other.

clear cascade
the dust on the waves
summer moon

So close to death, he still thought of haiku and of one particular poem composed months earlier that still needed editing. So after reciting what could have been his death-poem, he dictated this revision shortly before he died.

Basho's grave in Otsu, Shiga Prefecture

kiyotaki ya
nami ni chiri komu
ao matsuba

clear cascade
scattered on the waves
green pine needles

This verse was later carved on a stone, and in 1971 the stone was moved to a place where the Kiyotaki River flows into the Oi River. So Basho was correct in one sense. His so-called death-bed poem was, or was not, his death-bed poem. His obsession to write haiku and edit a haiku he had written a year earlier over-rode even the impulse to write a death-bed poem.

I can understand, to some degree, what he meant when he said that writing haiku had become his life's obsession. When I began writing haiku again after nearly sixty years, I thought I'd make a little book of 50 haiku. At some point, I lost count, and when I checked, I had written over 60. So I figured, okay, I'll make a little book of 100 haiku. Next time I checked, I had written 108, so I figured, okay, okay, I'll stop at 150, 150 sounds like a good round number. I checked again after another few weeks and counted 158. At that point, I figured, okay, we'll stop at 200. Soon, writing haiku had become an obsession. I thought about it day and night, writing haiku before falling asleep, writing haiku as I woke up the next morning, revising and rewriting throughout the day. I even wrote a few haiku complaining about the obsession to write haiku — it was exerting a stranglehold over me, I was becoming impatient with the rigidity of the 5-7-5 form, rebelling by composing one haiku in which the 5-7-5 form was inverted into a 7-5-7 form.

why is it five seven five?
seven five seven
works just fine, if you ask me.

After a few months, I wrote a haiku complaining about my need for elbow room, invoking a line from that cowboy song, "give me land, lotsa land, 'neath the starry sky above, don't fence me in." I wanted to write longer poems, but I couldn't. Everything was coming in three lines of 5-7-5 syllables. I got to 200 haiku and plodded on. When I'd written 250, I decided to stop at 300, no matter what. Cold turkey. I was like an addict declaring his last drink. I'm stopping at 300 I told the universe. Which I did. Sort of. My 300th haiku was a response to a haiku Issa had written, in which he mentioned "drops of ink." So my last haiku was a farewell to haiku.

I embrace these words.
Last haiku. Quick drops of ink.
These heartfelt scribbles.

That was to be my last haiku. For the next few days I fought the obsessive urge. While haiku came to me as I drove my car, as I made phone calls, as I fell asleep at night and woke the next morning, I resisted the urge to write them down. I let them float away. But I understood the obsession. It would always be with me. Finally, I wrote another haiku, not so much a revision, as Basho had done, but a recognition that once poetry had entered one's blood, it was impossible to let it go. Thus, the last haiku in my book ends with the same line I had used in the first haiku, coming full circle, as it were, completing the wheel of emptiness.

Okay, here's the deal:
waiting for the next haiku —
dum de dum de dum.

Then I began to write what I intended to be a short introduction to my book of haiku, maybe a few pages. At first, it was 10 pages, then it was 25, then it was 50, then 75, then 100, then … well, who knows. I'm still writing and revising, and it's over 125 pages so far. So much for haiku, so much for obsession, so much for poetry.

Mrs. Aime's *Jisei*

One day, Mrs Aime shared with us two melancholic poems by Saigyo Hoshi (1118-1190), poems that were personal for her. Perhaps she imagined they could stand in for her own *jisei.* Though we didn't understand the depth of the poems, we could see that she was moved as she read them, and we paid attention.

Even a person free of passion
would be moved to sadness:
Evening in a marsh, the snipe flying up.

Let me die in Spring
under the blossoming trees.
Let it be under that autumn moon.

Euclidian Geometry and Haiku

Even though I was no longer writing haiku, by the time I got to high school, haiku had become such a part of my thinking process, that, like Hamlet finding the shape of animals in the moving clouds, I found the spirit of haiku in the most unlikely of subjects: plane geometry. Mr. Zanca taught me that the fabric of the world is made of Euclidian geometry. When Mr. Zanca wrote an axiom or proof on the board, I found myself shaping them into the form of a haiku:

a line is either
parallel to a plane or
contained in the plane

I just found the following haiku in my old high school football playbook:

quarterback rollout
from single wing formation:
fadeout in the flat

Equations were also like lines of haiku.

a x plus b y
plus c z plus d
equal 0.

History, Football, Geometry, Haiku: Everything's Connected

Everything was connected. When Coach Palone drew diagrams on the blackboard during football practice, those diagrams with *x*'s and *o*'s and the football terms he used sounded like the recurring images in haiku: "post-pattern," "cross block," "single-wing formation," "the tight-T," "pulling guard," and "fade out in the flat."

When Mr. Hauth talked about Hegel's dialectic during history class, the 5-7-5 pattern of a haiku became thesis-antithesis-thesis. Mr. Hauth also introduced us to "Vico's Spiral" — the idea of eternal history and it's recurring cycles — Hegel called it "poetic wisdom," quoting the 18th century philosopher Giambattista Vico, who was also the first one to propose that the author of the *Iliad* and the *Oddysey* was not one man named Homer, but a conglomerate of different poets expressing the will of the entire people. Mr. Hauth then drew Vico's Sprial on the board and the image, even to this day, sticks in my mind as a haiku representation of history's dynamic.

In geometry class, when Mr. Zanca wrote on the board —

> Proving the Side-Side-
> Angle theorem was known as
> the ambiguous case.

— there it was again, haiku! Everything *was* connected. From fifth grade on, haiku became a lens that colored everything I was learning.

In Search of Lost Time

It was Mr. Hauth who filled my mind with historical dialectic, the thesis-antithesis-thesis of peace-revolution-peace, (or peace-revolution-war-revolution-peace), but it was Mrs. Aime who extended my reach for making meaning of experience through language. She taught us how to diagram sentences so thoroughly that, by eighth grade, I could see a sentence as both a mathematical and a geometrical structure. To this day, as I drive the freeways of Los Angeles listening to the news on NPR, some spoken sentence will float out of the speaker and arrange itself on the windshield into a well-diagrammed sentence.

The opening sentence of Marcel Proust's great novel, *In Search of Lost Time*— "For a long time I used to go to bed early"— rises in my imagination like a picket fence with broken slats, some tilted upwards, some pointed at the ground below. At the same time, I can imagine it in the configuration of a haiku:

For a long time
I used to go to bed—
early.

The last sentence to Proust's six-volume novel is a lumber yard full of slats extending in every direction.

> But at least, if strength were granted me for long enough to accomplish my work, I should not fail, even if the results were to make them resemble monsters, to describe men first and foremost as occupying a place, a very considerable place compared with the restricted one which is allotted to them in space, a place on the contrary prolonged past measure—for simultaneously, like giants plunged into the years, they touch epochs that are immensely far apart, separated by the slow accretion of many, many days—in the dimension of Time.

If diagrammed, the sentence would resemble a quadratic equation (see next page).

The game of writing haiku is fundamental to my work as a writer and teacher. More often than not, the haiku we wrote in fifth and sixth grades were less aesthetic endeavors than opportunities to score points with each other, a literary game of one-upmanship that included jokes, jibes, and obscene parlay-vouses. But the aesthetic seeped in, and continues to inform my experience of language.

Mrs. Aime and Shakespeare

Mrs. Aime passed away about thirty years ago, but she still hovers over me with her red pencil, ready to smack me if I violate some principle of grammar. I visited my old school the year before she died and she was still there, urging her students to excel. She saw me in the hallway with my wife, and without a

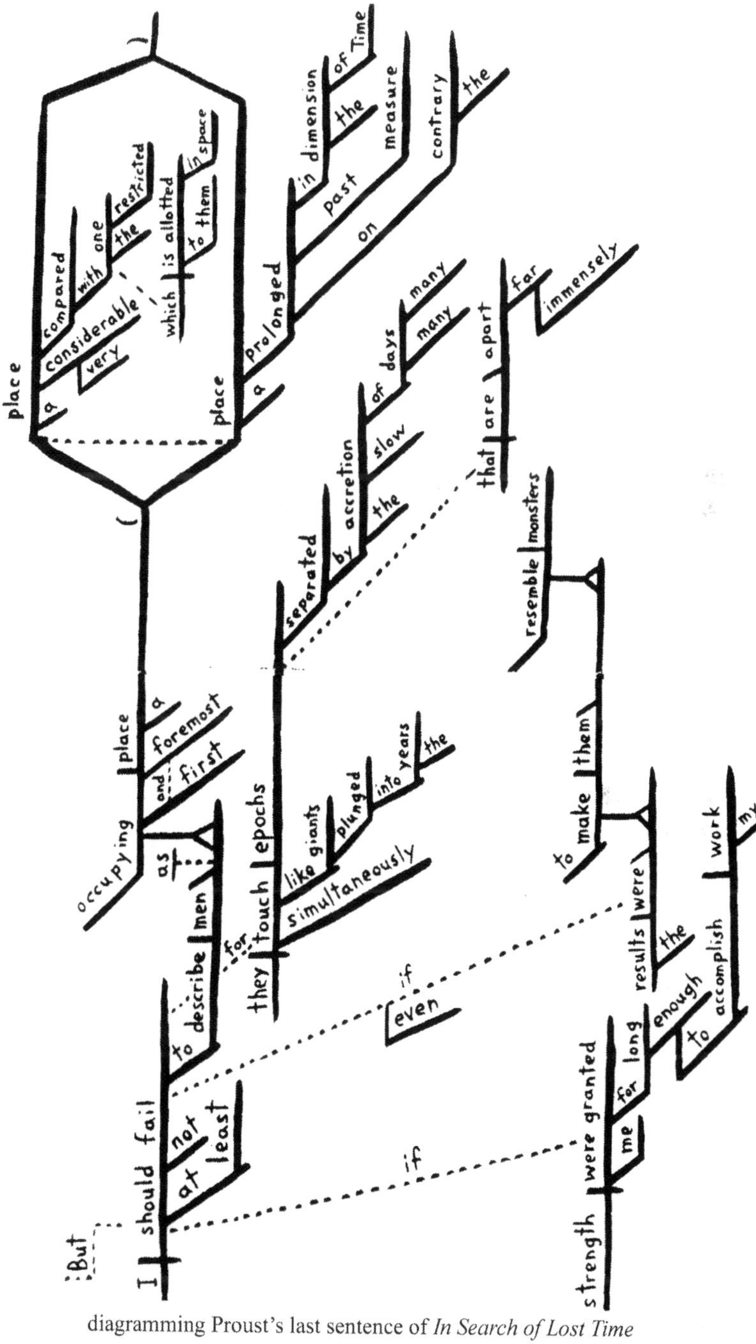

diagramming Proust's last sentence of *In Search of Lost Time* pause to verify my identity as her long-ago student, she pointed her finger at me and said, "And you . . .," then grabbed my arm and dragged me into her classroom as if I were late for class.

"This is Mr. Grapes," she said. "He's going to give us a lecture on Shakespeare." Then she sat in one of the empty desks and waited for me to proceed. Needless to say, I wasn't prepared, but did my best to invoke the spirit of Shakespeare, the poet and playwright I adore.

I bumbled my way through a short lecture, grabbing at whatever idea or image or quote bubbled up from my memory, as if I were constructing, slat by slat, a clubhouse shaped by Shakespeare's vision of humanity — the passions of love, the swords of conflict, and the dogs of war. "A horse, a horse, my kingdom for a horse," I exclaimed as desperate Richard III. "Lay on Macduff!" I yelled, holding aloft an imaginary sword. I presented Hamlet as a depressed Romeo, seeing the world as it was, not as he hoped it would be. Lady Macbeth was only sixteen, I told them, but she had more guts than the Scottish warrior who married her. Look how this king was a fool, I pointed out, and this fool, a king. "Was there a human emotion or plot contrivance Shakespeare did not cover?" I asked. "He creates a universe out of what?" I asked. "Words," I answered. Look how Prince Hal, now King Henry V, rejects Falstaff, his friend and father figure — with words more wounding than the polished steel of a sword: "I know thee not, old man."

More quotes followed. "O that this too too solid flesh would melt, thaw, resolve itself into a dew, or that the everlasting had not fixed his canon 'gainst self slaughter." From Hamlet to Falstaff's drunken speech on honor to Lear's mad challenge to the skies — "Blow winds, crack your cheeks!" — I did my best to impress her, but more importantly, to get to the spirit of Shakespeare's magic who dissappears in the body of every one of his creations and reappears in the heart of every one who sees them. I finished with Prospero's (and Shakespeare's) farewell to the stage: "But this rough magic I abjure, I'll break my staff, bury it certain fathoms in the earth, and deeper than did ever plummet sound, I'll drown my book." Then she asked me to read some of my own poems. By that point in time, I was breaking many of her rules, tossing proper syntax to the winds, but she nodded in approval.

I like to think she'd approve of these haiku, though not without some criticism of the few that don't adhere to form: there are five in this book in which I allow an extra syllable. If Matsuo Basho and Masoaka Shiki could do it once in a while, I figured, I can too. Mrs. Aime would understand the need to break free from established forms. Afterall, it was she who introduced us to Basho and Buson and Issa and, finally, that political radical, Shiki. Or, as I still nostalgically, think of them: Cough, Sneeze, Hiccup, and Buzoooooom.

You Say Hokku, I Say Haiku

Previously called *hokku*, the three-line "starting verse" of the longer renga, haiku was given its current name by Shiki at the end of the 19th century. Modern Japanese haiku tends not to follow the tradition of the seventeen syllables, though the use of juxtaposition (or "cutting") continues to be honored, if not in form, then in spirit.

The following haiku by Momoko Kuroda, one of Japan's most well-known haiku poets, recalls the poet's return to her village years after being evacuated in 1944, shortly before the nighttime firebombing from the B-29 Superfortresses that killed an estimated 100,000 people. Both the Japanese original and English translation of the haiku employ less than seventeen syllables, and do not adhere to the 5-7-5 pattern. (Compare it to Issa's haiku on page 79, and Basho's poems on pages 90, 143, and 279 about returning to their home villages.)

village of my youth —	*Nasu no mura*
that distant mountain cherry	*toyamazakurat*
his child evacuee	*sokai no ko*

The Trend Toward Shorter Haiku

In 1973, the Haiku Society of America noted that while writers of haiku in English most often used seventeen syllables, there was a trend toward shorter haiku. Buson was inclined to do without the *kireji*, or cutting word, relying as often on enjambment or punctuation marks — autumn moon *dash*, spring blossoms *colon*. In Japanese, haiku are traditionally printed in a single vertical line, while haiku in English often appear in three lines to parallel the three phrases of Japanese haiku.

But many contemporary haiku poets and translators of haiku into English are using the one-line form for haiku. Hiroaki Sato, who translated hundreds of haiku in *From the Country of Eight Islands* (University of Washington Press, 1981), is adamant about using the one-line format. John Ashbery was so intrigued by Sato's one-line translations that he wrote his own haiku using the same form. Marlene Mountain, Janice Bostok, and Jim Kacian are three contemporary American poets who champion the use of the one-line format.

But most mainstream contemporary poets are often unaware of the changes that have occurred in both Japanese and English haiku in the last fifty years, as if its development were taking place under the radar. Most assume that haiku's structure and essence have remained the same as it was four centuries ago when Basho composed his poem about the frog jumping into the old pond, but we have seen how even the four masters — Basho, Issa, Buson and Shiki — modified the form when it suited their purposes.

The last two lines of Basho's "Old Pond" haiku were actually composed first. He was almost forty years old, already in ill health, and this haiku marked a turning point in his poetic life.

furuike ya	old pond
kawazu tobikomu	frogs jumped in
mizu no oto	sound of water

The story of how the poem came about was told in a memoir by one of his disciples, who was there when it happened.

The Ten Philosophers

One evening, Basho and his friends, including his ten disciples — Etsujin, Hokushi, Joso, Kikaku, Kyorai, Kyoroku, Ransetsu, Shiko, Sanpu, and Yaha, also known as the "Ten Philosophers," a name derived from that of the ten pupils of Confucius — were sitting in the garden behind his house, discussing the art form and composing haiku as they drank sake. Writing haiku was a communal experience, often accompanied by convivial drinking. The sake was warm and served in small cups, called *sakazuki*. Each poet poured the sake for the one to their left, since it was customary not to pour for oneself. After several rounds of drinking and sharing poems, the disciple Etsujin composed two haiku. The first elicited much discussion and further drinking.

> Autumn evening;
> "Shall I light the lamp now?"
> someone comes to say.

Who was the person who asked to light the night-lamp? Was it Etsujin's wife, who grew old with him? Is her love the lamp she lights for him? They discussed the tantalizing ambiguity of the poem, then turned to Etsujin's second haiku.

> Another year goes away.
> I keep my hat on to hide
> gray hairs from my parents.

The haiku reminded Basho of a haiku he had written years earlier about his own parents.

> The voice of the pheasant;
> How I longed
> for my dead parents.

Basho was drawing together the "web of allusion" in which one haiku echoes another. Like most haiku, the image in Etsujin's poem suggests so many possibilities.

Kikaku: A Smartweed Eating Firefly

Eventually, after another round of drinks, they turned to a poem by Kikaku, whose poems were usually light-hearted and clever. Kikaku began writing haiku as a young boy, but reputedly had the temperament of a spoiled brat. He was a rich doctor's son who joined Basho's inner circle when he was only fourteen years old. Kikaku was a brilliant writer and became Basho's oldest friend. He was urbane, debonair, witty, with a quick sense of humor and generous spirit which added levity to Basho's more serious nature. He liked to show how clever he was. One day, while Basho and Kikaku were hiking, a red dragonfly darted past. Kikaku composed a haiku on the spot.

a darting dragon-fly — but wait!
pluck off its wings, and — ah ha!
a bright red pepper-pod!

Kikaku was delighted with his little joke. But Basho chided him.

"That isn't haiku," he said. "That is the wrong way, not to *say* it, but to *see* it. This is haiku." Then he recomposed what Kikaku had written.

a bright red pepper-pod — but wait!
put wings on it, and — ah ha!
a darting dragon-fly!

"A true poet," said Basho, "puts on wings, he doesn't take them off."

But Basho admired Kikaku's sense of humor and put up with it. By the time Kikaku was a young man, he was drinking heavily and consorting with prostitutes. His haiku thumbed its nose at etiquette. He likened himself to the brilliant firefly, staying up all night to enjoy the bitterness and danger of overindulgence and promiscuity.

At a grass hut
I eat smartweed,
I'm that kind of firefly.

Kikaku is making reference here to the Japanese adage "some prefer nettles." Basho gently rebuked Kikaku. "I prefer the simple life," Basho said, "a life in contemplation of nature." Kikaku laughed and read another haiku.

a man that eats
his meal amidst morning glories—
that's what I am!

The others complained at that point that Kikaku's haiku were "incomprehensible." Basho however, said that he found Kikaku's poems "swaggeringly elegant." Another round of drinks and a toast, after which Basho said, "Kikaku, you can express the most inconsequential things with great beauty." It was a backhanded compliment, but Kikaku was not deterred. Basho saw the "Buddha-nature" of things, while Kikaku was content to see things for their own nature. He accepted Basho's gentle rebuke and wrote a poem in which he rebuked himself.

A tree frog, clinging
to a banana leaf—
and swinging and swinging.

Basho's Banana Plant

Kikaku's clever image of the frog clinging to the banana leaf was typical of his "swaggering elegance." The humor is obvious, the image of the frog swinging and swinging, unable, perhaps, to let go. But Basho knew more was meant by the image of the banana leaf.

During the course of his life, Basho used some fifteen pen names, beginning with "Sobo" when he was just a young boy working in the home of the feudal lord and writing haiku with the lord's son, Yoshitada. "Basho" became his last.

In the winter of 1680, Basho's disciple Sugiyama Sanpu (1647-1732), a rich fish merchant, built a small, rustic house for him in the rural area of Fukagawa on the eastern shores of the Sumida River. Fukagawa was known as "the sea-level lowland" because it was on reclaimed land on the river's delta. It was exposed to the constant attack of sea wind from the Tokyo Bay as well as the danger of tidal waves from the ocean. It was a rough and wild place for a poet to live. In the spring, a student named Rika presented Basho with a banana tree to plant beside the new house. "The leaves of the banana tree," wrote Basho, "are large enough to cover a harp. When they are wind-broken, they remind me of the injured tail of a phoenix, and when they are torn, they remind me of a green fan ripped by the wind. The tree does bear flowers, but unlike other flowers, these have nothing joyous about them. The big trunk of the tree is untouched by the axe, too soft for lumber, utterly useless as building wood, resembling dragon scales. It's weed-like reeds are so rank, they choke the neighboring plants. But I love the tree, however, for its very uselessness. I sit underneath it and enjoy the wind and rain that blow against it."

"Basho's Banana Hermitage and Camellia Hill
on the Kanda Aqueduct at Sekiguchi" by Hiroshige

He became so fond of the banana tree that he changed his writing name from "Tosei," which meant "green peach," to "Basho," which meant "banana plant," and called his cottage "Banana Hermitage." The rare plant thrived and became "king of the garden," reaching as high as the roof. Basho likened himself to the plant — having neither utility nor beauty. When Kikaku used "banana leaf" in his poem, everyone knew he was invoking Basho himself. There was Kikaku, swinging at the feet of the master, clinging to the master's Buddha poems. It was hard to resist Kikaku's wit and his willingness to make fun of himself.

Sokan's Fan

At the time, haiku was still a mannered art, and Basho was encouraging his disciples to use everyday speech, rather than the elevated language used by military leaders and high officials of the court — formal imagery that focused more on clever juxtapositions than on profound insights or moments of Zen-like clarity. Basho recited a haiku by a poet who had lived a hundred years earlier, Yamazaki Sokan (1464-1551), as an example of a haiku more clever than enlightening:

If to the moon
one puts a handle — what
a splendid fan.

Sokan was referring to the *uchiwa*, the flat, round fan, not the *ogi* or *sensu*, the folding fan invented by a Japanese lady of the court in the 12th century. Sokan's haiku was charming, but Basho wanted haiku to function as something more than a parlor game with clever metaphors.

Teitoku's Slobber

At that point, Basho brought out a poem by Teitoku, the foremost poet of the Tokugawa days, who had died thirty years earlier. Basho pointed to Teitoku's haiku celebrating New Year's Day as another example of a poet being more concerned with the joke or clever image than with deeper insight:

This morning, how
icicles drip! — slobbering
year of the cow!

In Japanese, *taruru tsurara,* referring to dripping icicles, also has the meaning of "hang down," a word you'd use to describe a cow chewing its cud among the lowing herd. Basho admired the onomatopoeic cleverness, but felt the poem was more trick than magic. He dismissed haiku of this sort as "Teitoku's slobber."

Back to the Old Frog Pond

After such a proclamation, there was an uncomfortable silence. The ten philosophic poets took another sip of sake. Perhaps each poet was ruminating on his own limitations. Then, a sound was heard out in the garden. Basho looked up and said: "*Kawazu tobikomu mizu no oto*" (frog-jump-in / water-sound). Everyone recognized it as a possible ending for a haiku, needing only a first line. After the others made various suggestions for a first line, Kikaku suggested the first line should read *yamabuki*, since it was mid-spring and wild yellow roses were blooming near the fishpond outside Basho's hut. In classical poetry, "frog" and "*yamabuki*" were a designated combination, and *yamabuki* was one of the most frequently mentioned flowers. It can be translated as "yellow rose" or "globe flower"or "kerria rose." The most literal translation would be "mountain blossom." In haiku, the flower is often associated with water. A clever juxtaposition, Basho admitted.

In the end, Basho went for a simpler word/image in Japanese, for which a translation might be "old fishpond." Over the years, translators have found their own variations on that first line.

A lonely pond in age-old stillness sleeps,
apart, unstirred by sound or motion, until . . .
Suddenly into it a lithe frog leaps.
-Lafcadio Hern, 1850-1904

The quiet pond
A frog leaps in,
The sound of water
-Curtis Hidden Page, 1870-1946

old pond . . .
a frog leaps in
water's sound
-William Higginson, 1938-2008

Hern and Page translate the Japanese *furu-ike* as "lonely pond" and "quiet pond," but Basho meant old pond, and the word is deliberate. The spirit of illumination informed everything Basho wrote. Central to the cultivation of Zen is an appreciation of the given moment and the natural world, and of one's relationships to others. There is the belief that everything is connected to the whole and compassion is the spirit that guides one through suffering.

At this point in his life, Basho may have realized that he, too, had become set in his ways (like a stagnant old pond). Being open to change allows us to grow, to become reinvigorated. And what changes most of all is consciousness, the way we see the world and ourselves in it.

Water is often seen as a symbol of the unconscious. To take a journey on or into water represents a delving into the unconscious self. Ishmael's decision on the first page of *Moby Dick* to head out to sea tells us he is going to experience some life-changing revelation in the course of the tale. Though that may be a modern idea, it doesn't mean that Basho wasn't aware of what water symbolized, whether it be a raging river or a stagnant pond. The frog leaps into the water of the old pond (leaping into the consciousness of the old poet), stirring the water, and so the old pond once again swirls with life. The haiku may be *about* illumination, but the poem itself is an act of *satori*, Zen-like illumination.

Old Pond Call-and-Response

The call-and-response impulse in the history of haiku has enriched the tradition of the form. Poets not only pay tribute in this way to an oft-quoted haiku, but carry the original idea further. And in the case of a poem like Basho's "Old Pond," there have been affectionate parodies, as well.

Old pond—
after that time
no frog jumps in
-Kameda Bosai, (1752-1826)

Old pond—
something has PLOP
just jumped in
-Sengai Gibbon, (1750-1837)

Old pond—
the sound of water,
Basho jumps in
-Sengai Gibbon

Master Basho,
at every plop
stops walking
-Anonymous, (18th century)

Old pond paved over
into a parking lot—
one frog still singing
-Stephen Addiss, (1935-)

In "Old Pond," Basho's cutting word is *kawazu tobi-komu* — frog leap — which brings together the juxtaposed images of the old pond and the sound of the water. In Japanese haiku, a cutting word or image typically appears in the middle line, filling the role analogous to a *caesura* in classical Western poetry, or to a *volta*, or "turn" in sonnets, be they Alexandrian, Elizabethan, or Shakespearean.

Depending on which cutting word is chosen, and its position within the verse, it may briefly cut the stream of thought, suggesting a parallel to the preceding and following phrases. It may also signal an opposing idea or image in such contrast to the first that a third idea is suggested to the reader without the poet having to state it (recall Shiki's haiku in which he juxtaposes the persimmon with the sound of the temple bell). The cutting word or idea can also provide a dignified ending or resolution. Most English translations of haiku work best with the cutting word or cutting idea in the last line.

A Balloon Heavy as a Stone
A Stone Light as a Feather

For me, the most foreign aspect of writing haiku is the absence of a "gathering out leap," to take a line from Rilke's "First Elegy." There's not much to gather in haiku, and little room to leap. The form challenges the poet to construct a balloon heavy as stone, or a stone light as a feather — an impossible task. Because of the impossibility, the best one can hope for is light-footed haiku that attempt, per Buson's declaration, to capture a simple image as a painter would a peach. Shiki heard Buson's call and wrote:

> Ripening in fields
> that once were the samurai quarter—
> autumn eggplant.

This haiku achieves the impossible —it has both airiness and gravitas, the lightness of a balloon and the weight of a stone. The samurai's violent and glorious death is reduced over time to nothing more than an eggplant. Later in this essay, we'll see how Nick Virgilio responded to this haiku with one of his own, another example of the web of allusion. Some of Basho's haiku are similarly profound, yet are borne aloft by the simplicity of an everyday image.

> Sweep the garden
> all kindnesses
> falling willow leaves repay.

Basho's Narrow Road

It's a long way from the childhood pleasure of counting syllables to the awareness of a haiku's complexity. But the more one wrestles with the mechanics of haiku, the more one confronts its essential complexity. The challenge is to make the haiku internally sufficient, independent of context, so it will bear consideration as a complete work.

In Basho's masterpiece, *Narrow Road into the Interior*, he chronicles the journey he took through the villages and mountain temples of the northern interior of Japan. Each haiku is a distillation of the prose paragraph that precedes it. Unlike many books of haiku, Basho's travelogue presents a sequential narrative. A few translators have even suggested titles to each prose/haiku section, calling them "stations" along the way, such as "Departure" or "Shirakawa" or "Matsushima." Many haiku refer to characters or places that appeared in previous haiku. The emphasis is as much on the narrative as on the individual haiku. The sequence of prose and haiku contributes to the narrative of Basho's travelogue, which is also a journey into the spirit or soul. Some of his haiku illuminate other haiku, joining the two together. Some elevate the spirit, others sound the bell of profundity or epiphany.

Tennis Without a Net

Robert Frost once said (in response to the "free verse" versifiers) that writing poetry without the constraint of some formal device (rhyme, meter, sonnet, sestina, villanelle, etc.) was like "playing tennis without a net." That idea has always intrigued me. He was criticizing the contemporary poets who championed free verse. Frost wrote many poems that didn't rhyme, but there was always some formal constraint in his work, even if it was as minimal as the tension between natural speech rhythms and poetic meter.

In his introductory note to Frost's poems in the seminal anthology *The Voice That is Great Within Us* (1970), editor Hayden Carruth wrote: "Frost's poetic practice was based on what he called 'sentence sounds,' the natural tones and rhythms of speech cast loosely against standard poetic forms. Conventional as it may seem today, it was a new departure in its time, making Frost a distinctly modern poet." When I read that statement, I was encouraged by Frost's dictum that we eschew poetic language in favor of natural speech, while realizing that an awareness of formal structure contributed to the essential tension that exists, not just in poetry, but in all art.

Contemporary poets had the blessing of the man who read his poem "The Gift Outright" at Kennedy's inauguration. What I misunderstood at the time was that Frost hadn't abandoned traditional form — it still functioned deep within his poems. "Free verse" needs some constraint, even if the form is not outwardly visible. So his quip about playing tennis without a net captured my interest, though it resonated on a purely intellectual level, not a visceral or instinctive one. It was an intriguing idea, and as someone who played tennis often, I understood the concept of playing without a net, but wasn't sure why. What was so hard about playing tennis without a net?

An Imaginary Net

Then one afternoon I was meeting a friend for tennis at Poinsettia Park, just north of Santa Monica Boulevard. There were two courts, but one was occupied and the other's net had been cut and torn down. We didn't want to wait, so we attempted to play on the court without the net, and a strange thing happened. We couldn't do it. We tried to play with an imaginary net, hitting the ball low, but hitting the ball that low precluded the trajectory one needs for a clean return. And because there was no natural bounce, it was impossible to return the volley. No matter how hard we worked on it, we continued to hit the ball into the imaginary net. I don't know if it had to do with visual perception or with something psychological, but the tension between trying to hit above the line of the net, yet not so high that it went out of bounds on the back end of the court, was lost. We ended up waiting for the people on the other court to finish their game so we could play our game of tennis *with* the net.

Even in "free verse," therefore, some constraint is needed, whether it's internal meter and rhythm, or some other device, hidden or not from the reader. Hewing to the demands of the 5-7-5 syllable count is a physical constraint when writing haiku, but there's also a philosophical constraint. It has to do with the essence of haiku, that undefinable quality that makes a haiku a haiku, and not just a short poem. This is a problem American poets have been trying to solve for the last seventy years, starting in the 1950s, that post-war period in which all forms of art underwent a "post-modern" shift.

Mrs. Aime and Homer and Dante

What I couldn't appreciate at ten or eleven years old was that writing haiku, discussing its history and delights, was part of a larger dialogue occurring in American poetry. Mrs. Aime was one of the most passionate teachers I've ever known, and since I had her as a teacher from fourth through twelfth grades, I experienced the wealth of her knowledge, which ranged from philosophy to science, math, literature, religion, history, politics, and even good manners. Except for my father, she was the most influential teacher I've ever had.

She blamed her fiery temper and bursts of enthusiasm on her Greek-Italian heritage. You didn't want to get on her bad side or stand in her way as she strode between rows of desks to drag someone to the blackboard in order to rub their noses in what she had written in chalk. I know — I was one of those kids.

One winter, as I stood in front of the class reading my paper on "The Meaning of Hanukkah," she rebuked me for misunderstanding a finer point of the ritual and misapplying it to the tenets of my religion. Here she was, the Greek Orthodox teacher correcting the secular Jew on the meaning of his own religion. She seemed to know everything.

In eleventh and twelfth grades we were introduced to Homer and Dante, respectively, and I remember her reading passages from the *Illiad* in Greek and the first Canto of the *Commedia* in Italian. It was electrifying. She nearly cried reading that scene in the *Illiad* where Priam crosses enemy lines to ask Achilles for the return of the body of his slain son, Hector. "I kiss the hand," Priam says, kneeling before a seated Achilles, "the hand that killed my son."

When she recited Dante's opening lines in Italian, she sounded out *di nostra vita* — "of our life" — with such conviction that I felt she was inscribing those words on my forehead. "*Una selva oscura*," she whispered, "a dark wood." Then lifting her eyes from the book, she looked straight at us, as if warning us of dangers to come, and said, "*ché la diritta via era smarrita* — for the straight way was lost!" Those dark eyes of hers bore into mine; she was warning me that we often lose our way in this life, so I had better be prepared. And she was right. Many times I have felt lost, unable to face or comprehend the world, and Dante's words and her recitation of them have appeared like an admonishing oracle.

Mrs. Aime's husband had fought in the war (World War II), but what we didn't know was that he was a poet. Mrs. Aime was an olive-skinned beauty with dark hair and eyes so brown they seemed black. Whenever we saw her husband driving up in their beat-up Ford station wagon, we pigeon-holed him as the hen-pecked husband she ordered around, not understanding that beneath his gentle demeanor was a poet who had been scarred by war. It was he who introduced her to Japanese haiku.

Ridgewood Preparatory School Yearbook, June, 1960

Mrs. Troescher and the Walk-In Closet

I should take a short detour here to mention Mrs. Jane Troescher, my English teacher in 10th Grade. She was nowhere as rigorous as Mrs. Aime, nowhere as knowledgeable, nowhere as strict, but she gave me a free reign when it came to creative writing that I'll always be grateful for. It wasn't something she did intentionally. It was more of a fluke that it worked out that way. But it turned out to be a year of linguistic exploration before I even knew what the hell I was exploring. Without knowing anything about French symbolist poetry of the 1890s, or Russian structuralism of the 1920s, or even the language experiments with poetic syntax that was to come in the late 1970s and 80s, I embarked on a year-long spelunk into the arcane mysteries of linguistic fields and logical syntax.

Such a thing could never have happened with Mrs. Aime. She was a stickler when it came to proper grammar and syntax. She even gave us a list of "fumblerules," many of which I remember to this day. A fumblerule was a rule of language or linguistic style written in such an ironic way as to break the rule it was invoking. Here's a few:

Never use no double negatives.
Eschew Obfuscation.
Avoid clichés like the plague.
No sentence fragments.
Parentheses are (almost always) unnecessary.
English is the *crème de la crème* of all languages.

To use a metaphor that I will soon explain, Mrs. Aime was a Newtonian English teacher, while Mrs. Troescher opened the door for quantum linguistics – not by design, more by default. When Paul Dirac showed Neils Bohr an equation that seemed to violate the rules of Newtonian physics, Dirac said that it was "crazy," to which Bohr responded, "Maybe it's not crazy enough." When it came to literary narrative, Mrs. Aime knew exactly what she was doing, knew exactly what was allowed. Mrs. Troescher wasn't so sure. If you asked her a technical question about proper grammar or syntax, she sat there stumped, went into her walk-in closet and shuffled through handbooks and textbooks trying to find the answer. But it was just this lack of confidence on her part that allowed me the freedom to experiment.

Furthermore, with Mrs. Aime, there was no fooling around. She was a taskmaster who got down to business and brooked no disruption. She was my English Lit teacher all through Junior High and High School, except for that one year, my Sophomore year, the year I was fifteen, when Mrs. Troescher taught Sophomore English.

Where Mrs. Aime kept a tight reign on everyone, Mrs. Troescher kept no discipline at all. Oh, she'd huff and puff, yell our names, pound her desk, stamp her feet, but we paid her no mind. Class was a free-for-all. I probably danced rings around her with my foolishness, and not a day went by that I didn't frustrate her about something. But it was never mean-spirited. That's the funny thing about it. We all loved Mrs. Troescher, and she had great affection for us. There was always a sense of play about the disruptions. When she'd throw her hands up in exasperation, saying, "Jack Grapes, I don't know what I'm going to do with you," there was always a slight smile, as if the stern look on her face was covering an impulse to laugh.

One day I asked her a question about grammar, and as usual, she went into her walk-in closet full of books and papers and searched for a book in which she could find the rule. I was sitting in the front row, my foot only inches away from the door. I gave the door a push and it closed, locking her inside. We pretended we couldn't find the keys. "They're in the door,"she yelled. "Oh," we said. Then we tried every one of the two dozen keys she had on the ring, jangling like a tambourine.

Another day we got a coat hanger and wired her chair to the inside of her desk. When she went to pull the chair out, there ensued an epic struggle that lasted a good ten minutes. Finally, one of us crawled on the floor and untangled it. We expressed dismay. "Who could have done such a thing?" we wondered aloud.

Eschew Obfuscation, Espouse Elucidation

Another prank involved my hiding in the walk-in closet before Mrs. Troescher walked into the class. When she walked in, she dumped an armfull of books and papers on her desk and announced that she was giving us a vocabulary test. "The first word," she said, "is obfuscate." Gene slid a piece of paper

Ridgewood Prepartory School Yearbook, June 1960

under the door and in the dim light, I wrote down the word and its definition, then used it in a sentence. She called out a total of twenty words, which I wrote down, defined, and used in a sentence. When it came time to hand the papers up, I slid the paper back under the door to Gene, who handed it up with the rest of the papers. Mrs. Troescher marked me absent for that day, but was confused the next day when she handed out the page with my name and handwritten answers. I'd gotten a perfect score.

"Were you here yesterday?" she asked.

"Of course," I said, "how else could I have taken the test?" She opened the book where she kept roll and made a note, a perplexed look on her face.

"I must not have seen you," she said.

"I guess not," I said. "Maybe you weren't wearing your glasses."

She just stared at me, trying to figure it out.

"Who could have done such a thing?" I said, grinning impishly.

"Jack Grapes," she said, "I don't know what I'm going to do with you!"

"Ist Dass Ist Dass Troescher Babe!"

Eddie Haspel and I were always kidding around with her, especially when she'd first walk into class. We greeted her with a Germanic chant: "Ist dass ist dass Troescher Babe? Yah, dass ist dien Troescher Babe!" It drove her crazy, but we got away with it. Underneath all the tomfoolery, she liked me. And just as I learned more about the grammar and syntax of writing from Mrs. Aime, it was from Mrs. Troescher -- *ist dass ist dass Troescher babe!* -- that I expanded my creative process in ways I never could have imagined.

It all started with her announcement that she would give extra credits for creative writing, whether it was fiction, a poem, an essay, whatever. I jumped at the chance. That school year, every Monday, I handed in a sheet or two of creative writing. At first they were the usual prose stories, interspersed with an occasional poem. She never corrected a word, never made a suggestion, never did anything but hand it back to me the next day with a red check at the top of the page and gave me the extra credit. I knew that if Mrs. Aime had the same paper she'd have slashed it with red marks and dragged me across the carpet for sloppy syntax or confusing imagery. But Mrs. Troescher always returned the pages with a red check mark for extra credit, nothing more.

Attaboy!

Maybe, I thought, she was a bit intimidated by my creative work. Maybe she wasn't sure how to respond to the writing. I think she could never be sure if something I did violated a grammatical rule for effect and was intentional, or if I had just written a poorly constructed sentence. Then, after about two months of this, I began to wonder if she were reading the damn things at all! I wanted a pat on the back, I wanted some kind of praise for my imaginative writing. While I knew Mrs. Aime appreciated what I wrote, she was not one to give effusive praise. It was all about the meat and potatoes of grammar and syntax and clear sentence structure and all that other technical stuff. I was craving a response from the heart. I wanted Mrs. Troescher to make extensive comments extolling the virtues of the writing, of the story. With Mrs. Aime I'd learned to accept the knowing nod of approval, but with Mrs. Troescher, I was hoping for a few jumps of joy, an "attaboy" or two.

Maybe, I thought, she was reading them, but was hesitant to correct anything? How could I find out? Then I had an idea. What if I wrote a sentence that contained a grammatical error so obvious, she'd be forced to correct it? Then I would know for sure that she was at least reading what I'd written.

Red Check, Extra Credit

So I began to make errors in grammar on purpose. Usually it was something small, using the pluperfect tense instead of the past perfect or imperfect tense. These were small errors, something Mrs. Aime would have caught, but most people would have passed them over. After a few weeks of that, I got bolder. I made more egregious errors in grammar and syntax. I used run-on sentences or sentence fragments. Still, all I got was a red check and an extra credit. Okay, I thought, you wanna play tough, I'll play tough. By the end of October I was using words out of context, words that had no meaning. I even ventured into the area of total nonsense, sentences that seemed to make sense but didn't. Mrs. Aime would have strung me up by my you-know-whats, but not Mrs. Troesher. Red check, extra

✓ One Extra Credit

Jack Grapes
3rd Period
English
Nov. 18, 1957

Extra Credit Creative Writing

Further down the ladder, much to the disdain of galactic removal, however, the old buzzard refrained from punctuality. Emerson Gibralter knew his only hope was the unless attraction of Sophie Reynolds, who, as it were, memorized Hoover Damn into the consolidations of repose, suppose, and frequent alabaster images of betrayal. Unkind pencils volcanic distress. Which motorized amphibious assault spoke eventually to Robert Plato, the barber who offered apple pies to ten little Indians klepto forgiveness. He levitated the mackerel, sedfish unto removal once removed from constant nomenclature. "I'll have a rocking chair," blustered Mr. Thompson, already motivated toward nefarious palaces. Field mice whoever speaks. In the afternoon regions Captain Mouseketeer often between within. Not with standing his Mother the rabbit. She floated away unrhymed heavily muffled.

credit. Okay, time for desperate measures. With Thanksgiving a few weeks away, I felt I had to do something drastic. I took down a few of my father's technical books, wrote down arcane words and phrases, patched them together in sentences that had the flow of voice, but were totally meaningless in themselves. Red check, extra credit. The piece I handed in the week before Thanksgiving was clearly an exercise in goofball abstraction. I admit, it had a certain *joie de vivre* of nonsensical panache, syntactically and coherently speaking, bolstered by protagonist names like Emerson Gibralter and Robert Plato. But did it deserve a red check and extra credit? Apparently, it did.

A Game of Chicken

By spring break, I was playing with syntax dislocation and typographic deconstruction. I got the idea that I could insert haiku-like phrases that would float in space, disconnected from the surrounding text. I wrote haiku that made little sense, re-arranged the lines so they made even less sense, inserted them into a prose narrative that made no sense at all. I made certain words bolder using a pen with a bigger nib. At some point, the pages I was handing in looked more like scratch pads. If I were a painter, it would have been the equivalent of handing in a palette with smudged colors rather than a respectable painting on a respectable canvas. Even that was not enough to prompt her to question what I was doing. Red check: extra credit.

At that point, Mrs Aime would have hogtied me back into the traditional structure of clear, linear narrative and coherent imagery. If I had used a metaphor that bore no relation to the object being compared, Mrs. Aime would have probably cried out, "What the heck's come over you. I taught you better than that!" I wouldn't have heard the end of it for weeks. But without realizing it, Mrs Troescher was allowing me to discover the joy of linguistic deconstructions without knowing anything of what the French Symbolists had done, nor of what the Language poets of the 70s and 80s were yet to do. It became a game of chicken with Mrs. Troescher: Who would blink first?

Linguistic Deconstructions

Each week I experimented with linguistic meaninglessness. There was no linear thread, just a jumble of words and phrases and linguistic units, structural chaos. Each week I expanded the

✓ One Extra Credit

Jack Grapes
3rd Period
English
March 27, 1958

EXTRA CREDIT

magic red ball
eclipse lampshades
all perhaps in his MIND portrayed
as
pertaining to but not understood by
MISTER Fish gadzooks!
It was a dark and stormy night when
Renfro destablized the rhoddadendrum
who no salt was mentioned a carcass
levitation of rhino slippers.
mules hop-scotch
ebony free-thinkers
seven you bake
fabulous cakes and he found the
old man trace eleenental restrictions
my planet of safety zones. Etch.
"Not my wrench!" he declared. Whereas.
table salt plastic noodles
all nervous to display
the robin in the tree who sang in his sleep
Mercury megaphone
—.—.—

boundary of proper syntax and grammar. My only guideline was to test the waters to see how far I could go, to see at what point — assuming she was reading my creative pieces — Mrs. Troescher would finally break down and challenge what I was handing in. The elliptical nature of haiku — the juxtaposition of unrelated images, the fleeting phrases of conscious thought, the discontinuity of associations — all were devices I used to deconstruct linear narrative and logical syntax. The universe of literary matter was expanding into the energy density of the vacuum. It didn't faze her a bit. Red check: extra credit.

By the end of the school year, our undeclared tête-à-tête was technically a draw. It wasn't until a few years later that I understood what I had come away with.

The French Symbolist Poets

In my freshman year of college, we were introduced to the French symbolist poets: Charles Baudelaire, Arthur Rimbaud, Stéphan Mallarmé. They attempted to evoke the ineffable intuitions and sense expressions of man's inner life and experience. They wanted to liberate poetry from its expository functions and its formalized ideas by using metaphors and images that, despite lacking precise meaning, conveyed the poet's mind and hinted at the "dark and confused unity" of an inexpressible reality.

When we began to read Rimbaud's *Le Bateau Ivre* (The Drunken Boat), made up of short, haiku like stanzas, most of my classmates had trouble navigating the unusual imagery and confused consciousness of the writing. Since I had already been-there-done-that as a sophomore in high school, it was a snap for me. Rimbaud's poem seemed perfectly comprehensible to me. I read *The Drunken Boat* and gave Rimbaud a red check. Here's a few stanzas from that poem:

> And since then I've been bathing in the Poem
> Of star-infused and milky Sea,
> Devouring the azure greens, where, flotsom pale,
> A brooding corpse at times drifts by.
>
> I've touched, you know, fantastic Floridas
> Mingling the eyes of panthers,
> human-skinned with flowers!

And rainbows stretched like endless reins
To glaucous flocks beneath the seas.
I've seen fermenting marshes like enormous nets
Where in the reeds a whole Leviathan decays!
Crashing of waters in the midst of calms!
Horizons toward far chasms cataracting!

I can no longer bathe in your languors, O waves,
Obliterate the cotton carriers' wake,
Nor cross the pride of pennants and of flags,
Nor swim past prison hulks' hateful eyes!

Eventually, I came upon Stéphan Mallarmé's *Un Coup de Des Jamais N'Abolira Le Hazard* (A Throw of the Dice Will Never Abolish Chance) in which he co-opted typography to present a proliferation of meanings. Here's a snippet:

hesitates
corpse by the arm   separated from the secret
it withholds
rather
than play
as a hoary maniac
the game   in the name of waves
one invades the head
flows in the submissive beard
shipwreck this   pertaining to man
without vessel
no matter
where vain
from ancient time not to open up the hand
clenched
legacy amid disappearance
to someone
ambiguous
the ulterior immemorial demon
having
from nullified regions
induced
the old man toward this supreme conjunction with probability

Russian Symbolism and Language Poetry

We also read Russian symbolist poets such as Valery Bryusov, Vladimir Sergeyevich Solovyov, and Aleksandr Blok, then moved on to Vladimir Mayakovky and Sergei Yesenin. By the time I got to the stream of consciousness of James Joyce's *Ulysses* and the interior monologues of Virginia Woolf's novels, I felt right at home.

By the late 70s and 80s, the Language poets had become a dominant influence in American poetry. The Language poets were interested in changing the structure of the sentence. Linguistic units were often displaced syntactically so as to subvert traditional conveyance of ideas, story, linear meaning, and even the idea of an authentic voice. If traditional poetry painted a realistic picture or presented a coherent expression of ideas and feelings, just as traditional painters offered realistic pictures of nature or human figures, then one could say that Language Poetry used disconnected sentences and jumbled linguistic units the same way that cubist, post-modern, and abstract expressionists — painters like Jackson Pollock, Wilhem de Kooning, Mark Rothko, Arshile Gorky, Franz Kline, Hans Hoffman, Lee Krasner, Elaine de Kooning, Richard Diebenkorn, Helen Frankenthaler, and Joan Mitchell — painted canvases.

Like the abstract-expressionists, Language poets deconstructed typographical units so the reader was even further removed from the normal experience of linear storytelling. They thumbed their noses at intellectual property by borrowing, quoting, twisting, and distorting pieces of text from other writers. Personal expression was abandoned for the use of language as an object, a thing in and of itself. The sentence was not a device that shuttled meaning from writer to reader. There was no meaning, only language. Major figures in the Language poetry school were Ron Silliman, Lynn Hejinian, Barrett Watten, Charles Bernstein, Susan Howe, Clark Coolidge, Carla Harryman, Bob Perelman, Bruce Andrews, and Rae Armantrout (to name just a few).

For instance, Barrett Watten's poem "Complete Thought" consisted of numbered couplets that reminded me both of haiku, and those gnomic aphorisms of Malcolm de Chazal (see pages 110-112).

IX
Construction turns back in on itself.
Dogs have to be whipped.

XII
False notes work on a staircase.
The hammer is as large as the sun.

XIV
Everyday life retards potential.
Calculation governs speech.

XXIV
Thought remains in the animal.
Each island steals teeth.

XXXIII
A boot steps into an example.
Conviction is selected from space.

Or take this stanza from "Word of Mouth" by Ted Greenwald:

Bell who's holding   To
Spend all the time
Pending   Patent parent
Injection visions   De-
Cide to make incisive
Remark incision are

Much of what I read by these poets seemed familiar from that period of extra credit writings in my sophomore year of high school when I fused short aphoristic haiku-like snippets with lines of prose that lacked coherent syntax and meaning. Here's a piece by Hannah Weiner, from the definitive anthology of Language Poetry edited by Ron Silliman, *In The American Tree (1986,* which was dedicated, by the way, to Larry Eigner, see pages 183-184).

GET A SHOT THANKS A LOT MICHAEL LUBA *necessary* You *so what* realize *think of it Rosemary color* Wed was awful because you were just getting *sick again* The interference has a field day but doesn't *government* explain *neg* why *flu* DRINK NU says the tea YOU HAVE THE FLU JACK CONTROL YOURSELF DUMB You cant believe that the breakfront and table from *Jerry's apt* fit perfectly in yours *perfec* brown wood tall thin cabinet round holed screened bottom used to be over radiator, put milk cartons ms in it, *in your apt* SHOPPING GUIDE DOUBLeday and BLOOMingdales *nega* after you called Rhys what does it mean GO THERE SEE EDITORS Majorie calls SPEAKING THE SAME VOICES NO POETRY READING *bashful why not not conscious yourself take it easy* USE SOAP BIG PROBLEM NOT ALL PROBLEMS You mean there are pleasures IN LIFE GEORGE OMIT THE EDITING you thought you mentioned you read it over and you take out buts, ands, ifs, etcs. **AND NO PERIODS** and it puts in underlines MORE EFFORT and a few big words ALSO

The Fool's Business of Absence of Field

Even though I was to abandon haiku for most of my writing life, the writing of haiku in grammar school, and the way it allowed me to deconstruct sentences in those extra credit pieces I handed in to Mrs. Troescher when I was fifteen, helped me to reposition the goal posts at either end of the poetry field. In a manner of speaking, there was no field — structural, linguistic, logical, or otherwise — only an absence of field. There was no limit to what one could, or could not do.

When embedded in prose, sentences merrily roll along with the logic of language and speech in such a way as to obscure the structural implications of the sentence itself. In the words of poet Louis Simpson, the object was to make "words disappear," as if the words were less important than the idea or image or narrative being conveyed. Novelist William Gass, who also wrote essays on literature and the sentences that comprise it, said in a *Paris Review* interview that writing sentences "out of context is a fool's business, but I set about doing the fool's business." With poetry, the focus is not even on the sentence, but the smaller unit of the line.

When writing a poem, our attention is on the image and the melody of thought. When writing a poem, we are removed from that narrative overexuberance to place the world within the sentence, to make the sentence mean the world. But when writing haiku, we are so far removed from narrative that sentences hardly exist. Haiku avoids narrative. Even the line shuns semblances of conscious extension. We are reduced to Cezanne's cubist brushstrokes, snapshots of thought and imagistic phrases that appear to fall out of a photo album with no reference, no context, no narrative momentum. Haiku: those psychic thunderclaps composed of stones light as a feather, and feathers heavy as a stone.

The Surround of Sound vs The Bric-a-Brac of Haiku

I noticed quite early on that different writers wrote different kinds of sentences, and their influence on me had more to do with how they wrote sentences than with the narrative world they created. Writers like Earle Stanley Gardner and Ernest Hemingway wrote Western Union shorthand sentences – a little dab'll do ya. But the maximalist writers like Gertrude Stein, Henry James, Virginia Woolf, Malcolm Lowry, Ford Madox Ford, James Joyce, William Gass, and Marcel Proust delved into the core mysteries of sense making. They pushed the ability of great sentences to align with words in order to create and simulate the inner life of both writer and reader. Their sentences wore wide skirts that swayed when they walked, knocking down all the bric-a-brac of the tidy story. Gass called this "the surround of sound." Stories have plot, a beginning, middle and end; but character often remains unconcluded, like Strether at the end of Henry James's great novel, *The Ambassadors*. His future remains open since he represents the potentiality of character which cannot be exhausted by plot. It is completely appropriate to that novel that its structure, its very style — those sentences, like Proust's, which delay exact significance until the end, and even then, their significance is problematic — casts the reader upon his impressions like a boat forced to surrender to the tumultous river of the hero's experience.

The Everythingness of Sentences vs The Nothingness of Words

In high school, when I began to subvert the architecture of proper sentence-making in those creative writing pieces for extra credit, I reached a point where the nothingness of words replaced the everythingness of sentences, especially those long-winded sentences favored by writers like Proust and James. I was introduced to poets and writers in college who were fracturing the linguistic arc of the sentence, or even the melody in a line of poetry based on the literary philosophy of semantic displacement as advocated by the French and Russian symbolists. I had played with those toys when I was fifteen as a sophomore in high school. Eventually, my interests turned to the building of skyscrapers of speech from the narrative voice, rather than the fragile escapades of linguistic building blocks you knock over with a sneeze.

Haiku and Einstein's Cosmological Constant

And finally, why not mention my physics teacher Mrs. Hancock, whom we all had a crush on. As I had done with the postulates of Mr. Zanca's plane geometry class, I managed to find the sense of haiku in the formulas Mrs. Hancock pounded into our heads: the equations of motion, Newton's 2nd Law of Thermodynamics, angular acceleration, angular frequency, angular momentum, Hooke's law, Boyle's law, Bernoulli's equation, dynamic viscosity, volume continuity, and Archimedes' method of exhaustion.

But what made the biggest impression on me was something she said about the fate of the universe. Einstein had postulated a "cosmological constant" (usually denoted by the Greek capital letter Lambda as the value of the energy density of the vacuum of space). In his General Theory of Relativity, he couldn't abide by the implication of his own equations that indicated the universe was expanding. This didn't sit well with Einstein. He preferred a static universe, a universe that remained in a "steady state," neither expanding nor contracting. So he postulated a "cosmological constant," which would in effect "hold back gravity."

Fire or Ice

This number, once inserted into his equations, was designed to keep the universe – at least the universe in his equations — from expanding or contracting. The universe was in a "steady state," he maintained. Then Edwin Hubble discovered the red shift, which indicated that the universe was expanding, proving Einstein's General Theory of Relativity had been correct without the need to insert that cosmological constant. Einstein called that the "biggest blunder" of his life. Furthermore, said Mrs. Hancock, if the universe was expanding, it could also contract, assuming there was enough matter for gravity to overcome inertia. As Robert Frost had written in one of his poems, we could all end in fire or we could all end in ice.

Perhaps for the fun of it, if we could show the cosmological constant in the form of a haiku, it would look like this:

R_{\mu \nu} -\frac{1}{2}R\,g_{\mu \nu}
+\Lambda\,g_{\mu \nu}
= {8 \pi G \over c^4} T_{\mu \nu}

where R and g describe the structure of spacetime, T pertains to matter and energy affecting that structure, and G and c are conversion factors that arise from using traditional units of measurement. Basho would have approved.

God Plays Dice with the Universe

While I was writing those incoherent creative pieces for Mrs. Troescher, it was Mrs. Hancock who opened my mind to the possibility that, whether it was grammar or syntax, epic poetry or a three-line haiku, everything oscillated between the expanding linguistic structure of the big bang of language and the singularity of a one word poem. The universe was expanding, and would one day collapse back into its singularity. The same applied to all literary constructs, which could expand into volumes of epic poetry — endless narratives with endless sentences — or it could also contract back into three-line haiku, and if necessary, down to one line, one word, or even one letter. Anything was possible. Jackson Pollock, the big bang, and three-line haiku. Gravity was the same, whether in physics, art, or poetry. Like God, you could do anything you wanted. Or as Einstein complained to Neils Bohr when confronted with the anomalies of quantum physics, "God doesn't play dice with the universe!" To which Bohr responded, "Quit telling God what to do."

A Crumb of Bread

I assume everyone has had at least one teacher who made a lasting impact on their lives. I was fortunate to have many: Mrs. Aime, Mrs. Troescher, Mr. Zanca, Mrs. Hancock. While all of them taught me life-lessons, each taught me something about writing which has remained with me to this day. But my greatest teacher was my father. He was an amazing writer. All I have left of his writing is part of a short poem in that beautiful handwriting of his, on the back of a meal ticket – No. 1021,

W.H.M.S. Commissary – a meal ticket he'd been given during the depression, when he rode the rails and slept in flop houses and sold shoelaces office-door to office-door in those Manhattan skyscrapers. "Her mouth embalmed with the bitter dregs of . . . ." When he was dying in a hospital room, I asked him why he hadn't written about his life growing up on the lower-east side and his days as a young vagabond traveling about the country. "I was too busy trying to stay alive," he said.

I showed him my own attempts at writing, whether the detective novels I wrote in 8th grade or the complicated science-fiction stories I wrote in high-school. One day I showed him a short story filled with plot complications and clever twists and turns. We were sitting at the kitchen table and I sipped a cup of coffee while he read. Then he looked up and said, "Why don't you write a story about a crumb of bread?"

This was haiku in reverse. My dad was telling me that I could write pages of prose about something as trivial as a crumb of bread. Plot is irrelevant, my father was implying. Story doesn't matter. Details are important, the more specific the better. The writing is what's important. The sentences, the words. Whether a haiku or a 300 page novel, the smallest detail can be the most memorable. For instance, an image that has stayed with me from *War and Peace* comes from a scene where Prince Andrei is lying on the ground, dying. He looks up at the figure of Napoleon sitting on his horse. Andrei looks away for a moment and notices in the distance a soldier carrying a mop across a bridge. He looks back at Napoleon, then back at the bridge, and the soldier with the mop is gone. Only a cloud of smoke remains where the soldier stood.

> He heard the whistle of bullets above him, unceasingly and to right and left of him. He now saw clearly the figure of a red-haired gunner with his shako knocked awry, pulling one end of a mop while a French soldier tugged at the other. He could distinctly see the distraught yet angry expression on the faces of these two men, who evidently did not realize what they were doing. "Why doesn't the red-haired gunner run away as he is unarmed? Why doesn't the Frenchman stab him?" And really another French soldier, trailing his musket, ran up to the struggling men, and the fate of the red-haired gunner, who had triumphantly secured the mop and still did not realize what fate

Samuel J. Grapes, 1908 - 1962

awaited him, was about to be decided. But Prince Andrei did not see how it ended. He closed his eyes, then opened them, hoping to see how the struggle of the Frenchmen with the gunners ended, whether the red-haired gunner had been killed or not and whether the cannon had been captured or saved. But he saw nothing. Above him there was now nothing but the sky – the lofty sky, not clear yet still immeasurably lofty, with gray clouds gliding slowly across it. "How quiet, peaceful, and solemn; not at all as I ran," thought Prince Andrei – "not as we ran, shouting and fighting, not at all as the gunner and the Frenchmen with frightened and angry faces struggled for the mop: how differently do those clouds glide across that lofty infinite sky! How was it I did not see that lofty sky before? And how happy I am to have found it at last! Yes! All is vanity, all falsehood, except that infinite sky. There is nothing, nothing but that. But even it does not exist, there is nothing but quiet and piece." Prince Andrei lay bleeding profusely and unconsciously uttering a gentle, piteous, and childlike moan. Toward evening he ceased moaning and became quite still. He listened and heard the sound of approaching horses and voices speaking in French. He opened his eyes. Above him again was the same lofty sky with clouds and between them gleamed blue infinity. Horses and voices stopped near him. It was Napoleon. He stopped before Prince Andrei, who lay on his back with the flagstaff that had been dropped beside him. "That's a fine death!" said Napoleon. Prince Andrei heard the words as he might have heard the buzzing of a fly. Not only did they not interest him, but he took no notice of them and at once forgot them. His head was burning, he felt himself bleeding to death, and he saw above him the remote, lofty, and everlasting sky. He knew it was Napoleon – his hero – but at that moment Napoleon seemed to him such a small, insignificant creature compared with what was passing now between himself and that lofty infinite sky with the clouds flying over it. At that moment it meant nothing to him who might be standing over him, or what was said of him. Looking into Napoleon's eyes, Prince Andrei thought of the insignificance of greatness, the unimportance of life which no one could understand, and the still greater unimportance of death, the meaning of which no one alive could understand or explain.

I remember that scene, that image, those small details: the red-haired gunner with the mop, the lofty sky, the small, insignificant figure of Napoleon. The chapter recounts the battle of Austerlitz, also known as the Battle of Three Emperors, perhaps the most decisive engagement of the Napoleanic Wars. Tolstoy recounts the movement of troops, the rifle fire and cannon fire and bodies falling to the ground under a cloudless sky. And what do I remember? A man in the distance, walking across a bridge, carrying a mop. This is what my father meant when he told me to write a story about a crumb of bread. And that was what I had learned writing haiku when I was ten years old: how to make the smallest of details express the largest of ideas: a frog at the edge of a pond, a crow perched on the branch of a tree, a snow-hung gate, a plum-blossom, a little snail, persimmons, a half-eaten apple, the eyes of a hawk, the voice of the pheasant, the sound of the cuckoo, an icicle on the tip of Buddha's nose.

Haiku Flies Under the Radar

Haiku continued to inform my writing in high school and on into college, and beyond. I didn't always realize that. I assumed I was done with haiku, the preciousness of it. Haiku existed for me on the same level as limericks. After writing novels and short stories and poems that were expansive imitations of Eliot's "The Waste Land" and those "academic" poems I studied in college, haiku was the furthest thing from my mind. Even when I began reading those short, imagistic poems written by Ezra Pound, William Carlos Williams, and Robert Creeley, I didn't make a direct connection to haiku. It was as if the trash-compacter in my brain squeezed all haiku into such a small ball, that my consciousness overlooked it. The short line, the unadorned image, the aphoristic insight – these were part of a contemporary style having nothing to do with quaint, centuries-old haiku.

And yet, haiku was still a vital element within my conscoiusness, as it was in contemporary literature. By the same token, with respect to contemporary poetry, haiku was also flying beneath the radar. Throughout the 20th Century, as a result of Shiki's disciples and his disciples' disciples, Japanese haiku was breaking boundaries, exploring new ground both in form and content. All this was happening in Japan, but had no effect on American poets at the time because the only translations were done either before WWI or between the two

World Wars, and those translations didn't cover the work being done by Japanese poets in the twentieth century. It was only classical haiku that influenced the beat poets of the 50's, while most poets in the 60s and 70s were focused on the changes in American poetry as a result of the mimeo-revolution and Donald Allen's groundbreaking anthology, *The New American Poets* (see pages 253-255). When new translations began to appear in the late 70s and 80s, American haiku was revitalized, but I paid it no mind. My creative endeavors were on a completely different track.

Haiku and Zen Buddhism

After World War II, there was an increased interest in Zen Buddhism, accompanied by interest in Japanese culture in general, especially literature and poetry. The Beats began to include short Zen-like poems in their underground magazines. Some of this could be attributed to the influence of Pound's experiments in the 20s with Imagism, but the Imagist movement never became a major force in American poetry (except for the larger context in which it functioned as a product of Pound's dictum that modern poetry should be concise and clear and written in the language of everyday speech).

A few books on Japanese haiku were published in the 30s, but there was no significant influence. In 1932, *An Anthology of Haiku: Ancient and Modern*, translated and annotated by Asataro Miyamori, appeared. This was the big blue book with gold lettering on the cover that Mrs. Aime had on her desk. Miyamori's description of haiku was that it was a "peculiar form of wit, concentrated to the last degree — the shortest of Japanese poems." The big, green book that Mrs. Aime had in her stack was *The Hollow Reed* by Mary J. J. Wrinn, published in 1935, which included eleven pages of haiku information called "In the Japanese manner." The book was directed mainly to high school and college students. "Haiku consists of a primary statement of thought," Wrinn said, "out of which grows a secondary thought, corollary to it."

Harold Henderson was to become a major influence in the late 50's with his book *An Introduction to Haiku*, a dog-eared paperback copy of which I still have on my bookshelf with the original price of $2.50 stamped on the cover (see pages 18-19). In his earlier small book, *The Bamboo Broom* (a reference to the haiku by Issa), published seven years before the war in 1934, he first explored the possibility that haiku written in English could find its own form, its own essence. I'm convinced that my teacher, Mrs. Aime, had copies of both of Henderson's books, and probably that ground-breaking four-volume work by R. H. Blyth titled *Haiku*, published between 1949 and 1952, the years in which she was teaching us to write those short poems.

Brains & Eggs

Some of the poetry I was writing in college was influenced by the haiku-like poems of Gary Snyder, Jack Kerouac, Allen Ginsberg, Diane di Prima, and the other Beats, not to mention poems by Kenneth Rexroth in San Francisco who translated many classic Chinese poems. These Beat Generation and San Francisco Renaissance writers were writing haiku, though none of them used haiku as a main source of their creative output.

Even though Allen Ginsberg's poetry embraced the long-line form of Walt Whitman's poetry, we find in his journals, published in 1977 but written a decade earlier, a section of haiku entitled "Haiku composed in the backyard cottage at 1624 Milvia Street, Berkely 1955, while reading R. H. Blyths 4 volumes Haiku."

The sparrow shits
upside down
--ah! my brain & eggs

Looking over my shoulder
my behind was covered
with cherry blossoms.

My mother's ghost:
the first thing I found
in the living room.

On the porch
in my shorts;
auto lights in the rain.

The moon over the roof,
worms in the garden.
I rent this house.

quit shaving
but the eyes that glanced at me
remained in the mirror.

Gary Snyder's experience in a Zen monastery influenced his writing of haiku, and he was known to labor for years to get one perfect haiku.

This morning:
floating face down in the water bucket
a drowned mouse
– Gary Snyder

Ecstatic Tomfoolery

Jack Kerouac's facility for prose and poetry astounded both Snyder and Ginsberg. Ginsberg felt that Kerouac was the only American master of haiku at that time, "the only one in the United States who knows how to write haikus, the only one who's written any good haikus."

Kerouac did not consider himself a poet, but anyone who has taken any of his prose paragraphs, especially from *On The Road*, and read them aloud, knows that Kerouac had an ear for poetry that was as fine as any poet's. As he said of himself and Neal Cassady, the hero of *On The Road*, "We both got the secret of LINGO in telling a tale and figured that was the only way to express the speed and tension and ecstatic tomfoolery of the age." In 1971, City Lights Books pocket poets series published Kerouac's *Scattered Poems*, including many which were haiku. Ginsberg went so far as to say that "Kerouac thinks in haiku, every time he writes anything — talks that way and thinks that way. . . . Snyder has to labor for years in a Zen monastery to produce one haiku about shitting off a log!"

Kerouac proposed that the better equivalent for seventeen Japanese syllable sounds in English was three lines of twelve syllables. "Haiku must be very simple," he wrote, "and free of all poetic trickery and make a little picture and yet be as airy and graceful as a Vivaldi Pastorella." And, I might add, as concise as one of Chopin's "24 Preludes," many of which last no longer than a few seconds. Here are a few of Kerouac's haiku:

Shall I say no?
— fly rubbing
its back legs

Kerouac was familiar with the Japanese masters, and surely was aware of this poem by Issa, another good example of the web of allusion:

don't strike	*yare utsu na*
the fly! He wrings his hands!	*hae ga te wo suru*
he wrings his feet!	*ashi wo suru*

And this call-and-response back from Kerouac:

in my medicine cabinet
the winter fly
has died of old age.

Kerouac was familiar with Basho's masterpiece, *Narrow Road.* Where Basho made hiking trips, Kerouac made cross-country drives. One of them in 1959, with Albert Saijo and Lew Welch, was chronicled in *Trip Trap: Haiku Along the Road*, a combination of poetry and prose.

Thunder in the mountains —
the iron
of my mother's love
– Jack Kerouac

Drive, He Sd

Here's a few more examples of the haiku or haiku-like poems written by those poets in the 60s.

The madman
emerges from the movies:
the street at lunchtime.
– Allen Ginsberg

I know that I shall be the sea
and the mother
and never me.
– Sally Stern

What I know of the mind
seems to end here,
just outside my face
– Amiri Baraka (formerly known as Leroi Jones)

If castration rewarded
greatness
SUCH AN HONOR
to hear
"They're off!"
– Robert Hanlon

I KNOW A MAN
As I sd to my
friend, because I am
always talking,—John, I
sd, which was not his
name, the darkness sur-
rounds us, what
can we do against
it, or else, shall we &
why not, buy a goddamn big car,
drive, he sd, for
christ's sake, look
out where yr going.
– Robert Creeley

The Underground Mimeo Revolution

In my twenties, I was inclined to write poems that were expansive, like Eliot's *The Waste Land* or the poems from Robert Lowell's *Lord Weary's Castle*. At some point, I began sending my work out for publication.

There were three avenues of publication in the early 60's: commercial magazines such as *The Hudson Review*, *Harpers*, *The Nation*, *The New Yorker,* and *Partisan Review*; university presses such as *Poetry Northwest*, *The Chicago Review*, *The Sewanee Review*, *The Missouri Review*, *The Texas Literary Quarterly*, and *Field*; and privately funded journals such as *The Plumed Horn*, *Choice*, *Epos*, *Chelsea*, *Antaeus*, *Poetry*, *American Poetry Review*, and *Three-Penny Review*.

But a fourth avenue of publication opened up in the late 50s and 60s: the underground press, those mimeographed poetry magazines printed in garages or in the editors' kitchens. These were not readily available in bookstores, and had to be ordered

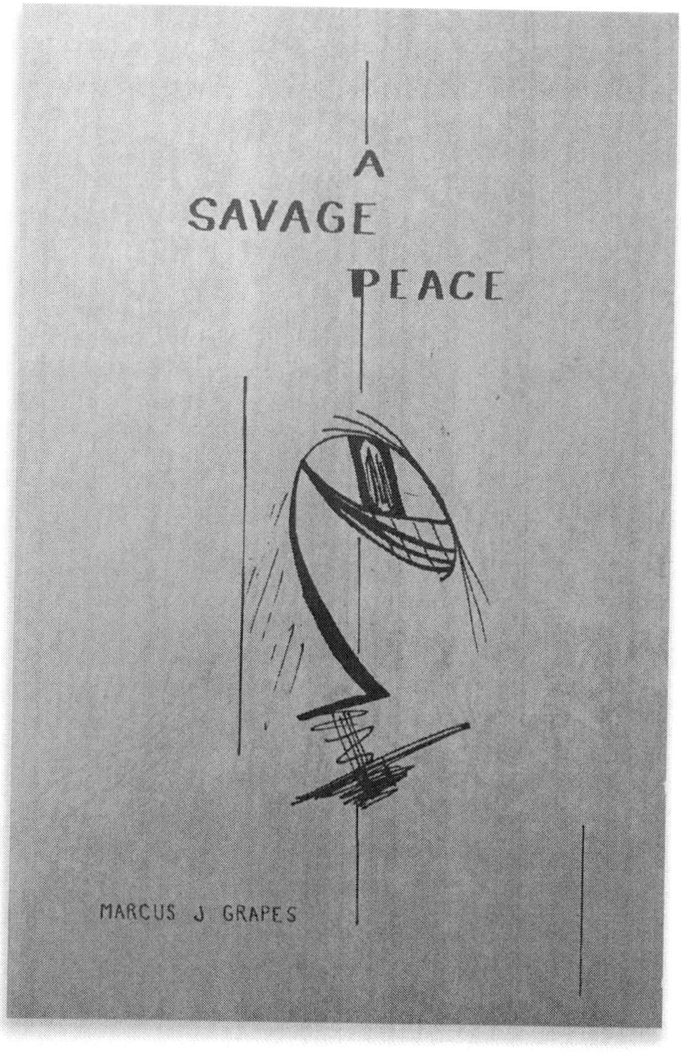

A limited edition of 100 copies, 1965
cover drawing by Susan Weinberg

by mail. Such small-press magazines were part of what is now called the "underground mimeo-revolution,"a movement that awakened American poetry from its academic slumber.

A few of those magazines were dedicated to haiku, or some American variation of haiku. I wrote a few poems that appeared in some of those mimeo-magazines which were publishing a new generation of poets such as Charles Bukowski, Harold Norse, Diane Wakowski, William Burroughs, Al Purdy, Carolyn Stoloff, Larry Eigner, Ed Field, Gregory Corso, Clarence Major, Kay Johnson, Diane DiPrima, Denise Levertov, and Robert Creeley. Most of those publications are now defunct, but I'm grateful to the editors who published those early poems of mine in *Poetmeat*, *Wormwood Review*, *The Outsider*, *Border*, *The New Lantern Club Review*, *Blitz*, *The Tiresian*, and *Olé*. Some of those shorter syllabic poems were included in my first collection of poetry, *A Savage Peace*, published in 1965.

*

your body blushes
when we kiss
or is it that
my beard is too rough

*

the frog beats the drum
past pools of black water,
past tombs of ancient dead

*

are we all to die
in a picnic world
to be buried in a potter's field

*

love
is a scarecrow
that scares all
but the crows

*

silly snow,
spreading your nakedness
on my front lawn.
even dreams melt.

Larry Eigner

Eventually, those poems came to seem trivial to me. They evoked the schoolroom, and I lost interest in short poems, haiku or otherwise. There were poets publishing in the late 60s and early 70s who were not strictly writing haiku, but the haiku sensibility informed their work, especially Larry Eigner, whose poetry I liked, but less because of its haiku nature and more because of its non-linear form and odd line breaks. From his 1978 book *air/the trees*:

the disappearance of matter
        where is the
         end of a poem
      tired eyes
          the sun travels
        and allows dream

**

the sky becomes
   endless
the clouds islands
      at this level we
         pass
            then leaves spread
            the hills' breasts

**

shhh goes the lawnmower
    should I stop
      the razor

Eigner was the author of over 40 books of poetry and critical writing. The titles of his book are as haiku-like and non-linear as his poems. Among his books are *air/the trees* (Black Sparrow Press, 1968), *readiness/enough/depends on* (Green Integer, 1974), and *windows/walls/yard/ways* (Black Sparrow

Press, 1994). I wasn't unimpressed by poets like Eigner and a few others writing short, eliptical poems, since a great deal of art in the mid-twentieth century was moving toward non-linear expression, a post-modern breaking of the three dimensional narrative plane. I was aware of the extremes of "high-modernism," but was more drawn to the authenticity of "popular-modernism," which seemed the more humanistic track to follow. I was moving toward poems that were informed by voice, poems that spread their arms and talked as if around a campfire in the wilderness, poems to ward off the wild things lurking in the dark forest of the unconscious.

The Spoken Word Nailed to Paper

In the summer of 1962, when I was 19 years old, I went to France and Italy, stopping in New York for a few days before flying to Europe. I spent $50 on a bag of books bought in Greenwich Village, carried them to Europe with me, and fell into the ocean of Beat poetry. When I came home (after receiving a phone call in Italy that my father had passed away), I spent the rest of the summer hanging out in the French quarter in New Orleans, listening to jazz and frequenting the coffee houses where beatniks and jazz hipsters read poetry while someone banged on bongos. One night someone brought in a black coffin and read aloud while lying in the coffin which had been placed on a make-shift stage.

One afternoon, I discovered a Bukowski chapbook, *Run with the Hunted,* being sold by an ex-con in the French quarter who sat on an orange crate selling his wife's paintings. Jon and Gypsy Lou Webb began publishing a literary magazine called *The Outsider*, which featured new American poets not considered part of the "northeast establishment." They also brought out Bukowski's first book, *It Catches My Heart in its Hands,* which won awards for its layout and design. Bukowski was a wind that blew away the preciousness of academia and the feigned be-bop of beatnik prose. As John William Corrington was to write in the introduction to that book, Bukowski's poems were "the spoken word nailed to paper." Haiku was in my rear-view mirror, getting smaller and smaller.

The Outsider (Loujohn Press), issue #3,
edited by Jon and Gypsy Lou Webb, Spring 1963.
featuring Charles Bukowski on the cover
(Note portrait upper right of Gypsy Lou by David Pallock

Modern Japanese Haiku After Shiki

Ironically, this was a period in which the haiku form in American poetry was being revived. As mentioned earlier, the Japanese poems that were translated into English in R. H. Blyth's four-volume *Haiku* series, published from 1949 to 1952, dealt mostly with pre-modern haiku, though Shiki was included, as well as a few of Shiki's disciples, but in most cases, Blyth gave them short shrift, limiting his translations to one per poet. As far as he was concerned, modern Japanese haiku was "clumsy, more modern than haiku."

Shiki succeeded in injecting new life into the form and restoring it as a vehicle for serious artistic expression. He advocated the use of modern themes and the use of colloquial diction, while retaining the 5-7-5 pattern and the use of a *kigo* (season word). As a young college student, determined to modernize haiku, he entertained numerous poets in his untidy college dorm.

At the time, there were many different "schools" of poetry, but all of them emphasized rules that bound haiku to the traditional form. Shiki and his followers wanted to bring about a poetic revolution that would shatter the stagnant form that constituted 19th century haiku. Write in a concise style, he advocated, get rid of trite motifs, appeal directly to emotion, use a modern tone, and eschew the rules that many of the schools set forth (except the 5-7-5- pattern and the season word). Shiki's untimely death in 1902 was a tragic loss for the new movement, which had already gained wide support because of the magazine he founded called *Cuckoo*, and his eager disciples who vigorously continued the movement toward the modernization of haiku.

Much like the shift in poetry after World War I among American poets, the influences and enthusiasms from abroad colored and shaped Japanese poetry during the Meiji period and beyond, reflected in its contemporary style. The so-called free-verse (*shintaishi*) had no basis in the Japanese tradition of haiku and *waka* (31 syllable poems), whereas in America, poets of the 20s took up where Whitman left off. Japanese poets felt no need to pay their respects to the themes and concerns of the past. Foreign forms, particularly French, took pride of place as younger poets searched for more authentic ways in which to express themselves.

But even in American poetry, the tension between those who

held on to the tradition of the "well-made poem" and those who pushed for greater freedom in style and content continued to play itself out (and in some ways, continues even today). The same is true for Japanese poets between the wars. Some haiku poets resisted change, especially as regards the standard seventeen-syllable form and the obligation to use a season word (*kigo*), while others pushed to introduce a more colloquial voice and more contemporary subject matter.

The majority of haiku translated into English in the decades following the war stopped at Shiki, or at best, included one or two poems by his disciples. The basic idea of the haiku was set: three lines of verse in a 5-7-5 syllabic pattern featuring a season word and a cutting pause juxtaposing disparate images. The work of those poets who followed Shiki — his disciples and the disciples of his disciples, were not to receive English translations until the late 70s. In the following chapters, I present a sampling of poets who were reshaping classical haiku in Japan, but whose work was not to appear in English translation until the 70s and 80s, or decades later. They had no direct influence on the American poets of the 50s and 60s, but did have an impact on the American haiku resurgence in the 70s and 80s, and continue to influence haiku poets today.

Takahama Kyoshi

Two of Shiki's outstanding disciples were Takahama Kyoshi (1874-1959) and Kawahigashi Hekigodo (1873-1937). Kyoshi wrote in the traditional haiku form as Shiki had, but following Shiki's prescription, infused his work with modern themes and colloquial diction. During his long life he produced a large body of work that continues to be highly esteemed. He wrote several novels, short stories, plays, and 40,000 to 50,000 haiku. Kyoshi took over the editorship of *Cuckoo* and moved the headquarters from Matsuyama to Toyko. He was instrumental in bringing many new writers and poets into the literary world, and was a dominant force in keeping haiku to the modernized, but traditional form Shiki had advocated, especially with the publication of his commentary on haiku composition, "The Path Haiku Ought to Take." In 1934 the *Complete Works of Kyoshi* was published in twelve volumes, but this edition soon became outdated as he continued his creative activities. In 1954 he was awarded the Order of Culture by the Japanese government, and died in 1959 at the age of 85. He was posthumously awarded the Order of Sacred Treasure, 1st Class.

The summer moon —
on the plate lies an apple
with its redness lost.

Cold as ice:
I go visit a sick friend
— already, he's dead!

Suddenly fire in the grass
a spider joins the flame,
itself the fire in the grass

I throw the gold-bug
into the dark night—
now just me in the dark night.

Kawahigashi Hekigodo

Hekigodo was a good friend of Kyoshi since middle school and remained close to him throughout his life. Like Shiki, he was the son of a Confucian scholar, well-tutored in the Chinese classics. Perhaps the best word to describe Hekigodo is "restless." He dabbled in mountain climbing, calligraphy, Noh dancing, traveled in Europe, North America, China, and Mongolia, and wrote journalism, literary and social criticism, and poetry. At Shiki's death in 1902, Hekigodo succeeded him as editor of the haiku pages in the newspaper *Nippon* and for a brief time was the most important figure in the Japanese haiku world. But eventually, he went beyond Shiki's attempt to modernize haiku by abandoning the strict reliance on the 5-7-5- pattern in favor of "free verse" or "free-form" haiku (*shinkeiko*). He felt that the traditional pattern was a "man-made rule," and wrote: "Any arbitrary attempt to mold a poem into the 5-7-5 syllable pattern would damage the freshness of impression and kill the vitality of language." As he grew older he became more isolated from the mainstream of literary and cultural activities and devoted more of his time to the study of traditional haiku, especially to that of Yosa Buson. He died in 1937 at the age of 64.

After the riot
another non-existent
moonlit night

A sleeping cow?
A boulder? Who knows?
Grass sprouts around it.

I hit the fly
with a fly-swatter
that before didn't exist

Oyster stew
served cold,
same old wife.

Takahama Kyoshi
1874-1959

Kawahigashi Hekigodo
1873-1937

Ogiwara Seisensui
1884-1976

Ozaki Hosai
1885-1926

Ogiwara Seisensui

Hekigodo's advocacy of "free verse" haiku was taken up by one of his students, Ogiwara Seisensui (1884-1976), who actaully had been experimenting with free form even before Hekigodo. Seisensui is remembered primarily as one of the most adventuresome haiku poets of his day. At the age of fifteen, he published an essay on language reform and specialized in linguistics at Tokyo University, becoming skeptical of the methodology of traditional haiku. Seisensui went even further with his radical experiments, breaking the last connection with traditional haiku by abandoning the use of the season word altogether. He shocked the haiku world by advocating that all haiku be transformed into free verse.

After a series of deaths in the family, Seisensui became a Buddhist mendicant priest for a time, and religious sentiment can be found in his work during this period. He founded the avant-garde literary magazine *Layered Clouds* in 1911 with fellow poet Hekigodo. The magazine soon came to serve as the main outlet for radical free-style haiku. Seisensui deftly used new media to promote his style, including lectures and his literary criticism on national radio. He died in 1976 at the sage of 92, leaving behind more than 400 books, including collections of haiku, essays, and travelogues.

Butterfly's wings,
most beautiful in the world;
ants pull them.

Blame the fence!
My neighbor's camellia
falls into my yard.

Morning with a baby crying
with all its might
and a crowing rooster.

I suck at
the sour tangerine of
memories of my wife

Ozaki Hosai

Two of Seisensui's students carried on his role in promoting the format of free-style haiku: Ozaki Hosai (1885-1926) and Taneda Santoka (1882-1940). Ozaki's haiku are permeated with loneliness, possibly the result of his heavy drinking and the isolation, poverty, and poor health of his final years. His interest in haiku began while still in high school where he met Seisensui. At Tokyo University he majored in law, but his real interest lay in philosophy, literature, and religion. Upon graduation he went to work for the Toyo Life Insurance Company (the predecessor to Asahi Mutual Life Insurance Co.) and married a young woman from his home town. He came to work "reeking of alcohol" and eschewed the wearing of a business suit, dressing in one of the only two items of clothing he owned, a tuxedo or a pair of pajamas.

When he began writing haiku, he chose the pseudonym Hosai, which symbolized the liberation he sought both in writing and in life. In search of complete spiritual liberation, he gave up all his material possessions at the age of 38, persuaded his wife to leave him, resigned his position at the insurance company, and became a lay mendicant monk at a Budhist training center. He went from one temple to another, serving as an acolyte-handyman. With ties to his former life severed, and without material possessions, he began to write haiku in earnest.

Hosai wrote free-verse haiku, devoid of all decorative words, just as his life was devoid of all superfluous activity. He finally settled down in a humble hut on the island of Shodoshima in the Seto Inland Sea, where was given the post of rector of a small hermitage at the temple of Saiko-ji. He subsisted on a diet of toasted rice and water, writing haiku that extended the form beyond the traditional language, rhythms, and seasonal imagery.

At the age of 41, he contracted tuberculosis and died. His only book of haiku, *Big Sky*, contains poems of his solitary final months, and was only published posthumously, now available in an English translation by Hiroaki Sato entitled *Right under the big sky I don't wear a hat*. Sato has been called by Gary Synder "perhaps the finest translator of contemporary Japanese poetry in English."

Trying to cast off
a slanderous heart
I shell the beans

From this lonely
body fingernails
begin to grow

Splendid breasts—
there! a mosquito!

I walk to the other side,
around the tombstone.

Opened the snow door and closed it, a woman's face

I take off a sock and throw away the pebble

The flesh getting skinnier, big bones indeed
Under the sun I didn't see for long I work

Spring's here says a big newspaper ad

A gun glinting in deep snow

Even nail-clipping scissors I have to borrow

I have no bowl   I receive   with my hands

Taneda Santoka

Seisensui's other disciple, Taneda Santoka (1882-1940), became known for the many walking trips he took, tramping thousands of miles through the Japanese countryside like Basho before him. These journeys were part of his religious training as a Buddhist monk, and became the literary inspiration for Santoka's memorable and often painfully moving poems in his quest for spiritual enlightenment.

Santoka was a master of the conventional-style haiku he wrote in his youth, but the vast majority of his works, and those for which he is most admired, are in free-form or free-style haiku. He also left a number of diaries in which he recorded the circumstances that led to the composition of a particular poem or group of poems, modeled surely after Basho's *Narrow Road into the Interior*. During his lifetime, his poetry attracted only limited notice. In *Modern Japanese Haiku*, Makoto Euda's translation into English of twenty Japanese poets published in 1976, Taneda Santoka is an understandable omission. In recent years, though, there has been an upsurge of interest in his life and writings.

His complete works were published in seven large volumes and Japanese bookstores now display numerous books of his poems, letters, and diaries, as well as critical studies and memoirs by those who knew him. His book, *For All My Walking*, was translated into English by Burton Watson (Columbia University Press, 2003). Hioaki Sato translated many of Santoka's haiku in *Grass and Tree Cairn* (Red Moon Press, 2002) and Scott

Watson translated close to 200 of Santoka's haiku in *Walking By Myself Again* (Bookgirl Press, 2011).

Santoka came from a wealthy land-owning family. When he was eleven, his mother committed suicide by throwing herself into the family well. He was raised by his grandmother. When he entered Waseda University in Tokyo, he began drinking heavily, and two years later dropped out of school due to a "nervous breakdown," which some believe to be a euphemism for frequent and severe drunkenness. By this point, his father was in such dire financial straits that he could barely afford Santoka's tuition. His arranged marriage to a girl from a neighboring village was not a happy one. He confessed in his diaries that the vision of his mother's corpse "being raised from her watery grave" had forever tarnished his relationship with women. After publishing translations of Ivan Turgenev and Guy de Maupassant in the literary journal *Youth* under the pen name Santoka ("Mountain-top Fire"), he joined a local haiku group led by Seisensui. Eventually, he became editor of Seisensui's literary magazine *Layered Clouds*, the same year his father went completely bankrupt and fled into hiding.

Santoka moved his family to the southern island of Kyushu and planned to open a second-hand bookstore, but it ended up being a picture frame shop instead. In a year's time, his brother committed suicide and his grandmother died. A year later, he divorced his wife and within another year, his father passed away. After a stint as a librarian, he lost his job again due to a "nervous breakdown." Then he was jailed as a communist. After his release, an extremely drunk Santoka jumped in front of an oncoming train, which managed to stop just inches away. He was brought to a nearby Zen temple, and at the age of forty-two, was ordained in the Soto Zen sect. Shortly afterwards, he began the first of his many walking trips.

During his trips, Santoka wore his priest's robe and a large bamboo hat known as a *kasa*. He had one bowl, which he used both for alms-getting and for eating. To survive, he went from house to house to beg. A day's earnings would go toward a room at a guesthouse or inn, food, and sake. It is clear from his diaries that he had mixed feelings about his lifestyle:

> Even if it means nothing to eat, I don't want to do any more of that hateful begging! People who have never done any begging seem to have difficulty understanding how I feel about this.

Loving sake, savoring sake, enjoying sake is not so bad. But drowning in sake, rioting in sake — that won't do! Running around drinking in this messy way — utterly stupid!

How I must look
from behind, going off
in drizzling rain?

got this far
drink some water
and go on

finish the last
of the sake
hear the wind

hangover
and blossoms
scattering scattering

Twenty years since I began writing haiku, and I realize more than ever: haiku writing is a practice that's easy to take up, but very difficult to really get anywhere in. It's like Buddhism in that respect.

wind blows right through me
plop
and I fall over dead

in the sweet taste of a ripe
persimmon, I remember
my grandmother

My sex drive is gone; my appetite is bit by bit disappearing. What will go next. I'm a man who has never known love. I've never loved a woman, never been loved by a woman. There were times when I thought that a woman's body was good, but somehow I could never come to like the woman herself.

more and more like him
my father
no longer alive

all withered —
grasses I walk over
going nowhere

After several more walking trips, Santoka published his first book of poems, *Rice Bowl Child.* He continued to live on the contributions of friends and admirers, whatever he could grow in his garden, and money sent from his son. In 1934 he set off on another walking trip, but soon grew seriously ill and had to return home. He attempted suicide but lived. Two years later, he began another walking tour, intent on following the trail Basho had described in *Narrow Road*, and returned after eight months only to embark on another walking trip. He died in his sleep,

Taneda Santoka
1882-1940

Mitsihashi Takajo
1899-1972

Sugita Hisajo
1890-1946

Hashimoto Takako
1899-1963

having published seven collections of poems. He was fifty-seven.

the deeper I go
the deeper I go
green mountains

somewhere
inside my head
a crow is cawing

asleep on the ground
sooner or later
peaceful as a clod of dirt

no desire to die
no desire to live
the wind blows over me

Heaven
doesn't kill me
it makes me write poems

waiting for what?
each day   each day
more fallen leaves pile up

Mitsuhashi Takajo

One of the most noted women haiku poets of the 20th century, Mitsuhashi Takajo (1899-1972) first wrote haiku under the tutelage of Yosano Akiki (1878-1942) and Wakayama Bokusui (1885-1928), both renga poets. Bokusui's poems were filled with romantic yearnings, but his later renga were more austere and experimental. Akiko worked in her parent's candy shop and began writing renga in her teenage years. Her first full-length collection of tanka, *Tangled Hair*, which appeared in 1901, formed her reputation as a poet of sometimes erotic romanticism completely new to Japanese poetry. She went on to write more poetry in various forms, a novel, as well as translating the classic *Tale of the Genji* into modern Japanese.

Both Akiki and Bokusui had a major influence on Takajo, as did her father, who wrote tanka, and her husband, a dentist, who wrote haiku and encouraged her to switch to haiku herself. A collection of her haiku was published in 1940, *Sunflowers*, followed by many other books, including those of literary criticism. Her third book, *The Bleached Bones*, an obvious reference to one of Basho's travel diaries, was published in 1952 and covered the war years, during which her only son was sent to the front and her husband fell gravely ill. Her last books of haiku showed the influence of avant-garde, experimental movements, where she strayed from the traditional form. These last haiku also dwelt on her sense of mortality.

a woman stands
all alone, ready to wade
across the Milky Way

the aged person
wanting to become a tree
embraces a tree

their lives last
only while aflame —
a woman and a pepper pod

falling leaves
falling leaves falling leaves
falling on my bed too

hard to die
can't stand living
this late summer night

with nothing to hold onto
I hold onto
a cold wind

The Return to Conservatism

If Haiku is not the classical 5-7-5 pattern, the classical form that had existed for centuries, then what is it? Jim Kacian, in his anthology *American Haiku,* defines haiku as "a kind of poem," which is about the best you can do before lapsing into abstract terms. American haiku poets have debated this question for the last fifty years, but they're only re-hashing the same debate that Japanese haiku poets experienced since the new direction it took after Shiki.

Many poets in Japan were worried that haiku was losing its basic impulse, and none more so than Kyoshi, a leading exponent of haiku's modernization and the editor of *Cuckoo.* This concern led him to suspend the publication of haiku in the magazine, though he resumed the practice a few years later and wrote several essays advocating a return to the 5-7-5 pattern and the use of the season word. He felt that haiku was a classical form of poetry, and without the traditional pattern, it was no longer haiku. "Its life depends on its classical flavor and its seventeen syllable form and its sense of the season," he wrote.

Kyoshi had no objection to a poem written in free-form, he said, just don't call it haiku. And if one chooses to write in a traditional form, one should observe the traditional rules that go with it. In time, he went even further, declaring that the haiku poet's duty was to observe a certain way of life that includes a "detachment of mind," which allows the poet to tolerate, or even enjoy, those moments in life that are tinged with sadness and suffering. Kyoshi didn't want to set haiku back centuries, only to return it to that point where Shiki had called for its modernization without giving up the syllabic pattern and the connection with nature.

Many poets who took up haiku regained their confidence in the traditional form, and contributions to *Cuckoo* increased every year, and many gifted poets emerged. Hegigodo died in frustration in 1937 and Seisensui continued his free-form experiments with his disciples, but Kyoshi gained an almost dictatorial power as editor of *Cuckoo*. Most of the haiku poets published after 1920 got their recognition through the help of Kyoshi. If any departed from the traditional forms, Kyoshi not only criticized them, but refused to publish their work in his journal, which amounted to a kind of "excommunication."

Sugita Hisajo

One of the haiku poets Kyoshi excommunicated was Sugita Hisajo (1890-1946), an early disciple of Kyoshi. Shiguta characterized herself as passionate and idealistic, and many of her poems are highly personal. She took the *haigo* (pen-name) "Hisajo," meaning "long-time woman" or "eternal woman." Upon graduation from college, she married a painter who was older than she, possibly a friend of one of her older brothers, who soon accepted a position as art master to a middle school, where he stayed for over 40 years. They had two daughters, one of whom later wrote of her parents that they were complete opposites. It was not a happy marriage, and when Hisajo's mother asked him to grant his wife a divorce for the sake of the kids, he refused. Hisajo struggled between her own fire of artistic temperament and the proprieties of social expectations, locked as she was into the role of obediant wife to a middle-school schoolmaster.

In the preface to her own magazine of haiku, *Clothes for Flower Viewing*, she wrote: "Devoted to art, I have not taken good care of my home. I am nothing as a woman. A vampire. A heretic. I have always been accused, pressured, and spat upon this way by people around me, so that I thought of suicide several times."

But Hisajo was a woman of vision, intellect, and innovative, ever daring, artistic skill. She struggled to write her haiku even if it meant neglecting domestic chores. In one of her haiku, she references Nora, the wife and heroine of the stage play, *A*

Doll's House, by Henrik Ibsen. Comparing herself to Ibsen's protagonist-housewife, she was relating to a woman's struggle in "a man's world," recognizing herself as an individual in the increasingly modern era. In 1936, for reasons that were not made clear, Kyoshi banished her from the *Cuckoo* circle, which devastated her. She stopped writing haiku and had several nervous breakdowns. Ten years later, she died in a mental institution. Her last haiku was found in her bed after her death:

gums itching
the baby bites my nipple—
spring's hazy sky

she mends socks
not quite a Nora
this teacher's wife

reading a play—
dishes left in the sink
this winter night

home from blossom-viewing
as I disrobe, many straps
cling to my body

haiku poet,
caring mother—
this summer I'm a wreck

I hate Kyoshi
I hate Kanajo—
my unlined sash

Hashimoto Takako

Until the disruption of the Second World War, Hashimoto Takako (1899-1963) led a charmed life of affluence. She married an architect, and their home was a local center of cultural activities where poets, artists, and musicians frequently visited. It was at one of those parties that she met Kyoshi and Sugita Hisajo, who encouraged her to write haiku. Her first guide was Hisajo, who became a close friend and confidant. Years later, when Hisajo was committed to a sanitarium, Takako visted her in the jail-like room and wrote this heartbreaking haiku.

myriad greens —
there on my forehead
the iron bars

Takako's husband died before the war and many of her poems reference his dying. After the war, Japan's social reorganization took away the last of the advantages she had enjoyed. "Between one person and another," she wrote, "there is no bridge." Her books of haiku began to appear regularly, and in 1959 she was awarded the Nara Cultural Prize. She died of liver cancer in 1963, and her last book, *The End of Life*, was published posthumously.

the typhoon passes —
quietly asleep
a man near death

in the moonlight
I sleep with one
who's alive dying

up close to his face
near death I say
the moon's shining

the fierce snowfall —
I'll die, having known no hands
other than my husband's

taking up chopsticks
I am all alone —
it snows and snows

fierce snow —
how many things
I leave unwritten

Natsume Soseki

Jack Kerouac, Richard Wright, and J.D. Salinger were highly influenced by Japanese haiku, but their main contributions to literature were as novelists. We can say the same about Natsume Soseki (1867-1916), who is best known for his novels *I Am a Cat*, *The Three-Cornered World*, *Kokoro*, and *The Grass at the Wayside*, as well as his unfinished work, *Light and Darkness*. From 1984 until 2004, his portrait appeared on the front of the Japanese 1000 yen note. He is often considered the greatest writer in modern Japanese history.

Soseki began life as an unwanted child, born to his mother late in her life, forty years old, and his father then fifty-three, into a household with five older brothers. He was soon given up for adoption, but returned to the family when the couple who had adopted him divorced. His mother died when he was fourteen and his two eldest brothers died when he was twelve, intensifying his sense of instability.

As a boy, he became enamored with Chinese literature and declared that he would someday become a writer. The family, however, disapproved, and he eventually entered Tokyo Imperial University with the intention of becoming an architect. It was there that he met Shiki, who tutored him in the art of

Natsume Soseki
1867-1916

Murakami Kijo
1873-1938

Iida Dakotsu
1885-1962

Takeshita Shizunojo
1887-1951

haiku, even as Soseki studied architecture in college. Soon he was publishing his poems and signing them with the name Soseki, which is a Chinese idiom meaning "stubborn." In his twenties, the Japanese government sent him to England to study at the University College in London, but he spent most of his time in his room, buried in books. His friends feared that he might be having a nervous breakdown. Later, he wrote, "The two years I spent in London were the most unpleasant years of my life. Among English gentlemen I lived in misery, like a poor dog that had strayed among a pack of wolves."

Despite his poverty, loneliness, and depression, he solidified his knowledge of English literature and returned to Japan where he taught literary theory and criticism at Tokyo Imperial University. He continued to publish haiku in *Cuckoo*, first when it was edited by his friend Shiki, and then when Kyoshi took over, but it was the public success of his satirical novel *I Am a Cat* that won him wide public admiration, as well as critical acclaim. In the 21st century, there has been a global emergence of interest in Soseki, with about 60 of his books being translated into more than 30 languages.

A vine climbing
on a charcoal kiln
slowly burns to death

Just as they were
before my birth,
I long to meet my parents

May I be reborn
into a man
as tiny as a violet

It comes to my shoulder
longing for human company
a red dragonfly

Murakami Kijo

A frequent contributor to Shiki's haiku magazine *Cuckoo*, Murakami Kijo (1873-1938) was another follower of Shiki. As a young man he studied law, but had to give it up when he became deaf due to an illness. He found work as a scribe, but was barely able to support his ten children. In 1927, the luckless Kijo lost his possessions and his home in a fire. He is often compared to the great master Kobayashi Issa because both men led lives of sorrow and hardship, and their work is characterized by a deep empathy. Kijo's haiku express resignation and acceptance of life's struggle. He published three collections of haiku in his lifetime, dying at the age of 64.

First autumn morning:
the mirror I stare into
shows my father's face

A winter hornet
without a place to die
staggers along.

Clutching a lump
of earth, it lies dying —
a grasshopper

Cold day in spring:
bumping into this and that,
a blind dog.

Iida Dakotsu

Even though his father was the richest landowner in the district, Iida Dakotsu (1885-1962) trained with Kyoshi and devoted his life to haiku. In his early twenties, he decided to give up school, sell his books, and return to his native village near Mt. Fuji, where he spent the rest of his life writing haiku. He picked the nickname Sanro, which means mountain hut, and his first book of haiku was titled *A Mountain Hut Collection*. He published nine more books after that, including *Mountain Echoes Collection*, *Spring Orchids*, and *Snowy Valleys*. He has been compared to Basho, since both poets wrote about nature and lived simply, finding solace in the natural world. Dakotsu was haunted by the deaths of three of his four children. His surviving son, Ryuta Dakotsu, also became a well-known haiku poet who helped his father edit the prestigious magazine *Unmo* and took it over after his death.

I wake from a nap.
Before my eyes, a hollyhock:
on it, a snake.

In the bath on the spring
equinox, my white towel
sinks immediately

Out for a swim:
the water that drowns people
smells fragrant to me.

the horse that loses the race
how its eyes stare at men
without looking away.

One of his son's haiku has intrigued me for years. I've found only a few translations, all different, and I'm still not sure what Ryuta Dakotsu meant, but I've cobbled together my own version:

Spring becoming visible—
color of the sky,
of the end of things.

Takeshita Shizunojo

Like many women haiku poets, Shizunojo (1887-1951) experienced the struggle between caring for her children and her calling as a poet. She was one of the few women haiku poets to appear in the early years of modern Japan and lamented being caught in that transitional period between the old customs and the modern world. She worked as a teacher at a primary school, and married the principal of an agricultural school who was taken into her family to work her father's estate. She didn't begin to write haiku until her early thirties when her poems were published in *Cuckoo,* the magazine that Kyoshi edited. But she felt restricted by the formalities Kyoshi required of the writers he published and felt the need to express herself more freely. When her husband died of a brain hemorrhage in 1933, she took a job as a librarian. After the war, she cultivated small parcels of land to help feed her mother and children. Her only book of haiku, *The Gusty Wind*, was published before her death at the age of 64 due to kidney failure.

the New Year, yet still
that same old winter hat—
my big husband

my husband gone —
flakes of spring snow
out of a blue sky

a pittance is what
I earn, along with
frequent heat rash

all of them, the writings
my husband left
in this seed bag

short summer night —
shall I throw away a baby
crying for my milk

those dumb menfolk
smelling of sweat
— I go and join them

grief and anger —
I spit out black, black
watermelon seeds

in the mosquito's
buzz, a thread of thought
begins in my mind

Akutagawa Ryunosuke

One of the most striking literary figures of the era between the two world wars was Akutagawa Ryunosuke (1892-1927). His short stories are considered classics. He was the first modern Japanese writer to attract wide attention abroad and most of his works have been translated. His writings, together with those of Natsume Soseki and Mori Ogai, provide foundational elements in the history of modern Japanese literature.

About seven months after Ryunosuke was born his mother had a psychotic break, and she remained in this condition until her death in 1902. In one of his autobiographical stories he wrote: "My mother was a madwoman. She would always be sitting by herself, her hair twisted around a comb, puffing away at a long-stemmed pipe. Once when I went upstairs to her room to say a word of greeting, she suddenly hit my head with her pipe. But most of the time my mother was an extremely well-behaved lunatic."

His suicide at the age of 35 stunned many of the writers of his generation. Some claimed it was the turning point of their lives, others were left silent, ceasing to write for years. Many lesser writers began to doubt the value of literature itself, if a man so favored with talent and fame by the gods, who was close to being a god himself, had spurned literature in favor of death, then what did their efforts mean? In what is considered his suicide note, he wrote: "In my present state, nature looks more beautiful than ever. You will doubtless laugh at the contradiction of loving nature and planning at the same time to kill myself. But the beauty of nature is apparent to me only because it is reflected in my eyes during my last hours. But I see that I am, after all, the son of a lunatic. At present, I feel disgust toward the whole world, myself most of all."

Silver this autumn day
is used to fill
this cavity in my tooth

Sick and feverish
in the gleam of cherry blossoms
I keep shivering

Mizuhara Shuoshi

There were many young haiku poets stifled by Kyoshi's conservative stance and power as editor of *Cuckoo*, but western ideas and literature after World War I had a growing influence on young writers and poets who continued to press for modernization. Several had sympathy for the symbolist movement, as well as for dadism and surrealism. One of the leaders of the new radical poets was Mizuhara Shuoshi (1892-1981), the eldest son of a doctor who ran a medical clinic. He followed in his father's footsteps, went to Tokyo University where he studied serology, obstetrics, and gynecology, graduating in 1926. He taught at Showa Medical College, practiced in his father's clinic, and in 1932 was appointed to the prestigious post of medical advisor to the Ministry of the Imperial Household.

Shoushi began writing haiku as an undergraduate, and his haiku was acclaimed in the pages of *Cuckoo*. But after a time, he grew dissatisfied with Kyoshi's conservative principles, which discouraged emotional expression and imaginative images, and Shuoshi became responsible for a trend towards greater emotional expression in haiku.

Kyoshi and the traditionalists believed that the use of metaphor, for instance, limited the freedom of imagination, while the more radical poets believed that metaphor encouraged it. Shuoshi thought that Kyoshi's dogma *kyakkan shasei* (objective sketch) based on Buson's imagist haiku (which Shiki so admired), yielded dull haiku that described one monotonous detail after another. He ridiculed Shiki's image of the poet, "notebook in hand, following after a cloud's shadow."

Shuoshi left the orbit of *Cuckoo* by publishing an essay titled "Truth in Nature and Truth in Literature," which called for the free expression of the poet's emotional response to the world. This essay was a declaration of independence, and a number of young poets followed him. They started their own haiku magazine, *Staggerbush*, and called for submissions that expressed the passion and subjectivity of modernism, with emphasis on abstraction, metaphor, and analogy. They named their radical movement Shinko Haiku (young and new).

The poets of Shinko Haiku expressed repulsion for a society where birth, relationships, and the authority of old men were more important than the quality of the individual.

Shuoshi's first book of haiku was titled *Katsushika*, published in 1930. He practiced medicine until he retired in 1952, then traveled a great deal, visiting old Buddhist temples that had held a special attraction for him since his student days. He published over twenty volumes of haiku, many on the

Akutagawa Ryunosuke
1892-1927

Mizuhara Shuoshi
1892-1981

Tomizawa Kakio
1902-1962

Nakamura Kusatao
1901-1983

subject of baseball.

Mountain moths do not
hover about a lamp; they
hover about the moon.

A dead vine, swimming
in the river pool, tries
to reach the other shore.

night game, our
team's good luck
heralded by lightning

a night game's
bright lights across
the great river

Tomizawa Kakio

Like T.S. Eliot and other American poets who believed the poet's life should not constitute the subject matter of their poetry, Tomizawa Kakio (1902-1962) used symbolism in his haiku, rather than details from his personal life. His poems expressed feelings of estrangement, melancholy, and ennui through surrealistic images. Because of this, his critics called his poems obscure.

Kakio studied economics and joined a shipping firm upon graduation, but spent a number of years in the engineer corps of the army fighting in China, and then during the war defending small islands on the northern front. After the war, he began several literary magazines that published both haiku and non-haiku poems, a daring anti-traditionalist undertaking. His haiku were eventually collected in three books.

Withered reeds —
I stuff them into my eyes
and trudge towards home.

Uttering a lie
with beautiful colors,
an icicle.

I keep rubbing an awl,
in the darkness of despair
I keep rubbing an awl.

Cage of a leopard.
Not a drop of water
Remains in the sky

Kingfisher. There stand
humble white tombs.

Within her eyes
ant, ant, ant, ant, ant.

A hail of nuts in the ripples
of thundering cannons.

Day of pollen,
the birds have no breasts

Kakatsuka Ippekiro

In the era of Meiji (1868-1912) and Taisho (1912-1926), many writers tried to incorporate the colloquial language into the traditional literary style. There was a lofty tone attached to the traditional style, a style equivalent to Shakespeare's Elizabethan English or 19th century Georgian verse. Writing in the spoken language, however, came to be seen as more suitable for the expression of modern ideas. There was a parallel development in the Western world after World War I where poets began using a more colloquial style. The five or seven syllables that constituted each part of a haiku were based on the traditional style; in the spoken language, each part may extend to 6 or 8 syllables.

Nakatsuka Ippekiro (1887-1946, no picture available) rebelled against tradition and introduced the colloquial style into haiku. He abandoned the seventeen syllable 5-7-5 pattern as well and initiated "the Free Form Haiku." He also rejected the use of kigos (season words) and questioned the usual operation of haiku magazines in which publishers and editors like Kyoshi wielded dictatorial power. Develop your own style, he exhorted young poets, find your voice and don't be restricted by traditional rules. Ippekiro's haiku were neither mysterious nor pretentious, yet they succeeded in presenting the essence of things.

The image of me
Out of the mirror
Came to the chrysanthemums exposure.

This is really a dilapidated house
Receiving a visitor
Under the burning sun.

A dog with a long flank is sad.
Rapes blossom.
Oh, my hand slips on the white hibachi,
Oh, my country.

Nakamura Kusatao

At the age of 29, Nakamura Kusatao (1901-1983) became Kyoshi's pupil, having written his bachelor's thesis on Shiki. His father was a career diplomat, and after studying German & Russian literature at Tokyo University, he changed his major and became a member of the teaching staff at the Seikei Gakuen schools. Kusatao wrote the lyrics to the school song of Matsuyama Kita High in collaboration with Denzaburo Futagami (a one-time principal of the high school). He taught at the Gakuen schools for the next thirty-four years. His first volume of haiku was published in 1936, *The Eldest Son*, and he went on to publish another six collections. In 1946 he founded a haiku magazine called *Myriad Green Leaves.* A follower of Kyoshi, he started his own group of poets whose haiku traced the uphill struggle to find solace in this life, while retaining an eternal youthful spirit.

Snow is falling now.
In my mind, the Meiji era—
So long ago.

The metaphors are
gone, and so is my faith . . .
sun over a moor.

Ants in the nighttime:
the one that has lost its way
crawls in a circle

A water lily: may something
other than death
cleanse my body!

From inside a cabbage
the faint crow of a rooster—
vast and desolate.

Eating grapes—
like one word, another word,
and still another.

thanks to the rainbow
apart from my wife
I do not know other women

In the sky there is primeval
blue, and from my wife
I receive an apple

Kaneko Tota

Called the grand old man of modern haiku in Japan, Kaneko Tota (b. 1919) started writing haiku as a boy. He studied economics and has worked for the Bank of Japan all his adult life. After World War II, he emerged as a flag-bearer for avant-garde haiku and started the haiku group "Kaitei" (Distance to the Sea) in 1962. His theories of haiku have gone through several phases.

Kaneko Tota
b. 1919 -

Yamaguchi Seishi
1904-1994

In the first, he stressed the importance of "plasticism" and "sociality." As a young poet, he emphasized such topics as labor disputes and the atomic bomb. By the 60s and 70s, he'd returned to classical haiku after heated debate between the conservative and avant-garde factions of his own group. A haiku poet, he wrote, should concentrate on his inner vision; it was okay to write about modern subjects, even using surreal or metaphorical elements, while retaining the seventeen-syllable form. There was always the possibilty, he said, that such form could yield the beauty of finality when nothing is really final in this life but death. The speed and fragmentation of the modern world has alienated modern man, Tota said, and we are estranged from nature and ourselves, anxious and frustrated. The fixed form of the haiku, which has been used for hundreds of years, gives us a framework within which to express our vision and moral truth. Today, Tota believes in "haiku for the masses," grounded in the work of Issa and Santoka. "To practice the modern in the grandeur of the old," is his current catch phrase.

> In 1970, I was very interested in the wandering poets Santoka and Issa. Although Issa is not usually considered a wandering poet, I was especially drawn to him. Even now I like him more than Basho, Buson, and Shiki. When I tried to see what drew me to him, I found an indescribable accessibility in his poetry. I do not want to use the term "mass appeal," but his haiku are so easy to understand. Take the following two haiku, for example:
>
> Carrying poppy plants /passing by / someone fighting
>
> Lice on paper scapegoats/ carried away/ by the stream
>
> Both are easy to understand and wonderful haiku. Two requirements of haiku are artistic quality and general appeal. Isn't it enough for a haiku to possess these two elements? Depending on how these two elements are joined, haiku can be compared with other forms of poetry.
>
> Since that time, I have tried to learn how to accept these two elements of quality and appeal. As a result, my haiku have changed a great deal. Plainly stated, I wanted to create

haiku that all could understand and love by all. My poems do not necessarily have to be loved, but I want them to be understood. With this in mind, I have continued trying to find my way. I used to think that quality mattered more than popularity, and that it was all right to write as I pleased. But I changed after the seventies. As a result, I fumbled about in various ways on my own. Some years ago, I asked some friends to show me some haiku loved by everybody and possessed of artistic merit. I wondered what would they come up with. We settled on three examples: Basho's "An old pond/ a frog jumps in/ the sound of water" was the first chosen. Another was Shiki's "Eating a persimmon/ the sound of a bell/ Horyu Temple." And the third was Kusatao's "Snow is falling/ Meiji/ so far away."

Tota has written over fifty books, including *Topography of the Dark Green Land*. Red Moon Press published a translation of an interview from 2011, and several other translations of his haiku will be issued in the coming year. Tota is a familar figure on television discussing haiku and other world matters. He rubs his body with a towel every morning, adding exercise to keep the body flexible. He walks to keep fit and enjoys the garden, which his wife planted with trees and plants brought from their home region in Chichibu forty years earlier. He lost his wife Minako to cancer and now lives with his son and daughter-in-law, who care for him.

A wild boar came
and ate the air —
mountain pass in spring.

bank clerks since
the morning —
fluorescent like squid

dead bones
dumped into the sea!
I chew a piece of pickled radish

above the crumbled bricks
a butterfly, its heart attached
here to the slums

factory dismissing workers —
vomitting cloudy autumn water
into the canal.

after a heated argument
I go out to the street
and become a motorcyle.

Yamaguchi Seishi

It is difficult to know in which period to place Yamaguchi Seishi (1904-1994) and his accomplishments as a haiku poet. After studying law, Seishi began working in Osaka, but because he was often sick, he was forced to stop working regularly and moved successively to a number of small towns near the Japan Sea. Seishi was a disciple of Kyoshi, who once called Seishi one of his more "out of the way disciples." Seishi's poems, especially his haiku, show a daring innovation of style and subject matter that are somewhat at odds with the more conservative Kyoshi. Together with three other poets, Shuoshi, Soju and Seiho, he created the "Four-S Epoch" of the Hototogisu School, founded and lead by Kyoshi.

By the early 1930s, Seishi had become famous for his unconventional poems, which combine a sensitivity to nature and the use of unusual, modern subject matter. He is now regarded as one of the most influential Japanese haiku writers of the 20th century. In 1993, Mangajin Inc. published the definitive collection of his works, 300 haiku, under the title *The Essence of Modern Haiku.*

miserable ant
climbing up a house pillar
higher and higher

at the deepest point
of grief, somebody nearby
breaks a withered branch

on a hook he hangs —
the wild boar, much as he lived,
with his dirty tusks

my own breath
is slightly white —
good to be alive

American Haiku

Very few of the Japanese haiku written between the two world wars were translated into English until the late 70s and 80s. It took a while for American poets to catch up to what the haiku poets in Japan were doing. While there had been haiku-like poems written in the 19th century by American and English poets, there really was no haiku tradition until Ezra Pound and the Imagists introduced a few translations of haiku, some by Pound himself.

Vorticism

Pound was also aligned with the Vorticists, a short-lived literary and artistic movement that flourished in England from 1912 to 1915. Founded by Wyndham Lewis, Vorticism attempted to relate art to industrialization. It opposed 19th-century sentimentality and extolled the energy of the machine and machine-made products, and it promoted a kind of cult of sheer violence. In the visual arts, Vorticist compositions were abstract and sharp-planed, showing the influence of Cubism and Futurism. Their literary compositions were often haiku-like, though unlike haiku, they were characterized by odd line breaks and disjointed and abstract imagery.

Vorticism not cnly sought to capture the mechanical dynamism of its age, but the stillness at its core. Pound coined the term in his essay "Vortex," which first appeared in *Blast*, published by Wyndham Lewis in 1914. Pound emphasized Vorticism's relationship to motion, noting that "the vortex is the point of maximum energy. It represents in mechanics the greatest efficiency." In poetry, Pound referred to this still point as the "unmoving pivot" or the "unwobbling pivot," from the Confucian *Doctrine of the Mean*, whose Italian title, *L'Asse che non vacilla*, translates as "The Unwavering Axis." In Pound's theory, the "unmoving pivot" could be found in the image (see page 103-106). Pound quoted the following poem by H.D. (Hilda Doolittle) as an example:

> Whirl up sea –
> Whirl your pointed pines,
> Splash your great pines
> On our rocks,
> Hurl your green over us,
> Cover us with your pools of fir.

Both William Carlos Williams and Ezra Pound, while still in college in Pennsylvania, vied for Doolittle's affection, even engaging in swordplay – they used walking sticks instead of foils – on her front porch to demonstrate their ardor. She eventually married Richard Aldington, another famous Imagist poet. In the 1930s, she befriended Sigmund Freud and became his patient in order to understand and express her bisexuality.

Mina Loy was another poet in Pound's Imagist and Vorticist circle, though it would also be safe to say that Loy was a modernist poet who defied conventional categorization. Often called a Futurist, a Dadaist, and a Surrealist, she was also a feminist, conceptualist, modern and post-modernist, an emblematic avant-gardist, the bohemian's bohemian, the nervy "impuritan" making the rounds of Village cafes and European salons, and in the end, none of the above. Her anti-career, if you like, was marked by so many seeming contradictions, counter-allegiances, and inconsistencies that she was often considered unbalanced. There was even a rumor circulating around Paris in the twenties that Mina Loy was in fact not a real person at all but a made-up persona. But she heard Pound's endorsement for imagist poetry, short poems that operated much the same way as haiku. In "Omen of Victory," she presents an imagistic echo of the haiku's transformation of imagery.

> Women in uniform
> relaxed for tea
> under a shady garden tree
> discover
> a dove's feather
> fallen in the sugar.

Of all the major literary figures in the twentieth century, Ezra Pound has been one of the most controversial; he has also been one of modern poetry's most important contributors. In an introduction to the *Literary Essays of Ezra Pound*, T. S. Eliot declared that Pound "is more responsible for the twentieth-century revolution in poetry than is any other individual." Four decades later, Donald Hall reaffirmed in remarks collected in *Remembering Poets* that "Ezra Pound is the poet who, a thousand times more than any other man, has made modern poetry possible in English."

The importance of Pound's contributions to the arts and to the revitalization of poetry early in this century has been widely acknowledged; yet in 1950, Hugh Kenner could claim in his groundbreaking study *The Poetry of Ezra Pound*, "There is no great contemporary writer who is less read than Ezra Pound." Pound never sought, nor had, a wide reading audience; his technical innovations and use of unconventional poetic materials often baffled even sympathetic readers. Early in his career, Pound aroused controversy because of his aesthetic views; later, because of his political views.

The Pisan Cantos

"The Pisan Cantos," written in 1945 while the poet was being held in an American military detention center near Pisa, Italy, as a result of his pro-Fascist wartime broadcasts to America on Radio Rome, was published in 1948 by New Directions and in the following year was awarded the Bollingen Prize for poetry by the Library of Congress. Imprisoned as a "dangerous war criminal" in one of the camp's "death cells," a six-by-six-foot wire cage open to the elements, Pound suffered a nervous collapse from the physical and emotional strain. Out of the agony of his own inferno came the eleven cantos that became the sixth book of his modernist epic, *The Cantos*, written as an Odyssean journey over the course of 50 years, loosely following the scheme of Dante's *Divine Comedy*. The honor came amid violent controversy, for the dark cloud of treason still hung over Pound, who had been transferred to St. Elizabeths Federal Hospital for the Criminally Insane and was to remain there for twelve years before being released in 1958 and sent back to his home in Italy. Yet there is no doubt that *The Pisan Cantos* displays some of his finest and most affecting writing, marking an elegiac turn to the personal while synthesizing the philosophical and economic political themes of his previous cantos. Despite the fractured postmodernist surface, *The Pisan Cantos* rejoin the most traditional impulses of elegy: grief transmuted into consolation, the work of mourning at last finding solace in the regenerative energies of Nature. What sets the poetry of the Pisans – typed on an Everest portable with a misaligned "t" – apart from the earlier Cantos, is its far greater alertness to the demotic cadences of American speech, and, as a corollary, to those of vernacular Italian, French, and British.

I have personally wrestled with *The Cantos* since I first encountered them in college, my own Odyssean literary journey. I can't say I've grasped the whole of them, but there are many shining moments of poetry, a haiku-like vision, a tone of compassion that reflects the man's heart at war with his protean mind. On the bookcase above my computer I've taped the following – the single most moving passage of the first Canto of the Pisans, and perhaps of the entire epic – as a reminder that my love of haiku as a boy and my love of poetry as a man remain the steadfast beacon that has guided me all my life:

Will you now bait him with nunneries?"

嗎

that sign is a horse and mouth.
Sitting in heaven he needs you to build him a roof?
"To unscrew φύσιν τοῦ θεοῦ
(Procopius and old Peabody) the inscrutable."
Antoninus and Leo got down the percentage
and, as Stock says, "the historians missed it".
Does god need a clay model? gilded?
hua[4] *t'ou,*[2]   these tongue words!
The maker of words ascending,
          whiteness of bones beneath.
The celestial wants your small change?
          or bears grudge when he does not get it,
(Cf/ Gemisto) a *hsiao jên*? 小
人

And the language in all their "classics"
          fan[1] *hua*[4]
If you don't swallow their buncombe
          you won't have to drive 'em out.

王
又
Ouang -iu- p'uh
          on the edict of K'ang -hsi
in volgar' eloquio taking the sense down to the people.
"Who display no constructive imagination;

702

The Cantos of Ezra Pound 1923-1958

What thou lovest well remains,
                                        the rest is dross.
What thou lov'st well shall not be reft from thee
What thou lov'st well is thy true heritage
Whose world, or mine or theirs
                        or is it of none?
First came the seen, then thus the palpable
    Elysium, though it were in the halls of hell,
What thou lovest well is they true heritage
What thou lov'st well shall not be reft from thee

Objectivism

Pound also founded the Objectivists, a group that touted free verse and highly concentrated language and imagery. Charles Reznikoff was associated with both the Vorticists and Objectivists, not to mention the Imagists, and his short poems had a haiku-like quality.

Among the heaps of brick and plaster lies
a girder, still itself among the rubbish.

Considering the "web of allusion," surely Nick Virgilio was aware of Reznikoff's poem when he composed his memorable lily poem.

Lily
out of the water . . .
out of itself.

When the United States entered World War I in 1917, Reznikoff joined the Reserve Officers Training Corps at Columbia University, but the war was over before he got any training. The war may, however, have been the reason why he printed, on the press which he had installed in the basement of his parents' home in Brooklyn, a small selection of his poems, which he called *Rhythms*. This little book appeared in 1918, and among the verses was "On One Whom the Germans Shot," lines inspired by Ezra Pound's memorial to his gifted friend, the sculptor Henri Gaudier-Brzeska, killed in battle in France in 1915. Those three lines are evidence of the thoughts of death which were haunting so many young men like Reznikoff during the war. When the poem was reprinted in 1920, Reznikoff removed the mention of Gaudier-Brzeska and dropped the title. Like a haiku, it has three lines, though the lines number more syllables than the 5-7-5 requirement.

> How shall we mourn you who are spilled and wasted,
> sure that you would not die with your work unended,
> as if the iron scythe in the grass stops for a flower?

Compare it to Basho's poem inspired by the sight of an infant abandoned on the side of a road (see page 279).

> roadside rose
> of sharon: devoured
> by my horse

Hokku-like Sentences

These movements were short-lived, losing energy with the onset of World War I, but the impulse behind them, to write short, imagistic poems, was similar to haiku's attempt to present a moment with clarity and surprise. Looking to break away from the Georgian verse that characterized 19th century English poetry, Pound called for poetry that was tuned to the spoken voice, that used clear images and resisted the flowery descriptions that he felt bogged poetry down. It was only natural that Pound and many other modern poets found in the concision of haiku the elements of precision they were advocating for modern poetry. Pound's famous poem written in 1913 appeared originally in a form that mimicked the Japanese breaks created by the cutting word.

> IN A STATION OF THE METRO
> The apparition   of the faces   in the crowd
> Petals   on a wet, black bough.

In his essay on "Vorticism" that was reprinted in the 1914 issue of *The Fortnightly Review*, Pound referred to this poem as being a "hokku-like sentence." One could claim that this was the first fully realized haiku in English. Pound was to use this technique of spacing and line breaks in the *Cantos*, though he never really wrote haiku, to speak of. His influence as an Imagist poet, nevertheless, led to what might be called a haiku craze, in which newspapers and magazines held haiku contests. Quite a few serious poets tried their hand at it, including Amy Lowell, Yvor Winters, e.e. cummings, Langston Hughes, Carl Sandburg and Wallace Stevens.

Swallows twittering at twilight:
Waves of heat
Churned to flames by the sun.
– John Gould Fletcher

Even the iris bends
When a butterfly lights upon it.
– Amy Lowell

About an excavation
a flock of bright red lanterns
has settled.
– Charles Reznikoff

the ceaseless weaving of the uneven water
– Charles Reznikoff

Thin air! My mind is gone.
– Yvor Winters

SUICIDE NOTE
The calm, cool face of the river
Asked me for a kiss.
– Langston Hughes

l(a
le
af
fa
ll
s)
one
l
iness
– e.e.cummings

High Modernism vs Popular Modernism

But the craze was not to last. In 1923, the publication of three books changed the course of American poetry just as it was beginning to claim a popular modern tone in which poets wrote in a natural, colloquial style. As a result of Eliot's publication of *The Waste Land*, Pound's *Draft of Thirty Cantos*, and Wallace Stevens' *Harmonium*, poets had no use for the simplicity of haiku, nor the popular modernism presaged by Whitman. The fourth book of poetry published that same year was William Carlos Williams' *Spring and All*.

The first three launched what came to be called "High Modernism," poetry of dense allusion and difficult interpretation of style and structure. As a matter of fact, interpretation was the key. Shortly after those books of poetry were published, three works of critical analysis followed, cementing the idea that poems were meant to be interpreted, analyzed, studied. Ambiguity and paradox became pegs on which literary analysis was hung. Those three books of literary criticism initiated what was called The New Criticism: Cleanth Brooks's *The Well-Wrought Urn*: *Studies in the Structure of Poetry*; W. K. Wimsatt's *The Verbal Icon*; and Robert Penn Warren's *Understanding Poetry*. The titles say it all: poetry was an object, an urn, a verbal icon to be studied, analyzed and understood.

The books of poetry by Eliot, Pound, and Stevens, along with those three books of literary criticism, widely influenced the teaching and study of poetry at the college level, spawning a generation of poets and teachers who dominated the university English departments well into the 1960s. When Eliot's *The Waste Land* caused such a sensation, William Carlos Williams declared that American poetry had been set back fifty years just when it was on the verge of carrying the Whitmanesque style of the American voice into prominence. Williams' book was forgotten, and when the new American poets of the 60s turned away from the academic verse of the previous decades, it was Williams' poetry they embraced, it was Williams who became their example, their guru, it was Williams who served as a living model of "popular modernism." In many ways, contemporary poets of the last fifty years can be called the wild children of Walt Whitman and William Carlos Williams. Before the publication of those books, haiku seemed on the verge of becoming an essential part of the American canon. But it was not to be. Haiku lost its appeal and seemed to wither on the vine. My own reluctance to write haiku stemmed from the same notion, that haiku was a dead end.

American Haiku Makes a Comeback

This is not to say there weren't publications that introduced Japanese haiku to American poets in the hope of reviving interest in the genre. Asataro Miyamori's *Anthology of Haiku, Ancient and Modern* came out in 1932 and included translations of many haiku poets before Basho, as well as his ten disciples, and a few contemporary poets including Shiki. This was the blue book with gold lettering on the cover that my fifth grade teacher had on her desk when she recited haiku. Not counting Pound's few translations, this was the first time in the West that Japanese haiku poets were introduced. A year later, Harold Gould Henderson brought out the first serious study of Japanese haiku in English, *The Bamboo Broom*. This book, too, sat on my teacher's desk as reference. It was an anthology of poems and poets from Basho to Shiki, in which Henderson defined haiku as "a poem intended to express and evoke emotion; haiku may be of many kinds, grave or gay, deep or shallow, religious, satirical, sad, humorous, or charming, but all haiku worthy of the name are records of high moments — higher, at least, then the surrounding plain."

In 1935, *The Hollow Reed* by Mary J.J. Wrinn was published, which covered all kinds of poetry from the couplet, the cinquain, the sonnet, the triolet, the rondel, the villanelle, to mention just a few. The 12-page chapter on haiku was titled "In the Japanese Manner." Had it not been for the political tensions of the 30s, and the war with Japan in the 40s, haiku might have flourished in the hands of American poets. But it didn't. The literary products of contemporary Japanese culture were dismissed, and it wasn't until after the war that interest in haiku returned, primed mainly by R.H. Blyth's four-volume study *Haiku* (1949-1952), followed by his two-volume *History of Haiku* (1963-64).

By equating haiku to the sensibility of Zen, Blythe influenced a generation that was becoming interested in Eastern philosophy and religion. Thousands of poems that had never been translated into English were made known to American poets and writers of fiction as well, but none more so than the poets of the emerging Beat Generation and the San Francisco Renaissance. Another influential book was Kenneth Rexroth's translations in *One Hundred Poems from the Chinese*, published in 1965, and his *Women Poets of Japan* (originally titled *The Burning Heart*) published in 1977. But it was Blyth's massive study that set the tone for post war classic and modern haiku.

Reginald Horace Blyth

In 1916, at the height of World War I, Blyth was imprisoned as a conscientious objector. After the war he attended the University of London, where he graduated in 1923, with honors. He adopted a vegetarian lifestyle which he maintained throughout his life. In 1925, he moved to Korea (then under Japanese rule), where he became Assistant Professor of English at Keijo University in Seoul. In 1937 he married a Japanese woman named Kishima Tomiko with whom he later had two daughters. He moved to Japan and took a job as English teacher at Kanazawa University. When Britain declared war on Japan in December 1941 following the bombing of Pearl Harbor, Blyth was interned as a British enemy alien. Although he expressed sympathy for Japan and sought Japanese citizenship, his request was denied. During his internment his extensive library was destroyed in an air raid.

After the war, Blyth worked diligently with authorities, both Japanese and American, to assist in the transition to peace. He functioned as liaison to the Japanese Imperial Household. His close friend, Harold Gould Henderson (who wrote *The Bamboo Broom* in 1934, *An Introduction to Haiku* in 1958, and co-founded the Haiku Society of America in 1968), was on General Douglas MacArthur's staff. Together, Blythe and Henderson helped draft the declaration "Ningen Sengen," by which Emperor Hirohito renounced his personal divinity and declared himself to be a human being.

Blyth died in 1964 of a brain tumor and complications from pneumonia, in the Seiroka Hospital in Tokyo. He was buried in the cemetery of the Shokozan Tokei Soji Zenji Temple in Kamakura, next to his old friend, D. T. Suzuki. He left the following death poem:

Sazanka ni kokoro nokoshite tabidachinu

I leave my heart
to the sasanqua flower
on the day of this journey

Reginald Horace Blythe, author of the four-volume *Haiku* (1949-1952) and *A History of Haiku* in two volumes (1963)

Blyth's Assessment of Women Poets

After early imagist interest in haiku the genre drew less attention in English, until after World War II, with the appearance of a number of influential volumes about Japanese haiku. In 1949, with the publication of Blyth's four-volume work, haiku was introduced to the post-war Western world. The work dealt mostly with pre-modern haiku, though Shiki was included. His two-volume *History of Haiku* published in 1964, continues to influence the writing of American haiku.

Present-day attitudes to Blyth's work vary: On the one hand, he is appreciated as a populariser of Japanese culture; on the other, his portrayals of haiku and Zen have sometimes been criticised as one-dimensional. Many contemporary Western writers of haiku were introduced to the genre through his works. Some noted Blyth's distaste for more modern themes, and his strong bias in favor of a direct connection between haiku and Zen, a connection largely ignored by modern Japanese poets. Blyth also did not view haiku by Japanese women favorably, downplaying their contributions to the genre, especially during the Basho era and the twentieth century. In just over 800 pages of text in his two volume *History of Haiku*, Blyth devoted a total of 16 pages to haiku by women, and even these pages are run through with negative comments. "Women are said to be intuitive, and as they cannot think, we may hope this is so, but intuition, like patriotism, is not enough." With respect to a verse ostensibly by Chiyo-Jo, he wrote, "Chiyo's authorship of this verse is doubtful, but so is whether women can write haiku."

Fudoki Spirit

Although Blyth did not foresee the appearance of original haiku in languages other than Japanese when he began writing on the topic, and although he founded no school of verse, his works stimulated the writing of haiku in English. At the end of the second volume of his *History of Haiku* he remarked, "The latest development in the history of haiku is one which nobody foresaw, the writing of haiku outside Japan, not in the Japanese language." Blyth admitted that he wasn't fond of the inevitable changes occurring in contemporary Japanese haiku. He wrote:

> Modern poetry since Shiki has been, like the world itself, in a state of confusion. It may be said, with too much truth, that his-

tory is confusion itself, and indeed none but a presumptuous nit-wit would attempt to write a history of anything at all. . . . Indeed, it is not that Basho wanted to write haiku, so he travelled all over Japan visiting famous sites and tasting the special products of various places. This is really putting the cart before the horse. . . . Haiku had to be written to let off steam. With Buson and Issa, and all the host of lesser poets, the *fudoki* spirit [a hard word to translate, it can refer to the "self and soul and home and shrine and myth and folklore and ancient history" — the collective history and experience of one's being.] infused and inspired their work; they were conscious of it, as they were not, fortunately, of the pantheism and Zen and so on. However, when we come to the Meiji Era [1868-1912], the spirit of place, the spirit of time weakens, and haiku with it. Shiki was a kind of atheist, an agnostic, which is really a don't-want-to-know-er. A man of violent poetic energy must believe in something, even superstition, even Roman Catholicism. Actually, the best haiku of Basho and Buson and Issa have little or nothing to do with historic places or famous mountains or special products or local customs. They are "a pure delight" in the particular thing, quite apart from romantic or emotional associations, but the point is this, that to be wise you must have been a fool, have been sentimental, have been vulgar, have been cruel, have been snobbish, have been a savourer of the *fudoki*. You can't transcend such things if you have nothing to transcend. Thus, the best old haiku rise out of the *fudoki*. The best modern haiku emerge as from a vacuum, or from the narrow hopes and fears and loving and loathing of the individual poet. Like Shakespeare, Basho spoke for humanity, of humanity and by humanity; there is nothing eccentric in his view of nature, nothing egoistic in his view of himself.

Having thus indirectly blasted all modern haiku, we are now in a position to be agreeably surprised by the wealth of sensitivity and sincerity of the haiku poets during the last sixty or seventy years.

Fusei Hits the Spot

Blyth translated a few poems by Shiki, questioning whether or not Shiki was deep or shallow. He then translated one poem each by Soseki, Kyoshi, Hekigodo, Fusei, Bosha, Otsuji, Kijo, Ryunosuke, Seisensui, and others, along with short acerbic comments such as, "With Hekigodo we get long, stumbling, unmusical, more-than-seventeen-syllabled 'haiku' that can hardly be called hokku, 'the first verse,' because each one tries to include everything within itself." He notes with some sarcasm that Seisensui "freed haiku from its three-hundred-year-old form." He translates a haiku by Akutagawa Ryunosuke, claiming that "it shows how unpoetical a writer of some genius can be." Grudgingly, he admits that, even though Fusei's popularization of haiku was undesirable, "to use a suitable vulgarism, he hits the spot."

Form Versus Content

As poets and translators of poetry in all times have wrestled with the tension between form and content, Blyth closes his book with a similar struggle to come to terms with that tension. It is a tension inherent in all art, that impulse by the artist to both accept the challenge to work within prescribed aesthetic principles and the impulse to subvert those very principles. Because Blyth's account of that struggle is so telling and heartfelt — how could he not know that "form and content" always change, yet remain essentially the same — I quote his closing remarks (which I imagine my 5th grade teacher, Mrs. Aime, must have read as a mission statement, guiding her toward the teaching of haiku to her young, impressionable charges).

> The two problems of human life are loneliness and boredom, and they are one problem. Haiku is the chief way of not being bored, that is, not being lonely. Thus, haiku should be the chief subject in primary and secondary schools in every country in the world. But it should be prohibited in the universities, and on no account should children ever be examined on them, or forced to explain them. How about my own explanations? Some say they are better than many of the original haiku. Some say they should be omitted. I myself agree with both views.
>
> But wherever haiku are composed, the problem of the form must arise. Europeans and American have to decide whether their haiku are to be in [a specific form] or free verse, what some rude people call "a dribble of prose," or in five, seven, five syllables as in Japanese. [No question that] a strict adherence to 5, 7, 5 syllables in English has produced some odd translations of Japanese haiku.

> The philosophic significance of 5, 7, 5, in Japanese syllables, may be this. Seventeen such syllables are one emission of breath, one exhalation of soul. The division into three [lines] gives us the feeling of ascent, attainment, and resolution of experience. The haiku form is thus a simple and yet deeply "natural" form, compared to the sonnet, blank verse, and other borrowed forms of verse in English. The ideal, that is, the occasional, attainable haiku form in English, would perhaps be three short lines, the second a little longer than the other two.

Free Verse Haiku: The Suchness of Things

In an attempt to be fair, Blyth gave the opposition a chance to speak. J.W. Hackett had won the Japan Airlines Haiku Contest in 1964 (see page 25). Blythe allowed him to make a case for the free verse form.

> I regard "haiku" as *fundamentally* existential, rather than literary. Or if you will, as primarily an experience, rather than a form of poetry. Basho's statement that: "Haiku is simply what is happening in this place, at this moment," shows that he regarded intuitive experience to be the *basis* of Haiku. And Now, his criterion, is my own. If the Haiku experience can be expressed in seventeen syllables, all well and good. If not, then the experience should be rendered freely, in the manner best serving its comprehension and effect. Even the Japanese masters strayed from 5-7-5, as do many modern Japanese poets. It seems clear that the whole matter of syllables and lines is an arbitrary one, and should be. For Haiku is more than a form of poetry: it is a Way — one of living awareness. Haiku's real treasure is its touchstone of the present. This, together with its rendering of the Suchness of things, gives Haiku a supra-literary mission, one of the moment.

The Essence of the Mush

Blyth's closing paragraph is not a rebuttal, but an attempt to deal with the abstractness of haiku's nature, an abstractness that confounds any attempt to define, not just haiku, not just poetry, but all art. For instance, either a sonnet is a sonnet or it is not a sonnet, and yet, Ted Berrigan wrote a book of poems called *The Sonnets*, which do not conform to the traditional sonnet form, be it Petrarchian, Elizabethan, or Shakespearean. The poems contain fourteen lines, with the last two lines forming a couplet, except there is no rhyme scheme. If they do not adhere to the strict form in terms of the rhyme scheme, what then makes them sonnets? That they have fourteen lines? That they exhibit the "turn" or "volta" in line eight? By the same token, is a haiku a three line poem, or a three line poem containing seventeen syllables, and must the seventeen syllables be in a 5-7-5 sequence?

Berrigan was a prominent figure in the second generation of the New York School of Poets. *The Sonnets* weaves together traditional elements of the Shakespearean sonnet form with the disjunctive structure and cadence of T. S. Eliot's *The Waste Land* and Berrigan's own literary innovations. The product is a composition, in the words of Berrigan's editor and second wife Alice Notley, that is "musical, sexy, and funny."

Like those who are drawn to the haiku form because of its structure, Berrigan was initially drawn to the sonnet form because of its inherent challenge; in his own words, "the form sort of [stultifies] the whole process [of writing]." The procedure that he ultimately concocted to write *The Sonnets* is the essence of the work's novelty and ingenuity. After attempting several sonnets, Berrigan decided to go back through what he had written and take out certain lines, one line from each work until he had six lines. He then went through the poems backwards and took one more line from each until he had accumulated six more lines, twelve lines total. Based on this body of the work, Berrigan knew what the final couplet would be; this process became the basis for *The Sonnets*.

Addressing claims that the method was mechanical, Berrigan explained that some of the seventy-seven sonnets came to him "whole," not needing to be pieced together. The poet's preoccupation with style, his concern for form and his own role as the creator as evinced by *The Sonnets* pose a challenge to traditional ideas about poetry and signify a fresh and innovative artistic approach. The only other structural form to the sonnet aside from the particular rhyme scheme, number of lines, and final couplet, is the first part, composed of six lines, and the second part, composed of six lines, in which the second part creates a "turn" from the first part, either in idea or theme. The last two lines then encapsulate the previous twelve lines, somewhat like Hamlet's final two lines to one of his soliloquys,

"The play's the thing wherein I'll catch the conscience of the king."

But if one doesn't adhere to the structure or form, what inherently makes Berrigan's sonnets "sonnets?" Berrigan recognized the eternal possibilities for invention in a genre seemingly overwhelmed by the success of its traditional form. By imitating the forms and practices of earlier artists and recreating them to express personal ideas and experiences, Berrigan demonstrated the potential for poetry in his and subsequent generations. As Charles Bernstein succinctly commented, "Part collage, part process writing, part sprung lyric, Ted Berrigan's *The Sonnets* remains one of the freshest and most buoyantly inspired works of contemporary poetry. Reinventing verse for its time, *The Sonnets* are redolent with possibilities for our own."

So what makes them sonnets? Any attempt to explain it in abstract terms will naturally fall into mush, but isn't all literature and all art a kind of mush, the mush not of numbers and reports and cosmological equations, but the mush we all recognize as the essence of this undefinable life. Blyth, like most of us, uses words as a defense against meaninglessness, but his attempts to describe the mush of haiku in such abstract terms only leads to more mush.

> The problem for haiku in any language as for life itself in any age, is how to put thought completely into sensation, how to make sensation thought-full. In addition — and this has only too often been forgotten by the Japanese haiku poets themselves — sensation must be intense, though not violent, the thinking all-inclusive and subtle, not parochial and complicated. But after all, which is more important, to write (haiku) or to live? Thoreau answers:
>
> > My life has been the poem I would have writ,
> > But I could not both live and utter it.
>
> It is this which makes life an unwritten poem. Writing haiku, and the desire for (more and more) enlightenment is the last infirmity of the noble mind. We must not write haiku, we must not write, we must not live, to fulfil ourselves, or to share our experiences with others. We must not aim at

immortality or even timelessness; we must not aim. Infinity and eternity come of themselves or not at all.

Blyth's translations influenced the work of many San Francisco and Beat Generation writers such as Jack Kerouac, Gary Snyder, and Allen Ginsberg, as well as poets who were part of the international "haiku community," many of whom got their first taste of haiku from Blyth's books. Blyth did not relate to Japanese haiku that focused on modern themes, though.

Borrowed Water

But something was afoot in American poetry, a resurgent interest in haiku, which seemed to operate beneath the radar of the modernizing impulse in mainstream American poetry. In 1956, as the beats were publishing their free-verse poems in anti-establishment magazines, many of which were produced in garages and kitchens, the Writers Roundtable in Los Altos, California was founded by Helen Stiles Chenoweth to further creative writing among adults interested in haiku. As Chenoweth put it, the poets used "the Japanese tone poem referred to as haiku to appreciate the syllabic content of words." They read and discussed the four classic Japanese haiku poets and wrote American haiku.

Meanwhile, in 1963, the first journal outside of Japan dedicated to haiku was founded in Platteville, Wisconsin. *American Haiku* was edited by James Bell and Don Eulert. It's impossible to overstate the influence this semi-annual journal had on the development of American haiku. Its first issue was dedicated to Harold Henderson, author of *Bamboo Broom* and *The Introduction to Haiku*. *American Haiku* was the first magazine to devote itself solely to the publication of haiku and featured poets who were to become major contributors: James W. Hackett (who you will remember was the only contemporary non-Japanese haiku poet to receive Blyth's approval), Larry Gates, O Mabson Southard, and Nick Virgilio. Many of the poets who were part of the Writers Roundtable were published in the magazine. A few years later, James Bell contacted the Writers Roundtable and encouraged them to publish a collection of their haiku, which resulted in *Borrowed Water*, the first anthology of haiku written exclusively in English and featuring 300 haiku.

Borrowed Water was a beautifully produced book. It was printed on high-quality linen bond, different colors for different sections: Spring in muted pink, Summer in vibrant yellow, Autumn in pastel green, and Winter in light gray. A final section was printed on textured pink paper. I bought a hardcover copy for $2.95 while still in college, and though I was attracted to the beautiful production design by Keiko Chiba, which featured Japanese watercolors, I wasn't impressed by the poetry. The haiku seemed precious, light, and lacking in depth or darkness, hardly approaching the work of Gail Pratt, Walter Seltzer, or the early experiments by the Beat Poets. If this was haiku, it was not a form I was interested in exploring. Most of the poems referenced the scent of lilacs, rainbows, petalled snow, dewdrops, dandelions, wet sand, promenading sea-gulls, hovering birds, small orchards, and lines like "from whence butterflies." I had done that when I was in fifth and sixth grades, and these haiku did not contain the majesty or heart of Basho's and Issa's best work, the vividness of Buson's poems, or the modernity and bluntness of Shiki's. A few of them were okay.

Name faded in stone
required Braille of fingertips
that spring, to free it.
– Joy Shieman

Library shelves packed with
books the boy cannot read—
his fingers touch them.
– Catherine Neil Paton

Poet sent in space
describing infinity,
forgot re-entry.
-Joy Shieman

Watching busy ants —
my clumsy shadow cover
their entire world.
– Margot Bollock

These haiku were quite wonderful, but what the rest of them lacked, in my estimation at the time, was the desolation of *sabi*, the profoundity of *yugen*, and the great sadness of *mono no aware*. Certainly these qualities existed in the haiku of the masters, but the poets of the Writers Roundtable did not appear to pick up on those aspects of Issa's and Basho's poems; rather, they emphasized their delicacy.

I was not in the mood for poetry that was quaint. Nor did I resonate with the academic poetry I was being taught in college.

Borrowed Water: A Book of American Haiku by the Los Altos Writers Roundtable (Charles E. Tuttle Co., 1966)

I was on the prowl for something more vibrant, poetry that was capable of expressing the deeper contradictions of the world I was experiencing at the time. Haiku was not making it for me, and whatever was going on in American haiku after that, I lost track of it.

The Haiku Society of America

Part of the problem for American poets attracted to the writing of those short poems "in the Japanese manner" was the lack of English translations of the poets writing after Shiki. In the winter of 1968, Harold Henderson and Leroy Kanterman brought together two dozen poets, who met at the Asia House in New York City with the intention of forming a haiku group to read and discuss haiku. Coming from outside the city were William Higginson and the New Jersey poet, Nicholas Virgilio. With encouragement from the Japan Society of New York, they named themselves The Haiku Society, held monthly meetings and drew up a series of bylaws with membership open to all those interested in haiku upon payment of nominal dues.

Henderson was named honorary President and took an active interest in the group until his death in 1974. Word of the Society spread and soon members joined from all over the country. Meetings concentrated on discussion and criticism of haiku, including historical research and a series of programs on punctuation and techniques, as well as the question of syllable count that has proven to be a continuing point of dispute within the haiku poets' community. Minutes were sent out to all members, which became a valuable resource for haiku poets and scholars. The name was changed to The Haiku Society of America. *A Haiku Path* covering the history of its first twenty years was published in 1994.

The formation of the Haiku Society of America renewed interest in haiku and a considerable body of literature on Western haiku began to emerge. In 1969, Eric Amann's *The Wordless Poem* appeared as a special issue of *Haiku Magazine*. A year later, William J. Higgenson's essays were collected and published. Translations of Basho's travel diary *Oku-No Hosomichi* were available, but they were unsatisfactory, often wordy and sentimental.

In 1968, Cid Corman published a spare, sensitive rendering, which he titled *Roads to Far Towns*. At a meeting of the

Haiku Society, he read from the work and discussed aspects of American and Japanese haiku. By the 1970s, translations into English of modern Japanese haiku poets began to appear. *The Anthology of Modern Japanese Poetry* was published in 1972, translated and compiled by Edith Marcombe Shiffert and Yoki Sawa, and included the work of many of Shiki's disciples: Kyoshi, Seisensui, Dakotsu, Shuoshi, Takako, Seishi, and Shigenobu. And two years later, the *Penguin Book of Japanese Verse*, which included many modern and contemporary poets was published. *Modern Japanese Haiku* appeared in 1976 in which Makoto Euda translated twenty poets. This in turn brought the modernizing impulse of Shiki and his disciples — not to mention the disciples of his disciples — to the attention of a new generation of American poets who were in the process of their own modernizing revolution. In 1981, *In the Country of Eight Islands* appeared, edited and translated by Hiroaki Sato and Burton Watson. Sato published another book in 1983 titled *One Hundred Frogs: From Renga to Haiku in English*, which dealt with haiku, as well as with the often ignored renga or linked verse form out of which haiku grew. Sato translated many renowned Japanese poets, most notably Basho, and discussed at length modern Japanese and Western haiku. What makes this book so delightful is his in-depth analysis of Basho's poem about the frog in the pond, presenting a compilation of over one hundred translations and variations of the poem.

In 1983, Donald Keene's two-volume work *Dawn To The West* appeared, part of his four-volume study of the whole of Japanese literature.

Soon, numerous magazines and journals appeared, including *Dragonfly*, *Haiku*, *Haiku West*, and finally, what was to become the journal of record, *Modern Haiku* edited by Robert Spies, Charles Trumbull, Lee Gurga, and Paul Miller respectively.

Speculations, Pops, Shorts, and Weirds!

Robert Spiess became known as "the gatekeeper." He was not only the editor of *American Haiku*, but the poetry editor of *Modern Haiku* for some twenty-four years and published nearly a dozen collections of his own haiku and two more of his epigrammatic "Speculations." It was becoming almost fashionable to give nick-names to haiku that departed from the 5-7-5 pattern. It was theorized that in English, a haiku could better approximate the Japanese *onji* symbol sounds by using twelve to seventeen syllables. Jack Kerouac introduced many poets to haiku when his book *Dharma Bums* was published in 1958, but he also theorized that the Japanese haiku of seventeen syllables may not be appropriate for English haiku, because "American speech is something else again . . . bursting to pop." He even called his haiku "Pops." Auden called his haiku "Shorts," Allen Ginsberg called his haiku-like short poems "American sentences," and Nick Virgilio called the haiku he wrote that departed from the classical form, "Weirds."

How Suite It Is

An expansive view of poetry might shrug off the reduction of form altogether. What difference does it make what we call a short poem? Lee Perron has written a wonderful suite of poems titled *North American Suite: Day Dreams at Night*, which is composed of twenty-one poems arranged as Largo, Cantabile, Scherzo, Dolorosa, ma non troppo, Ostinato, and Coda. I quote four of the individual poems, not in the order in which Perron displayed them:

❊

new haven
old port
lost coast

❊

passing time
ghost boats
fall river

❊

daydreams of sedition
wild hog hill
fat chance

❊

a way that cannot be told
day dreams at night
night dreams in the soil

Strictly speaking, they're not haiku; some have fewer syllables, some more. I asked Perron if he had a name for the short poems. His response: "I wanted to start off with simple nouns and adjectives in section one, then bring in more complexity and grammatical variety as the sequence develops. I don't have a word for these kinds of poems. As I write, I remind myself I want to make the shortest possible poem that fully conveys the fleeting awarenesses." This could be a 17th century Japanese haiku poet talking about his work, in terms of essence, not necessarily the formal 5-7-5 17-syllable structure.

Speaking of definitions, Perron reminded me of a Midwestern magazine published since the '70s and '80s called *High/Coo*. The editor, Randy Brooks, defined high/coo as "fully Americanized haiku." He later called his publication a quarterly of short poetry, because it contained a lot of poems that were just not like haiku, or senryu, or any other Japanese form. "A bold, if quirky undertaking," wrote Perron. Brooks has a web site called Brooks Books. Among the haiku poets he's published are Raymond Roseliep and Lucien Stryk.

The Call for a Stylistic Revolution

Harold Henderson wrote a letter in 1963 to James Bell, who edited *American Haiku*: "If there is to be a real '*American Haiku*,'" Henderson wrote, "we must—by trial and error—work out our own standards." Henderson was suggesting that the 5-7-5 form of seventeen syllables in three lines might not be the best form for the English expression of the essence of haiku, though attempts to define just what that essence is continued (and continues) to be debated.

There were groups forming across the United States that considered themselves followers of either Basho or Buson, or another of the classical poets, while still experimenting with line and syllable counts. John Willis, another prominent haiku poet featured in *American Haiku* and *Modern Haiku*, argued for a stylistic revolution— even shorter haiku with an emphasis on action as opposed to Buson's and Shiki's emphasis on static imagery. Along with his wife, Marlene Mountain, he often employed the one-line format. And when he did evoke the usual quaint image from nature, there was an emotional aura that deepened the experience.

After the founding in 1968 of The Haiku Society of America,

dozens of magazines devoted to haiku were being published, and various poets came to be recognized as major practitioners of the form: O Mabson Southard, Robert Spiess, Clement Hoyt, Michael McClintock, John Wills, Anita Virgil, J. W. Hackett, William J. Higginson, Nicholas Virgilio, Foster Jewell, George Swede, Mabelsson Norway, Eric Amann, Winona Baker, Gary Hotham, Elizabeth Searle Lamb, Alan Pizzarelli, Raymond Roseliep, Virginia Brady Young and Arizona Zipper formed the tip of a very large iceberg that encompassed not just American haiku, but haiku being written all over the world in German, French, Spanish, Portuguese, Italian, and many other languages, including, of course, Japanese.

Haiku in the Western World Comes of Age

A landmark work in modern American haiku was published in 1974, *The Haiku Anthology*, edited by Cor van den Heuvel (W. W. Norton & Co). This anthology brought together thirty-eight well-known American and Canadian haiku poets. A two-day festival in Glassboro, New Jersey was organized featuring readings, workshops, and seminars. Publication of the anthology was the first recognition of original Western haiku by a major commercial publisher, marking a kind of coming of age for the genre in the Western world. Cor van den Heuval dedicated the publication to R. H. Blyth, who had died in 1964, and Harold G. Henderson, who passed away a few months after the festival, marking the end of one era and the beginning of another.

Red Moon Press

In 1993, Jim Kacian founded Red Moon Press, now the largest publishers of haiku and haiku-related books outside of Japan. Kacian also edits *Frogpond*, the journal of the Haiku Society of America. Kacian also brings out the annual *Red Moon Anthology*. He's a strong advocate, along with such poets as Marlene Mountain and Janice Bostok, of single-line haiku in English. Cor van den Heuval's *The Haiku Anthology*, published in 1974, was followed by a second edition in 1986, and a third revised edition in 1999, which included over 800 English language haiku and senryu by 89 poets.

Also in 1993, *Haiku Moment, an Anthology of Contemporary North American Haiku* appeared, edited by Bruce Ross (Tuttle Publishing), containing over 800 haiku by 185 poets. In his introduction, Ross boiled much of the history of North American English-language haiku down to the push-pull between subjective and objective haiku, dividing this history into four stages.

The first stage began in the 1910s with Ezra Pound's manifesto on Imagism which criticized 19th century sentimentality and clichéd figurative expression. His poem "In a Station of the Metro" characterized poetry that presented objective images. This stage continued into the 20s and 30s with William Carolos Williams' Objectivism, as exemplified by his poem "The Red Wheelbarrow," and Wallace Stevens' call for revelatory realism, as exemplified by his poem "Thirteen Ways of Looking at a Blackbird." In that respect, Williams resembled Basho in his direct engagement with nature, and Stevens invoked the imaginative renderings of experience found in Buson, what Stevens called "the supreme fiction." This first phase was also influenced by those translations of Japanese haiku that appeared in the 30s that my 5th and 6th grade teacher had shown us: *Haiku Poems Ancient and Modern* by Muyaniru Asataro (1932), *The Bamboo Broom* by Harold G. Henderson (1934), and *The Hollow Reed* by Mary J. J. Wrinn (1935).

The second important phase, according to Ross, centered on the Beat movement of the 50s. As Pound had reacted to the sentimental abstract verse of the Romantic era, the Beats reacted to the cerebral academic poetry that dominated this period by writing haiku and other poetry focused upon emotional vividness and the subjective response to the present moment, the "haiku moment." Ginsberg combined Romantic sensibility with vivid imagery to create Blake-like poems on nature, love, and social criticism, while Kerouac melded Christian and Buddhist spirituality that breached the moodiness of classical Japanese haiku. Gary Snyder was influenced by the Zen Buddhism found in the work of D. T. Suzuki and Alan Watts, and in the four-volume translation of Japanese haiku begun in 1949 by R. H. Blyth. Also influential in this second phase, according to Ross, was Donald Keene's *Anthology of Japanese Literature* (1955).

The third generation of American haiku poets dates from

the late 50s and early 60s with English-language introductions of haiku by Kenneth Yasuda and Harold Henderson and the establishment of English-language haiku journals and magazines beginning with *American Haiku* (1963), *Haiku Highlights* (1965), *Haiku* (1967), *Haiku West* (1967), *Modern Haiku* (1969), *Dragonfly* (1973), *Cicada* (1977), and *Frogpond* (1978). The establishment of the Haiku Society of American in 1968 was a significant watershed that led in 1974 to Cor van den Heuvel's pioneering *The Haiku Anthology* (1974), which was followed by the equally significant *Canadian Haiku Anthology* (1979) edited by George Swede.

The fourth phase of American haiku began in the late 70s, and continued through the 80s and 90s in which the structure and form of haiku was extended, modified, and in many cases, all but obliterated. Many haiku societies sprang up with centers in Seattle, San Francisco, Santa Fe, Dubuque, Raleigh, Rochester, New York City, Boston, Toronto, and Ottawa. This period also saw the production of dozens of important books of haiku criticism and translations, including Geroge Swede's *The Modern English Haiku* (1981), Hiroaki Sato's *One Hundred Frogs* (1983), William J. Higginson's *The Haiku Handbook* (1985), *From the Country of Eight Islands, An Anthology of Japanese Poetry*, translated by Hiroaki Sato and Burton Watson (1986), further editions of Cor van den Heuval's *The Haiku Anthology* (1986 and 1999), and Makoto Ueda's *Modern Japanese Haiku* (1976). It would be almost impossible to list all the publications of books by individual haiku poets, but a partial list would include: Lee Gurga's *The Measure of Emptiness*, John Wills' *Reed Shadows*, Rod Willmot's *Sayings for the Invisible*, Nick Virgilio's *Selected Haiku*, George Swede's *High Wire Spider*, Robert Spiess's *The Cottage of the Wild Plum*, Raymond Roseliep's *Rabbit in the Moon*, Bruse Ross's *Thousands of Wet Stones*, Lee Richmond's *Diary of a Winter Fly*, Jane Reichold's *Thumbtacks on a Calendar*, Alan Pizzarelli's *The Flea Circus*, Penny Harter's *The Monkey's Face*, Gary Hotham's *As Far as the Light Goes*, Patricia Donegan's *Without Warning*, Michael Dudley's *A Man in a Motel Room*, and David Elliott's *Wind in the Trees*.

In 2003, Makoto Ueda followed up his earlier book of translations with *Far Beyond the Field, Haiku by Japanese Women.*

In 2013, another anthlogy of haiku appeared, *Haiku in English*, edited by Jim Kacian, Philip Rowland, and Allan Burns, with an introduction by Billy Collins. The book contained more than 800 poems by over 200 poets from around the world. Also included was an insightful historical overview by leading haiku poet, editor, and publisher Jim Kacian.

Experiments in form and presentation, as well as attempts to define haiku's essence, have been debated to the point of meaninglessness — any short poem may be thought of as haiku, and many poems that do follow the 5-7-5 pattern are dismissed because they don't have the proper "essence," all of which tends to relegate haiku to the category of "worthless fragments," as some in the literary establishment call them. The majority of haiku are dismissed as light verse whose only value is as an educational aid to interest children in poetry.

How Short Can a Haiku Be?

I admit, as a college student and beyond, I had the same attitude, yet here I am, after all these years, writing haiku. Once I decided, however, to make a small book of short syllabic poems, a question arose: Which form do I use? The haiku, the senryu, the tanka, the renga? And if I choose to write haiku, will it have three lines? Four lines? Two lines? One? And what syllable count shall I choose? Seventeen? Twelve syllables, as advocated by Kerouac? Or even down to one syllable per line, such as this one by Raymond Roseliep:

light
lights
light

And then there are these one-line or two-word haiku by George Swede:

After the search for meaning   bills in the mail

Night begins to gather   between her breasts

stars   crickets

A One-Word Haiku Worth $500

It's hard to imagine anything shorter than Roseliep's three line, three word haiku, but a few decades ago, Aram Saroyan, son of William Saroyan (the author of *The Daring Young Man on the Flying Trapeze*), wrote a book of one-word poems, one poem per page. He became well-known for these minimalist poems, a famous example of which is the one-word poem "lighght." (That poem was included in *The Haiku Anthology*, which won an NEA award amounting to $500 for each poet. Senator Jesse Helms objected to the amount of the award on principle, dismissing contemporary poetry as worthless. He singled out Saroyan's award because, he said, $500 for one word was too much, and furthermore, he complained, it was not "a real poem" and was not even spelled correctly.)

The World's Shortest Poem

Where do we go from Saroyan's one word poem? — a book containing isolated letters of the alphabet? Well, Saroyan's other well-known and somewhat controversial "poem" was a four-legged version of the letter m, cited in the *Guiness Book of Records* as the world's shortest poem. It looked as if the letter "m" and the letter "n" were in the process of separating. Some have cited it as a pun on "I am," implying the formation of consciousness itself. What's next? A book with one punctuation mark per page? I know I'm reducing the question to the point of absurdity, but the truth is, I respect the endeavor of any poet to wrestle with form, whether it be haiku or epic. The real difficulty, in my view, is not one of form, but of essence — what makes a poem a haiku, apart from the number of syllables and lines? Once we attempt to make a distinction, the waters turn to quicksand.

When is a Short Poem a Haiku?
When is a Haiku just a Short Poem?

I was at a dinner party recently and shared with someone the fact that I was working on a book of haiku.

"What's haiku?" she asked.

"Haiku is a poetry of simplicity," I said, "a direct observation of something in nature."

She was puzzled. "What's so special about that?" she said.

"Poets do that all the time."

She asked more questions and I answered each one with another definition:

"Haiku presents those timeless moments, the immediate experience of the *now* in which all of life is reduced to the smallest image."

More questions, more answers:

"It is the silence that surrounds haiku that matters."

More questions, more answers:

"Some haiku are about nature, others are about human nature." She found that interesting, but still not clarifying.

"Well," I said, "there's the haiku moment, the haiku mood, the haiku spirit." This sounded like one of those television commercials for Viagra — I could imagine a couple in bed shuffling under the sheets with the announcer intoning: "They're having a haiku moment."

An Open Door Which Looks Shut

R. H. Blyth, the great translator of Japanese haiku, wrote that a haiku is "an open door which looks shut." He explained that to see what is suggested by a haiku, the reader must share in the creative process, being willing to associate and pick up on the echoes implicit in the words. A wrong focus, or lack of awareness, and he will see only a closed door.

In Cor van den Heuval's introduction to a recent edition of *The Haiku Anthology*, he writes: "The haiku poem is refined into a touchstone of suggestiveness. In the mind of an aware reader it opens again into an image that is immediate and palpable, and pulsing with that delight of the senses that carries a conviction of one's unity with all of existence."

At that dinner party, I was grateful for my companion's interest, yet frustrated by my inability to give a definition that made sense to her. I did my best to paraphrase Cor van den Heuval's definition, but I could feel the words dissolving into abstraction. It was like trying to describe wetness to someone who had never touched water by telling them it was two hydrogen atoms and one oxygen atom. I realized how ephemeral the "essence" of haiku was.

Ornate Rings on Crooked Fingers

There are many contemporary haiku groups. American groups,

in particular, emphasize haiku's spiritual quality, relating it to the philosophy of Zen. They would be in the Basho club, you might say, citing haiku as a way of life more than literature.

American haiku poets are not rigid about the three-line 5-7-5 structure and allow for considerable deviation from that classic form, but as far as the essence is concerned, they come down on the side of "immediate experience with nature." Other groups who might consider themselves followers of Buson stress imaginative creation or the evocation of scenes in which human nature confronts nature itself, that "haiku moment" mentioned above. Buson, who was a painter, focused on poems that captured visual images, and Shiki emphasized that as well.

Some schools favor a more poetic approach, and others favor everyday language. There are drawbacks to both. R. H. Blyth warns that too many ornate rings on the finger can distract from what the finger is pointing at, while others counter that a plain-spoken style can be likened to a crooked finger pointing in the wrong direction. Even the distinction between haiku and senryu has been the subject of contentious debate. Though haiku and senryu have similar structural forms, unlike haiku, senryu is primarily concerned with emotion and is usually humorous, often ribald or vulgar. But who's in charge of maintaining the distinction? Will I get a critical slap on the wrist because a poem I call a haiku is decreed a senyru? So many poems called haiku seem more like senryu to me, and vice-versa. Does it matter? Does anybody care?

Lost in the Haiku Moment

At that very long dinner party, I explained these different points of view, but my companion was still confused, and I reluctantly resorted to the basic definition of its classic form, knowing that even that had become debatable. I told her, simply, that haiku consisted of three lines of poetry in a 5-7-5 syllable pattern. Finally, we were on solid ground. She perked up and nodded her head.

"But," I added, "many of those writing in English feel that it can be less than seventeen syllables, which more closely approximates the actual length of a Japanese sound symbol." Finally, I ventured, "Many poets who champion free verse aren't sticklers about the 5-7-5 form, they call them 'liberated haiku,' which dismisses the necessity for counting syllables or lines altogether."

"Then they're just short poems," she concluded.

"Yeah," I said, "I guess you could say that — they're short poems." We each took a sip of wine. Then I couldn't resist the urge to try again.

"But sometimes a short poem is not a haiku, it's just a . . . short poem."

"Then what makes a short poem a haiku?" she asked. And we were back where we started.

"Ah," I said, "it's the haiku way that makes it a haiku, the haiku spirit."

"Inscrutable," she said, and took another sip of wine.

"Yes," I said, "mysterious."

"The sound," she said, "of one hand clapping."

"That's a Zen koan," I said.

"No," she said, "It's a haiku." Then she polished off the last of her wine and glided off to the kitchen to get herself another drink. I finished mine and stayed where I was, lost in the haiku moment.

Touchstone of Suggestiveness

In Cor van den Heuvel's foreword to the third edition of *The Haiku Anthology*, he writes the following description of haiku (italics are mine for emphasis).

> The idea that haiku is anything written in three lines of 5-7-5 syllables dies hard. Many are not even written in three lines. *What distinguishes a haiku is concision, perception and awareness — not a set number of syllables.* A haiku is a short poem recording the *essence of a moment* keenly perceived in which Nature is linked to human nature. . . . The poem is refined into a *touchstone of suggestiveness.* In the mind of an aware reader it opens again into an image that is immediate and palpable, and *pulsing with that delight of the senses* that carries a conviction of one's unity with all existence. The period, beginning in the fifties and early sixties with the first experiments of Jack Kerouac, J. W. Hackett, Nick Virgilio, and others, and which is now being crowned with the mature works of a number of outstanding haiku poets, may someday be looked upon as the Golden Age of North American Haiku."

What Cor van den Heuvel says about haiku — "concision, perception, and awareness"— could apply to any form of poetry, a cinquain, for instance. "Recording the essence of a moment keenly perceived" could apply to a villanelle or sestina. "A touchstone of suggestiveness" could apply to the quatrain or ghazal. "Pulsing with that delight of the senses" could describe the triolet, the canzone, the rondeau. If I had to work backwards from the description alone, I might come up with an ode, a tanka, a pantoum, an elegy, an epithalamium, or even a sonnet, whether that sonnet be the Italian or Petrarchan variety (rhyme scheme: abba abba abab cc), Spenserian (abab bcbc cdcd ee), or Shakespearean (abab cdcd efef gg). There are so many examples of every kind of "suggestiveness, perception, and moments keenly felt," that it would be hard to say what passes for a haiku and what doesn't. Even when the poet adheres to the 5-7-5 formula, some critic declares, "That's not a haiku" because it fails to capture the proper "essence." What then sets haiku apart from other forms, in terms of essence, and how will I know it when I see it?

Matsushima Ya, Matsushima Ya!

Most Americans writing senryu assume they're writing haiku, and why not? It follows the same 5-7-5 form. Like senryu, many classic haiku are humorous, the kind you'd compose at a drinking party, such as this one by Yamazaki Sokan, who wrote the haiku about putting a handle on the moon and turning it into a fan (p. 147).

> Even at the time
> when my father was dying
> I still kept farting.

Basho wrote humorous haiku, though at times it's hard to know whether he meant to be funny, serious, or ironic. Basho pays homage to one of Yasuhara Teishitsu's haiku (another example of the web of allusion) about one of Japan's scenic wonders, Matsushima ("Pine Island"), an area twelve miles wide, in which some eight hundred small islands are densely forested with thousands of pine trees whose branches, blown by the salt-sea winds, are twisted into countless shapes.

Matsushima!
Ah, Matsushima.
Matsushima!

In Japanese, the cutting word "ya" adds an element of humor.

Matsushima ya,
a Matsushima ya,
Matsushima ya!

Kore Wa, Kore Wa!

Basho's haiku about his own speechlessness when viewing Matsushima is an affectionate nod to Teishitsu's haiku written many years earlier. Teishitsu destroyed all but three of his 3,000 poems. We're lucky this one survived, for it's an exquisite evocation of inarticulateness when trying to express the inexpressible. Teishitsu wrote his haiku about Mt. Yoshino, a large hill in Southern Japan, which has four groves of a hundred thousand white mountain cherry trees that bloom for three days in early April, billowing with intense whiteness (see page 285).

Teishitsu foregoes description to express his speechlessness at such a sight: *kore wa kore wa* is somewhat untranslatable. It could mean "look at that! and that!" Or it could be translated simply as "Wow! Wow!"

kore wa kore wa	"Ah," I said, "Ah!"
bakari hana no—	That was all I could say—
Yoshino yama	cherry blossoms at Mt. Yoshino.

What Teishitsu did for Mt. Yoshino, Basho attempted to do for Matsushima. Basho called Teishitsu's poem "the finest haiku ever written," yet all it seems to say is: "There's nothing I can say." One is reminded of the great Chilean poet Nicanor Parra's "anti-poems," which often touch on the essence of haiku. The following poem by Parra is titled "Hot Cakes."

What's she selling,
the woman near the Hotel Metropol?
Hot cakes. Right?
An anthology of Chilean poetry
(translated by Margarita Aliguer)

Oh, Rachmaninoff!

In his pocket-sized book, *Lunch Poems,* Frank O'Hara echoed that experience of speechlessness when he repeated, "Oh, Rachmaninoff!" There are three lines within that poem that lean toward haiku-ness.

> Thundering window of hell,
> will your tubes ever break
> into powder?

O'Hara's note on the back cover of *Lunch Poems* could describe the experience of writing haiku.

> Often this poet, strolling through the noisy splintered glare of a Manhattan noon, has paused at a sample Olivetti to type up thirty or forty lines of ruminations, or pondering more deeply has withdrawn to a darkened ware- or firehouse to limn his computed misunderstandings of the eternal questions of life, co-existence and depth, while never forgetting to eat Lunch, his favorite meal.

The Singularity of Nothingness

There are times when, writing or editing a poem, trying to be concise, to excise the clutter, to pare it down to its essence, that I feel a yearning to reduce poetry to the singularity of nothingness, leaving in poetry's wake the ineffable mystery of existence. Haiku is the vessel that invites such attempts. Maybe haiku's resistance to definition best expresses its essence. In Japan, at the beginning of the 20th century, Shiki tried to reinvigorate the form, and his success at achieving that goal is exemplified by the work of his followers, as well as by the hundreds of haiku magazines in Japan today. Japanese poets continue to wrestle with the requirements of both form and essence. Take this haiku by Ozaki Hosai (see page 190-192), a student of Ogiwara Seisensui, who was himself a disciple of Shiki.

> right under the big sky   I don't wear a hat

In reaction to the narrowly defined, highly stylized form of his day, Shiki pushed for greater realism in haiku. Like his idol,

Buson, he wanted poets to paint pictures. Is that poem by Hosai a picture? Yes, but it's more. Imagine a photograph of a man standing alone in a field. The man is not wearing a hat. Would such a photograph have the same impact as Hosai's haiku? The photographer would have to emphasize something that doesn't appear in the picture, which is impossible — the missing hat, which cannot appear in the picture, is the point of the picture.

But he isn't just not wearing a hat. The poem implies that he's *choosing* not to wear a hat. If the poet had written, "I am not wearing a hat," it would be an incidental statement. "I don't wear a hat" is a declaration that evokes the negation of the hat under the big sky. And do not the words "big sky" impact us in a way that an image of the sky cannot? The words convey something beyond the picture — the poem itself evokes the experience of speechlessness.

Disjunctive Tension

Richard Gilbert talks about "disjunctive tension" in haiku as the source of its power. An effective haiku, he says, extends beyond easy consumption, resisting attempts to define it. Haiku is a poetry of unresolved tensions — disjunctions — in both the poet and the reader, and no matter how that idea is articulated, it remains central to the genre in both Japanese and English language haiku communities. The poet might use the juxtaposition of contrasting images, but the disjunctive tension is created by a subtle use of language, a particular word or phrase that says more than the obvious meaning. How haiku works remains a mystery, but when it works, we feel it.

What is the *Essence* of Haiku

So how to describe the essence of haiku in a way that distinguishes it from other poetic forms? Better minds than mine have tried. Perhaps that's why I have returned to haiku. And I'm not alone. As English language haiku approaches the end of its first sixty years, a number of contemporary poets have emerged as major figures: Nick Virgilio, Anita Virgil, Gary Hotham, Marlene Mountain, Alexis Rotella, George Swede, Alan Pizzarelli, Michael McClintock, Raymond Roseliep, and Rod Willmot. To see how far haiku poets have strayed from the 5-7-5 form, here are a few included in Cor van den Heuvel's *Haiku Anthology*:

lily:
out of the water
. . . out of itself
– Nick Virgilio

rain in gusts
below the deadhead
troutswirl
– John Wills

A bitter morning:
sparrows sitting together
without any necks.
– J.W. Hackett

flea . . .
that you
Issa?
– Raymond Roseliep

home early—
your empty coat hanger
in the closet
– Gary Hotham

not seeing
the room is white
until that red apple
– Anita Virgil

The Map Is Not the Territory

In their introduction to *Haiku 21*, an anthology of contemporary English-language haiku published in 2011 (Modern Haiku Press), Lee Gurga and Scott Metz call for the drawing of a new map defining haiku's territory. "You may think you know what haiku is," they write, "we did, too." They go on to admit that "reading through ten years of published haiku over the period of a few months surprised us . . . . Haiku is more varied and more interesting than you might have imagined." Among the

800 haiku in that book, I was able to find one or two that adhered to the 5-7-5 three-line formula. Here's one by Peter Yovu:

mosquito she too
insisting insisting she
is is is is is

And at least half of them consisted of one line:

out of nowhere isn't
– Marlene Mountainas

if it were a lie the moonlit sea
– Peggy Willis Lyles

calling the bear who might be there "mister"
– Jim Kacian

the rain song of our broken machine grief
– Lorin Ford

mental health day cleaning my handguns
– John Edmund Carley

Furthermore, state the editors, "many of the ideas admired and promoted most by 20th century English-language haiku poets have, in effect, created 'narrow definitions' of haiku, that are, by and large, historically inaccurate." They point to the influence of Haruo Shirane's *Traces of Dreams: Landscape, Cultural Memory and the Poetry of Basho* (Standford University Press, 1998), Cor van den Heuval's *The Haiku Anthology* (W.W. Norton & Company, 1999), and Richard Gilbert's *Poems of Consciousness: Contemporary Japanese & English Language Haiku* (Red Moon Press, 2008) as essential reading for anyone wishing to further explore the forms and essence of modern haiku, and to that list we might add Kacian's anthology, *Haiku in English* (W.W. Norton & Company, 2013).

Avant-Garde Haiku

Poets at the end of the 20th and the beginning of the 21st centuries have embraced a haiku that relies as much on imaginative expression as it does on direct experience or "ordinary reality" — the dictum that Buson established and Shiki revived. Stretching those boundaries allowed for innovative language, surreal elements, and variations of syllabic form so radical that the line between haiku and short poems has practically been erased.

The description of haiku put forth by R.H. Blyth's 1952 four-volume series has been viewed as a romantic ideal that confines American haiku to the notion of the "haiku moment." The idea of the "haiku moment" has been challenged by Philip Rowland in his "From Haiku to the Short Poem: Bridging the Divide," published in *Modern Haiku* (2009), which was based on a talk he gave at the Haiku North America conference in 2007. Rowland doesn't strictly write haiku himself, but his short-form poetry is experimental and imagistic. He is also the founder and editor of *NO/ON: Journal of the Short Poem*. Rowland argued for a more robust haiku, as opposed to what he referred to as "the haiku of watery pebbles," or, I might add, the haiku of "borrowed water." "How often is our poetry," he wrote, "a poetry of the quick fix, or short cut: a neat preemption or failure to think further and really explore what the language can do?" In his estimation, there is no need to maintain a rigid separation between short poems and haiku. Allow them instead, he advises, to "cross-fertilize."

The New American Poetry

If there is a consistent theme to the evolution of haiku in America and Japan, it is that haiku and short poems have indeed "cross-fertilized." Along with Ezra Pound, poets such as William Carlos Williams, Amy Lowell, and Wallace Stevens wrote haiku-like poems that didn't conform to the traditional structure, and the same can be said of the Japanese poets influenced by Shiki. In the post-World War II era, the Beats fused jazz-like improvisation with imagistic snapshots to create a variety of short poems that cross-fertilized with haiku. In the 1960s, poets devoted solely to writing haiku in English coalesced around Harold Henderson and the New York-based Haiku Society of America. While there was cross-fertilization, there was also a parting of the ways — haiku poets were often marginalized, as New York poets, influenced by haiku and Pound's imagist idea entered the post-war, post-modern movement in American poetry, and in so doing, left haiku in its wake. Like Shiki, the new American poets dismissed traditional academic poetry and sought to create something new. True, there were many haiku-like poems included in Donald Allen's groundbreaking anthology, *The New American Poetry* (Grove Press, 1960), but the idea of haiku as a strict form was brushed aside. The haiku stream became a small tributary and remained so until the end of the last two decades of the 20th century.

Allen's 1960 groundbreaking anthology brought to the fore a new generation of poets, a generation that was rebelling against the stultified forms and academic verse that dominated English departments and the writing of poetry between the two world wars. Poetry had became fodder for literary criticism, and literary criticism dictated the kind of poems poets should be writing. A poem was not meant to be a spoken-word experience, but an object-d'art with hidden meanings and literary references. The movement was referred to as "High Modernism." But in the decade following World War II, there was a cultural shift, and as rock 'n roll overthrew swing, as the hot-rod overthrew the sedan, as the mini-skirt replaced petticoat junction, the poets of the 60s overthrew academic poetry.

The forty-four poets in Allen's anthology were categorized according to various "schools" that emerged after the war, and each school carried a banner for a particular kind of poetry.

First were the "Black Mountain" poets associated with two magazines of the period, *Origen* and *Black Mountain Review* — Charles Olson, Robert Duncan, Robert Creeley, Denise Levertov, and Paul Blackburn.

The second group, called the "San Francisco Renaissance," was noted for poets such as Jack Spicer, Kenneth Rexroth, Lew Welch, Brother Antonious, Robin Blaser, and Lawrence Ferlinghetti.

The third group, "The Beat Generation," received the lion's share of publicity in *Life* magazine's issue that featured Allen Ginsberg, Jack Kerouac, Gary Snyder, Philip Whalen, Gregory Corso, and Diane DiPrima.

A fourth group, the so-called "New York School" tended to overlap both the Beat Poets and those associated with the

San Francisco Renaissance, but it was in New York that they established a spoken-word, bebop style — poets such as Frank O'Hara, Barbara Guest, Kenneth Koch, Edward Field, James Schuyler, and John Ashbery.

The fifth and last group had no identifying name. They were more eclectic, having no regional distinction or stylistic prediliction, including poets from the Mid-West, the South, New England, the Southwest, the Northwest and California: Stuart Perkoff, Michael McClure, David Meltzer, John Wieners, Gilbert Sorrentino, and LeRoi Jones (Amiri Baraka).

The differences in subject matter and style were initially debated, but within a decade, all were just thought of as contemporary American poets. It no longer mattered which school one belonged to — there was overlap and blending among all of them. Today, the theoretical and stylistic territory they battled over is largely forgotten. Contemporary poets trace their voice and style to those trailblazing post-war poets, hardly realizing how entrenched academic verse of the pre-war period was until those poets of the 60s knocked down the walls and brought the freshness of the spoken word to paper.

Form as an Extension of Content

What the new American poets had in common was a focus on the "breath-line," informed by jazz, speech-based improvisation, and personal experience, a "poetics" influenced by impulses that went beyond the essence of haiku. Contemporary poets who came after them may be unaware that the free form, personal poetry they're writing today emerged from a battleground of opposing "poetics" in which differing sides fought for their rightful place in American poetry.

Perhaps the statements of poetics made by these poets were as vague as those regarding the "essence" of haiku, but such debate among writers and artists is a positive force that leads to innovation. In this case, it led to poets exploring the range of the spoken voice in poetry — a far cry from haiku-like snapshots. I was energized by the poetic zeitgeist of the 60s, reading not only the poems but the statements of poetics. I was done with haiku by that time, devouring instead poetry that mirrored that expansion of self-expression so particular to my age and to that era. Those manifestos lit a fire under me.

PROJECTIVE VERSE: COMPOSITION BY FIELD: FORM IS NEVER MORE THAN AN EXTENSION OF CONTENT: THE LAW OF THE LINE: But breath is man's special qualification: a projective poet will, down through the working of his own throat to that place where breath comes from, where breath has its beginnings, where drama has to come from, where, the coincidence is, all act springs.

– Charles Olson, "Statement on Poetics"

In 1955 I wrote poetry arranged by phrasing or breath groups into little short-line patterns according to the ideas of measure of American speech I'd picked up from W.C. Williams' imagist preoccupations.

–Allen Ginsberg, "Notes for Howl and Other Poems"

I am mainly preoccupied with the world as I experience it. My formal "stance" is found at the crossroads where what I know and can't get meets what is left of that I know and can bear without hatred.

– Frank O'Hara, "Statement on Poetics"

This poetry is a picture or graph of a mind moving, which is a world body being here and now which is history, and you.

– Philip Whalen, "Statement on Poetics"

SUFFER ALL THAT MATTERS
IS FIRE. WHAT HURTS IS!
CRUEL, WHAT PAINS IS AGONY!

– Michael McClure, "Statement on Poetics"

There cannot be anything I must fit the poem into. Everything must be made to fit into the poem.

– LeRoi Jones [Amiri Baraka], "How You Sound??"

The Merging of Haiku and Modern American Poetry

It is only now, in the last decade or so, that haiku has merged with mainstream American poetry, due mainly to the efforts of a few people. William J. Higginson brought out fresh translations of contemporary Japanese poets. Robert Spiess, long-time editor of *Modern Haiku*, promoted a literal approach to haiku, in particular, the emphasis on juxtaposition.

Makoto Ueda, Hiroaki Sato, and Richard Gilbert have

translated into English many contemporary Japanese poets, making known to an American audience the aesthetics of heretofore unknown poets such as Ogiwara Seisensui (who was a disciple of Shiki), Hosai Ozaki (who was a student of Seisensui), Santoka Taneda (who wrote "free verse" haiku, also a student of Seisensui), and Ippekiro Nakatsuka (who initiated "the Free Form/Free Style Haiku" known as *Jiyaritsu*). Their work brings to haiku stream-of-consciousness, extreme subjectivity, and confession-like seriousness. They did not adhere to fixed forms, such as the *kigo* (seasonal references), or old literary expressions, and their influence on American haiku poets was enormous.

Sato's decision to translate haiku into English in a single line has been especially galvanizing. It wasn't as if American haiku poets weren't already writing one-line haiku — Marlene Mountain, John Wills, and Matsuo Allard had been doing that since the mid-1970s — but Sato's insistence on this structure, which more closely resembles Japanese haiku, influenced many poets of the last two decades to experiment with the one-line form.

Gendai Haiku

American haiku poets were eventually introduced to the battle of poetics in Japanese poetry, much like the one among American contemporary poets. There was an experimental school of haiku and senryu in Japan called the *gendai* haiku, written during and after World War II by poets known as the Shinko, New Style or New Rising. Their anti-traditional haiku was opposed by Takahama Kyoshi and his Objectivist/Realist poetics, which focused on cultural and political realism, leftist politics, and surrealism. In recent years, contemporary Japanese poets who proclaim that haiku should concern itself with "the totality of human reality" — poets such as Tohta Kaneko, Saito Sanki, Uda Kiyoko, and Ban'ya Natsuishi — have appeared in English translations. Makoto Euda's *Modern Japanese Haiku*, a compilation and translation of twenty modern Japanese poets, was published in 1976. It begins with a selection of work by Masaoka Shiki, as well as more recent poets such as Natsume Soseki, Ogiwara Seisenui, Takahama Kyoshi, Kato Shuson, and Tomizawa Kakio.

Translations of Japanese Women Poets

Another influence on American haiku has been the translations of Japanese women poets. Except for the work of the 18th century poet Chiyo-ni (or Chiyo-Jo, who changed her name when she became a nun), the work of female poets in Japan was largely unknown in the West. I talked about the haiku Chiyo-Jo wrote after her son's death on page 69-70. Here are four more by her:

just for now
I spread the morning snow
over the dust

this morning
my energy can only defeat
a butterfly

the adonis blooms
from the place
your hand cannot touch

the samurai doll's face
doesn't know love
either

The poems by these Japanese women have challenged and inspired American poets. Also influential was Hiroaki Sato's translations of the haiku of Kamiyama Himeyo in *Modern Haiku* 36.1 (2005). Kamiyama's first book of haiku, *Blood's Rhythm*, was published in 1996, followed by *The Sun God* in 1998, *Jacob's Ladder* in 2001, and *Resentment Before Birth/ Forest of Stillborns* in 2003. She often writes one-line haiku, but uses seventeen syllables and season words in most of her poems, and sometimes she plays with staggered lineation.

Is color stolen
    by Cézanne
        white hydranga

love love love
  love raised to the nth power tonight
    ends

Poems of Consciousness

In the book *Poems of Consciousness* (2008), edited and translated by Richard Gilbert, dozens of contemporary Japanese poets experiment with space and lineation, deftly employing techniques favored by the *gendai* and avant-garde movements. One of them, Uda Kiyoko, started writing haiku in 1954 at the age of nineteen.

Mugi yo shi wa ki isshoku to omoikomu

wheat?
—realizing death as one color
gold

Onishi Yasuyo talks about senryu as "extraordinary literature," capable of expressing human pathos and the nature of being.

Sogekihei no futokoro fukaku sarusuberi

in the deep bosom
of a sniper? —
myrtle blossom

Yagi Mikajo, born during the post-war haiku movement, was the first woman in Japan to graduate from a medical college, and the first female opthomologist in Japan. She founded her own optholmology clinic. An eco-feminist radical poet, she wrote *zen-ei* (avant-garde) haiku, controversial at the time for their sexual, erotic content.

Mankai no mori no inbu no era kokyû

full bloom
in the forest's genitals
respiration of gills

Tsubouchi Nenten writes haiku that exhibit a playfulness with language and persona. His haiku are "literary constructs," without autobiographical elements. Nenten also uses *kakakoto*, "broken language" or "baby talk," as a feature of his work

sakura chiru anata mo kaba ni narinasai

cherry blossoms fall? –
you too must become
hippo

Kaneko Tota is close to a hundred years old at the time of this writing, and practically a national treasure in Japan (see page 210-213). He was one of the main leaders of this post-war group and pioneered *shakaisei* haiku, poetry of social consciousness. He coined the term "intellectual wildness," which filtered its way through the poets who studied at the Naropa Institute in Boulder, Colorado — poets such as Gary Snyder, Patricia Donegan, Anne Waldman, and Allen Ginsberg.

It was Waldman and Ginsberg who founded the Jack Kerouac School of Disembodied Poetics at Naropa in 1972. The school cultivates contemplative and experimental writing practices based on master Choyan Trungpa's literary experiments as part of Buddhist meditation. Trungpa coined the term "crazy wisdom," which he applied to "crazy-wise" teachers he saw as "holy fools" and "saintly madmen," such as the 9th century poet Han-shan who, when asked about Zen, would laugh hysterically. These literary and spiritual concerns were embodied in Kaneko Tohta's haiku. Though he worked throughout his literary career for the Bank of Japan, Tohta was one of the most radical of the post-war haiku poets.

Genbaku yurusu kani katsukatsu to gareki ayumu

never, atomic bomb never –
a crab crawls click, click
over rubble

Contemporary American Haiku

Richard Gilbert studied in Japan for many years. He asserts that Basho was less like a mendicant monk and more like a beat poet of the Sixties. In keeping with the post-war modernization of radical poetics, a recent book by Arashiyama titled *Rogue Basho* dispels the image of Basho as a pilgrim in search of enlightenment. According to Arashiyama, Basho created that persona in much the same way that Robert Frost created the persona of the wise old farmer poet. Arashiyama reminds us that Basho was ambitious in his pursuit of fame. Some of the poetry in his first book was considered obscene, and he associated with criminals.

In his review of Fay Aoyagi's first collection, *Chrysanthemum Love* (Blue Willow Press, 2003), William J. Higginson praised the freshness and modernity of her verse, calling her one of "a new generation of American haiku masters." Aoyagi combines surrealism with personal and mythological elements. "I am not interested," she wrote in her introduction, "in Zen and the oriental flavors to which some Western haiku poets are attracted. I love the shortness and evocativeness of haiku. I don't write haiku to report the weather."

Other literary journals in the last decade or so have broadened the definition of haiku to include the experimentation found in language poetry, Olsen's projective verse, found haiku, dada, and surrealism. One such journal is the quirky *ant ant ant ant ant*, founded twenty years ago and still edited by Chris Gordon. Another online journal is *Roadrunner*, edited by Scott Metz and Paul Pfleuger, which publishes experimental haiku. By selecting judges from the mainstream tradition for their Scorpion Prize, the editors reinforced the connection between English-language haiku and the larger world of contemporary poetry.

The *NO/ON*: journal of the short poem, edited by Philip Rowland, publishes senryu and haiku alongside other short poems, emphasizing the view that the differences between them are negligible, except in the minds of those promoting a rigid definition for their own purposes. Rowland himself doesn't strictly write haiku, but his short-form poetry is experimental and imagistic. He encourages haiku poets to integrate techniques found in mainstream contemporary poetry, especially those of poets such as Larry Eigner, Robert Grenier, and John Ashbery. Grenier, who edited and published Larry

Eigner's posthumous poems, wrote fragmentary verse that shares the same strategies of haiku. Eigner himself fashioned many of his early poems on the Projectivist verse of the 20s, which were haiku-like in their imagistic details. Nobel laureate Seamus Heaney once said that Old Irish verse was similar in many ways with hiaiku. Cid Corman translated many haiku, including Basho's *Narrow Road into the Interior*, and his own poems have a haiku-like sensibility. For years, he edited *Origen*, which included Projectivist and Objectivist work. Robert Bolden's poems are minimalistic, quite unlike any other haiku poet. Some of his work anticipates the kind of effects found in the poetry of the L=A=N=G=U=A=G=E school. Alice Walker and Rita Dove used the basic haiku stanza form in their longer poems. Michael McClure was noted for his odd typographical disjunctions resembling the Vorticist poems of the 20s, and his haiku-like short poems are unique. Even William J. Higgenson, one of the charter members of the Haiku Society of America, and who codified some of the haiku rules in his 1985 book *The Haiku Handbook*, endorsed the 5-7-5 three line traditional form, but cautioned readers that such a formulation should not be taken as the final word on the matter. His book is one of the most widely read English-language haiku books in the world. A contemporary imagist haiku poet, Anita Virgil, writes haiku that is also experimental with striking images and often erotic content. Like Basho, she maintained a narrative arc and point of view over the course of an entire book in both *A 2nd Flake* and *One Potato Two Potato*. I just got an email from Bill Mohr who mentioned *Hummingbird*, which is currently edited by CX Dillhunt. "The saddle-stitched magazine," Mohr wrote, "was founded over twenty years ago by Phyllis Walsh, and it almost folded after she died, but it's a tribute to the inspiring quality of her editing that her admiring readership refused to let it expire." You can subscribe to it at: Hummingbird, 7129 Lindfield Road, Madison, Wisconsin 53719.

Thus, the so-called "haiku moment" and the "way of haiku" have met with challenges from poets and critics over the last sixty years, leading to new ways of conceptualizing these short poems. Whatever haiku has been, whatever it is now, the possibilities of what it will become is anyone's guess.

The Haiku Moment

Read enough definitions of haiku, and the definitions themselves become meaningless. If you were to look up the word haiku in the *Daijiten*, the Japanese encyclopedic dictionary, you'd find examples, but no definition. The only fact that all practitioners agree on is its original function as the pretext for a drinking party. You hung out, you drank sake, you wrote haiku. As Richard Gilbert points out, the foundation of haiku lies in its being a communal experience, not much different from what I experienced in fifth and sixth grades. Attempts by translators and critics to define haiku are almost haiku in themselves:

starting points
for trains
of thought.
– Harold Henderson

Japanese literature
stands or falls
by haiku.
– R. H. Blyth

bridge the flat intervals
between high
moments.
– Sir Arthur Quiller-Couch

In the Eye of the Beholder

In his anthology, *Modern Japanese Haiku*, Makoto Ueda writes that the disjunctive principle asks the reader to actively participate, since the haiku poet completes only half the poem. These unresolved tensions are what make haiku the property of the reader, as well the poet. Haiku may be about an ephemeral experience, but the experience of haiku arises from the consciousness of the reader. Thus, the act of reading haiku is also a communal act. Roland Barthes pronounced haiku essentially "wordless." He said it consisted of unspoken associations, silences between *kerij* — those "cutting words"

— the faint shape of meaning that blooms from the communal consciousness. So we're back to the "haiku moment," "the haiku spirit." To further complicate matters, there are different kinds of haiku: grave or humorous, deep or shallow, spiritual or skeptical, charming or satirical, sad or glad, mad or — like Teitoku's slobber— just plain bad. It's like trying to define pornography: I can't define it, but I know it when I see it.

Japanese Haiku & the Web of Allusion

It's easy today to find English language translations of Basho, Buson, Issa, and Shiki, but translations of 20th and 21st century Japanese haiku poets are far rarer, especially a substantial body of work by a single author. But the recent translations of modern Japanese poets have shown us that Japanese haiku poets today do more than riff on nature. They carry on a dialogue with poets who came before them, a call-and-response to a particular poem or to characteristic references found in previous haiku.

American haiku is still young. We do not have the rich cultural tradition from which Japanese poets draw. Consider a haiku by Momoko Kuroda, whose work deals with issues central to modern Japan: post-war identity and nuclear politics, including the Fukushima Daiichi nuclear disaster in 2011. Momoko's haiku, written while standing before the Miidera temple, is a response to a haiku by Basho, who was responding to a haiku by the 9th century T'ang Dynasty poet, Jia Dao. We can trace this web of allusion from Jai's haiku to Basho's haiku to Momoko's haiku, almost as if they were in the same room having a conversation.

Jia wrote both discursive *gushi* and lyric *jintishi.* He also wrote *youxia* poetry, defined as poems celebrating "wandering force," but the terms "soldier of fortune" or "knight errantry" better capture that spirit. For example, Jia's poem "The Swordsman" echoes the Western medieval spirit of knight errantry (parodied by Cervantes in *Don Quixote*).

> For ten years I have been polishing this sword;
> Its frosty edge has never been put to the test.
> Now I am holding it and showing it to you, sir:
> Is there anyone suffering from injustice?

Jai also wrote hundreds of haiku. Basho was familiar with the following haiku by Jia:

> Birds rest in the trees by the pond.
> A monk knocks on the temple gate
> under the moon.

Basho's haiku, written a thousand years later in response, references the same season word, the same temple by the pond, and the same autumn moon, except Basho writes his haiku in first person.

> Miidera temple
> I am tempted to knock at the gate
> —today's moon.

Four hundred years after Basho, Momoko enters the conversation. Her response also references that sacred place.

> at this temple
> by the edge of the lake
> I wait for the moon

Anyone familiar with Japanese culture would recognize Momoko's references. The web of allusion in her poem allows the reader to intuit the differences between her haiku and those haiku by the other two poets. In Jia's haiku, he creates a disjunction between the free-spirited birds and the monk seeking seclusion and repose. In Basho's haiku, he struggles with spiritual yearnings — he is "tempted" to knock at the gate, but remains outside, isolated beneath the moon. Momoko stands at the edge of the lake, seeking spiritual renewal. She isn't struggling with temptation, but rather "waits" patiently for the moon, that ancient symbol of life, death, and rebirth. As the shadow side of the sun's light, the moon represents the mystery and fear within our souls.

The Web of Allusion: Basho to Shiki

Shiki would have been aware of Basho's travel diary *Narrow Road into the Interior*, which contains several of Basho's most famous poems. In the course of Basho's journey through the interior of northern Japan, he came upon a small village and found that the local temple had preserved among its greatest treasures the sword of Yoshitsune, Japan's favorite hero. He hiked up to Takadate, the "Castle on the Heights," where Yoshitsune and his last faithful followers were killed in battle. Standing on a slight rise behind the castle, Basho could see the plain of Hiraizumi, all green fields and wasteland, where in former ages the Fujiwara clans lived in splendor. Thinking of bygone glories, Basho sat down and wept, then wrote the following haiku:

Natsu-gusa ya
tsuwamono-domo ga
yume no ato.

It is almost impossible to find English equivalences for the Japanese words, which convey more than simple nouns. *Natsu-gusa* evokes the grasses and plants of summer that seem to sprout overnight; *tsu-wamono*, which literally means "the strong ones," was a name given to medieval warriors, an archaic term even in Basho's time, somewhat like knights errant or chivalric warriors; *domo* and *ya* and *ga* are cutting words that add syllabic resonance; *yume* means "dream" but has overtones of "splendor" (recall Wordsworth's poem "Intimations of Immortality" — "in darkness lost, the darkness of the grave, though nothing can bring back the hour of glory in the flower, of splendor in the grass"). *Yume* conveys the sense of "lives that have vanished like a dream;" *Ato*, which means what is left behind, the aftermath, a relic, is a surprising way to end the haiku, reminding us that glorious deeds and splendor in the grass are nothing more than the aftermath of dreams (see also page 289). Following is Harold Henderson's first attempt at translation:

summer grasses:
the afterward
of strong men's dreams

Henderson admits that his "literal" translation was somewhat clumsy and left out important resonances. Basho was a samurai by birth, well-aware of the passing of those martial times in which his father lived. Now, samurai were no longer doing deeds of glory. Thinking of his father, and of his ancestors, Basho infuses the poem with a sense of his own grief for the passing of those bygone days. Twenty-five years after Henderson published that first translation, he tried once again to find the equivalent English.

summer grass:
of stalwart warriors splendid dreams
the aftermath

Henderson confessed that he hoped "some genius could find the proper English" for the haiku. A recent anthology features this translation by Makoto Euda:

summer grasses
where stalwart soldiers
once dreamed dreams

An earlier attempt by Curtis Hidden Page sacrifices the economy of Basho's words for an extended phrasing, ending not with the word "dreams" but the more striking word "slain," which offers a rhymed closure with "again."

Old battlefield, fresh with spring flowers again
All that is left of the dream
of twice ten thousand warriors slain

My own version goes something like this:

ancient battlefield overgrown
with summer grasses
overgrown with soldiers' dreams

Battlefields and Graveyards

Basho was not the only poet to write about battlefields and graveyards transformed and forgotten. General George C. Patton composed "Through a Glass Darkly" (a reference to 1

Corinthians 13:12), which alludes to his belief in re-incarnation (though he remained a devout Christian) and to the many ancient battles of history. He knew intimately each battlefield. As portrayed in the movie *Patton*, he takes his staff on an unexpected detour to the site of the ancient Battle of Zama fought in 202 BC, which marked the end of the Second Punic War. There, a Roman army led by Scipio Africanus defeated a Carthagenian force led by Hannibal. Here's a portion of that scene from the movie.

Three men in W.W. II uniforms (two Generals) traveling down a North African road in a jeep.

General George S. Patton (George C. Scott): "Hold it! Turn right here."

Driver: "But sir, the battlefield is straight ahead."

Patton: "Please don't argue with me Sergeant. I can smell a battlefield."

General Omar Bradley (Karl Malden): "He was out here just yesterday George."

Patton: (points with his riding crop) "It's over there, turn right, damn it!"

(The jeep goes off road and then comes upon some Romanesque ruins. Patton gets out, followed by Bradley.)

Patton: "It was here. The battlefield was here. The Carthaginians defending the city were attacked by three Roman Legions. Carthaginians were proud and brave but they couldn't hold. They were massacred. Arab women stripped them of their tunics and their swords and lances. The soldiers lay naked in the sun, two thousand years ago; and I was here."

(Patton, on bended knee, pauses, smiles knowingly, turns to a sometimes bemused Bradley and says:)

Patton: "You don't believe me, do you Brad? You know what

the poet said,

'Through the travail of ages,
midst the pomp and toils of war,
have I fought and strove and perished,
countless times among the stars.
As if through a glass and darkly,
the age old strife I see,
when I fought in many guises and many names,
but always me.

Patton: "Do you know who the poet was?"

Bradley [smiles slightly and shakes his head, no.]

Patton: "Me."

The Web of Allusion: Shiki responds to Basho

Shiki loved his country, its history and traditions, and probably wrote more about them than previous haiku masters. Like Basho who wept before the battlefield where Yoshitsume lost his life, Shiki laments the lives lost on forgotten battlefields.

Of those who pass
with spears erect, there are none.
Plumes of pampas grass.

Shiki had never seen the processions that celebrated the battles of the Tokugawa Shogunate, but he probably heard them described by older Japanese men who had been there. He could have visualized them from the illustrations by Hiroshige, who had died less than twenty years before Shiki's birth. The long cortege of retainers, those carrying spears, and the long poles with colored tufts at the end — these images are alluded to in Shiki's haiku, in which he says nothing more remains but the plumes of pampas grass, the plumes a reminder perhaps of the long poles which acted as identifying standards. In another haiku, he references Atsumori, a gallant young samurai of the 12th century who was killed in battle at the age of fifteen.

Atsumori's tomb –
and here there is not even
a cherry tree to bloom!

Most Japanese readers would recognize the traditional connection between young samurai and falling cherry blossoms. Shiki didn't even have to mention the blossoms. The reader would feel, as Shiki did, that we so often allow the past to slide into oblivion. The battlefields where brave warriors died are transformed over time into inconsequential grass and waste lands. Here's Shiki's response 200 years later to Basho's haiku:

Ripening in fields
that once were the samurai quarter –
autumn eggplant.

From Basho's reminder that summer grasses are all that remain of samurai warrior's dreams, to Shiki's eggplant ripening under the sun, we come to Nick Virgilio's haiku conflating American Civil War battlefields with the slave quarters being bulldozed behind Southern plantation ruins

Nick Virgilio Responds to Shiki's Response to Matsuo Basho

Nick Virgilio was born and raised in Camden, New Jersey, and is considered one of the pioneers of American haiku. A legend to some, an inspiration to others, he spent countless hours alone in his cellar typing away on his Remington typewriter. Among his more traditional haiku are elegiac poems in which he evoked the deep sense of loss that affected him and his family when his youngest brother was killed in Vietnam. (See *Nick Virgilio: A Life in Haiku*, Turtle Light Press, 2012.)

Virgilio would have been familar with those haiku by Basho and Shiki that touched on the impermance of glory, the uselessness of war, and the forgotten lives marked by fading letters carved on graveyard tombstones.

The webs of allusion are many. Gabi Greve, a medical doctor from Germany has lived with her husband for decades in the remote mountains of Okuyama, Japan, not far from the village where Issa lived. Head of the *World Kigo Database*, at the time of this writing, she translates contemporary Japanese poets, and operates the Daruma Museum. One of her own haiku touches upon a familar theme.

graves of the unknown
pilgrims faces faded
into stone

The residue of loss is also the theme of Thomas Gray's famous poem, "Elegy Written in a Country Churchyard," a poem published in 1751 and translated into Japanese in the late 19th century. (see also page 41)

Let not Ambition mock their useful toil,
Their homely joys, and destiny obscure;
Nor Grandeur hear with a disdainful smile
The short and simple annals of the Poor.

The boast of heraldry, the pomp of power,
And all that beauty, all that wealth e'er gave,
Awaits alike th' inevitable hour:-
The paths of glory lead but to the grave.

Virgilio begins his response to Shiki's response to Basho with his own reference to an old graveyard in Camden, a small lot of bare ground trampled by trespassers. Virgilio says he tried to capture the destined anonymity of most human beings with a first draft he wrote on a bus as it passed the graveyard.

the grassy graveyard . . .
not a blade where children played,
near the battleground

Virgilio admits that the graveyard was not actually grassy, and the idea of it having been a battleground was something he made up for the sake of the haiku in which images of children playing are juxtaposed with men dying on a battlefield. Some months later, he approached the same theme in a poem with a plantation setting:

the plantation ruins:
a bulldozer levels
the slave quarters

Months later, he tried another version in which the two experiences are fused.

near the battleground
where children play in the grass:
the graveyard of slaves

After several more versions, he came up with this:

where cattle graze
near the grassy battleground:
the grave mounds of slaves

This final version juxtaposed cattle with slaves, the pastoral peace of a grassy field and the grazing of a lowing herd with the clash of battle and the blood of dying soldiers.

Haiku Anthologies and Journals

Such a web of allusion is part of Japanese haiku's long tradition. Everyone who loves haiku should read Basho, Buson, Issa, and Shiki, but English-language readers will be challenged and moved by the haiku written throughout the 20th and into the 21st centuries. Contemporary publishers of small presses and now websites continue to publish collections of Japanese haiku by old and modern masters alike.

For starters, check out *Far Beyond the Field: Haiku by Japanese Women*, compiled and translated by Makoto Euda (Columbia University Press, 2003), *Modern Japanese Haiku*, compiled and translated by Makoto Euda (University of Toronto Press, 1976), *Japanese Women Poets: An Anthology* edited by Hiroaki Sato (M. E. Sharpe, 2008), as well as *Modern Haiku*, an independent journal of haiku and haiku studies edited by Paul Miller (*Modern Haiku* Press, editor Lee Gurga). Perhaps the best place to start for haiku in English would be the recent aforementioned anthologies: Cor van den Heuval's *The Haiku Anthology* and Jim Kacian's *Haiku in English*. Online you can find the internet blog of Fay Aoyagi (http//fayaoyagi.wordpress.com/), which includes English translations of over a thousand contemporary haiku, and Dr. Gabi Greve's *World Kigo Database* (http//worldkigodatabase.blogspot.com/) with translations of contemporary Japanese haiku poets.

International Haiku

With interest once again on the rise, the response to modern haiku on an international level is unprecedented. Styles and forms arise so fast, nomenclature can't keep up. There are hundreds of "haiku schools" advocating a variety of styles, some with no form at all. Classification in such cases depends on "haiku taste"— a rather abstract concept. No matter what the structure, if it "tastes" like haiku, it's haiku.

Some fall into the category of *garakuta* — "garbage haiku" or "junk haiku." Even the term Shiki famously used, *tsukinami haiku*, to mean formulaic or hackneyed, is still being used. Other terms include "Spam-haiku" and "headline haiku." Haiku-like poems resembling doggeral verse (but written in the 5-7-5 three line form) are called "pseudohaiku" to make sure they're not taken for real haiku (whatever real haiku is). Senryu and haiku wear the same clothes so often, it's hard to tell them apart. Many of Basho's and Issa's haiku crossed the border into senryu, which, despite their wit, offer profound insights into human nature. As one haiku poet put it: "Haiku grazes the realm of senryu, and senryu grazes the realm of haiku."

Must haiku today contain a *kigo*, a seasonal reference, to be properly called a haiku? As Faye Aoyagi put it, "I'm not interested in discussing the weather." Many literary critics encourage poets to create definitions on the how of haiku, rather than the what and why. What is it that haiku actually do, and how do they do it? In an interview a few years ago, Robert Haas, former Poet Laureate of the United States, was asked to describe the qualities in haiku that had influenced his own work as a poet.

> The power of the image, the power of simplicity, the power of discrimination, the implicit idea that anything can contain everything, something about negotiating nothingness in the sense of not ultimately having a place to stand (or sit) in our observation of the world. . . .Haiku is still acclimatizing itself,

> in this country, to the cultures of American poetry. It might be useful to let the tradition of Japanese haiku, as well as surrealism and language poetics to enter the practice of haiku, if only to take away the sort of easy *wow!* poem that tends to be the first stage of our attempts to appropriate that form.

Despite the growth of American haiku, not to mention worldwide haiku, haiku today is neither at a dead end nor a fork in the road. In many ways, though it has gone through so many innovative changes within such a short form, haiku continues to appear as the local, one-lane road that runs parallel to the interstate highway of mainstream poetry. We can see it from the car, and writing it may serve as a pleasant pit stop for a while, but the side road of haiku still seems quaint and limited, if not at times downright trivial. But to invoke one of Issa's haiku, there's always a yet and a yet lurking as a qualifier at the end of every such pronouncement.

The Everything of Nothing

Sixty years after discovering haiku as a ten-year old, I began to read Basho again, the old master himself, and his loneliness and sense of suffering moved me in a way it couldn't have when I was a child without true understanding of such suffering. If there is to be some consideration of essence, then, here it is: what informs haiku is compassion, that traditional Japanese way of thinking about the nature of being, so contrary to Western philosophy's focus on having and doing, defining and categorizing, constructing and excluding. At the beginning of this essay, I mentioned certain aesthetic principles that define haiku — the sense of desolation and solitude of *sabi*; the feeling of powerlessness and loneliness caused by the sight of austere beauty, or *wabi*; the sense of mysterious profundity or grace, called *yugen*; the lightness of *karumi*; the refined style of *iki*; one's understanding of *mujo*, that sense of impermenance, and the contemplation of the pathos of things in the world whose beauty fades, *mano no aware*. But without compassion for oneself and others, those aesthetic principles would be empty.

In Japanese haiku, one finds the "everything" of the world contained in the "nothingness" of a stone, a crow, a bottle cap, a willow leaf, an apple on a table, a pond in the forest. Japanese haiku have a quality of dailiness, the moment seized and presented simply. The very "thingness" of the thing pokes at existence. It's true, the stone at the edge of a pond tempts us to make it more than a stone — that's our Western sensibility — but the essential can be found in objects as they are. What's left is the irreducible mystery of the images themselves, and our acceptance of our own limited place in this world.

A Windswept Spirit

Basho says that the language of haiku can be called aesthetic madness, but its total effect can be one of elegance, even when invoking the image of a crow picking mud snails from a rice paddy. Reading the following statement by Basho, I felt as if I were reading about myself.

> One need not be a haiku poet, but if someone doesn't live inside ordinary life and understand ordinary feelings, he's not likely to be a poet at all. In this mortal frame of mine, there is something, and this something can be called, for lack of a better name, the poetic spirit (*furabo*), a windswept spirit. This something in me took to writing poetry years ago, merely to amuse itself at first, but finally making it its lifelong business. It must be admitted, however, that there were times when it sank into such dejection that it was almost ready to drop its pursuit, or again times when it was so puffed up with pride that it exulted in vain victories over others. Indeed, ever since it began to write poetry, it has never found peace with itself, always wavering between doubts of one kind or another. At one time it wanted to gain security by entering the service of the court, or at another it wished to measure the depth of its ignorance by trying to be a scholar, but it was prevented from either by its unquenchable love of poetry. The fact is, it knows no other art than the art of writing poetry, and therefore it hangs onto it more or less blindly.
>
> (translation by Robert Haas)

Basho's Walking Tours

In Basho's most famous collection of haiku, *Oku-no Hosomichi* or *Narrow Road into the Interior* — a collection of fifty haiku, each preceded by a short prose commentary — he chronicles his six-month journey in the spring of 1689 when he was 45 years old and in frail health. It was his last such journey. He and his traveling companion, Kawai Sora, started out from Edo (Tokyo) and ended at the sacred shrine of the Sun Goddess at Ise. With that small book, one of the major texts of classical Japanese literature, Basho transformed a parlor game into high art. Kenji Miyazawa once suggested, "It was as if the very soul of Japan had itself written it." The haiku evoked deep philosophical thinking, without being ponderous. They were soulful and playful, eliciting countless interpretations and endless debate.

Technically speaking, the form in which he wrote is called *haibun*, short prose and poetry combined — Basho was not afraid of breaking with tradition. This epic and dangerous journey on foot, propelled by a desire to see the places about which the old poets wrote, was an effort on Basho's part to "renew his own art."

Specifically, he was emulating Saigyo (1118-1190), whom Basho had praised as the greatest *waka* poet. (Japanese poems composed in classical Chinese are known as *kanshi*; poems written in Japanese are called *waka*.) Basho made a point of visiting all the sites mentioned in Saigyo's verse. Despite the difficulty of the journey, he was committed to that poetic ideal of wandering.

He traveled for about 156 days, covering almost 1,500 miles. While the poetic work itself is seminal, the poet's travels have inspired many to follow in his footsteps, tracing his journey for themselves. In one of the book's most memorable passages, Basho suggests that "every day is a journey, and the journey itself home." This was not his first walking tour. He had made several such journeys before, chronicling each one with a travelogue.

The Journal of *Bleached Bones*

In the winter of 1662, a great fire reduced to ashes the greater part of the city of Yedo in just a few hours, and unfortunately, Basho's "Banana Hermitage" fell victim to the flames. The conflagration reminded Basho of the vanity of life and human impotency. Through the subscriptions of his pupils, his hut was reconstructed and a banana tree was planted in its garden, and in compliance with his pupils' earnest request, he came back to Yedo.

That same year, he had written a haiku which established his break with the Danrin school of poetics, and established his own style. The poem was published in several haiku journals. (for a slightly different translation, see pages 30 and 103)

Kare-eda ni	a lonely crow
karasu no tomari-taruya	on a leafless bough
aki no kure	one autumn eve.

Basho later changed the word *tomari-taruya* to *tomari-keri*, which means the same thing, but has a smoother sound and echoes the last line's *aki no kure*. The solitary crow on a leafless bough suggests the dreariness of life and probably symbolized the poet's frame of mind. But depending on the translation, it can also imply transformation and rebirth in old age or impending death. Where his "old pond/frog" poem suggested that one's stagnant consciousness could be revived with the transformative leap of a frog — itself a symbol of transformation — Basho's crow poem suggests the possibility of magic and creativity in the midst of wintry silence. The crow is a spirit animal associated with life and magic (see page 298-300); it is often a harbinger of rain or death, though the idea of death implies the power for deep inner transformation, the void or core of creation. One translation has the crow "settling" on a "dead branch," in "late autumn." Thus the crow's appearance in a haiku has an ambiguous meaning: It can be a harbinger of death, but at the same time, it can imply transformation, a gestating truth finally revealing itself. An old anonymous medieval poem titled "Counting Crows" goes this way:

one is for sorrow
two is for mirth
three is for death
four is for birth
five is for silver
six is for gold
seven for secrets
yet to be told

Basho's earlier verses were recited often and struck a popular chord, but now they became poems of the mind with greater depth of feeling. Basho's characteristic style — serious, quiet, refined and naturalistic — came to be referred to by his disciples as *Shofu*, "The Legitimate Style." (The Chinese character for *sho* can either mean an abbreviation of Ba-sho or signify the word for legitimate). His reputation as a poet and teacher rose and his pupils steadily increased, but Basho was not content to remain in Yedo. He idolized and emulated the wandering Chinese poets Li Po and Tu Fu, as well as the itinerant Japanese poets Saigyo and Sogi. Like them, he yearned to make a pilgrimage both to visit the historic sites of the Empire and to meet other poets in the provinces in order to spread his doctrines of naturalistic writing with deeper philosophical implications.

When he was forty, accompanied by his friend and disciple Namura Chiri (1649-1716), he made his first such journey, going south from Edo, passing Mount Fuji, Mount Koya, down to Osaka and across to Kyoto. He wore the same traveling garb he was to wear on all his subsequent journeys: a large, basket-work hat, paper-clothes (made of pure Japanese paper, soft and tough, and generally worn by the poor), and a light-brown cotton coat with a pouch round his neck, carrying in hand a walking stick and a rosary of one hundrd and eight beads. The pouch contained two or three anthologies of poetry, a flute and a tiny wooden gong. In a word, he looked like a Buddhist pilgrim.

Touring many a day along the Tokaido Highway, Basho and Chiri went to the province of Ise where they worshipped at the Great Temples, the most sacred of all Shinto sites dedicated to the Sun-Goddess and to the Goddess of Food. From there they turned northward. On the way, he stopped at his native village where he was re-united with his brother, whom he hadn't seen in sixteen years, and to visit his mother's grave. She had passed away the previous year, and Basho was grief-stricken to learn of her passing.

After several more months of travel, he returned to the Banana Hermitage in the Spring. During his long tour, poets he met in the villages along the way called on him to hold a poetry workshop, and most of them became his pupils, helping to spread the Basho style throughout the provinces he had visited. It was to be the beginning of a wayfaring life.

His account of the trip was written over the course of eight months. This first travel-journal was titled *A Travelogue of Weather Beaten Bones*. "Weather-beaten bones" can also be translated as "bleached bones."An undertone of sadness pervades this book, which consisted of alternating passages of prose and poetry, often called *haibun.* The prose opening is followed by two haiku:

> I set out on a journey of a thousand leagues, left my ramshackle hut beside the river during the eighth month of 1684, and placed my trust in my walking stick and in the words of the Chinese sage [he's quoting Kuang-wen (1127-1279)], who said, "I pack no provisions for my long journey—entering nothingness under the midnight moon." The voice of the wind was strangely cold.

> Weather-beaten bones,
> the cold wind pierces
> my body straight to the heart.

It's a compelling way to begin a travel diary, imagining oneself dead by the roadside. This poem is typical of Basho's work in which we see that elegant sadness in response to the impermanence of all things. After passing an infant abandoned on the road, he expresses his shock at witnessing such a sight, how fleeting and capricious life is.

> roadside rose
> of sharon: devoured
> by my horse

Eventually he arrives at the village where he was born.

> After ten autumns,
> it is strange to say Edo
> speaking of my home

He is saddened by the deterioration of his childhood home, with the "forgetting grass" by his mother's room withered with frost. His brothers and sisters had aged as well. His brother hands him several strands of his late mother's hair.

should I take it in my hand
it would melt in these hot tears:
heavy autumn frost

Later on his journey, he walks a few hundred yards down a woodcutter's path to the remains of Saigyo's thatched cottage, which once stood near the Inner Temple. He notices the "clear trickling water" falling from one of the eaves.

With clear melting dew
I'd try to wash away the dust
of this floating world

Despite the stunning views of valleys and hills, white clouds embracing mountain peaks, the sound of temple bells and wood being cut outside the shacks of local woodsmen, Basho can't help but notice signs of impermanence, the *sabi* of desolate beauty.

> I went to Atsuta Shrine to worship. The grounds were utterly in ruins, earthen walls collapsed and overgrown with weeds, stones with the names of gods no longer worshipped, mugwort and longing fern growing wild among the Remembrance Grass. Somehow, the place touched my heart, more so than if the shrine had been perfectly maintained.
>
> I spent the night in Ogaki as a guest of the poet Bokuin. When I left my home at the start of this journey, I was prepared to end up as bleached bones on a roadside.

somehow, I'm not dead yet
as I near journey's end —
this autumn evening.

Leave it to Basho to end his melancholy travelogue with humor:

Home in time for summer robes —
though still some lice
I've yet to pick!

A Visit to Kashima Shrine

Three years later he wrote *A Visit to Kashima Shrine*. Rather than alternating short prose with haiku, this travel journal consisted of a long prose introduction and a series of haiku, many written by Basho's own disciples. Where the tone of *Bleached Bones* is characterized by sadness, this travelogue is characterized by humor. The opening paragraph sets the scene with an amusing portrait of the three travelers — a pretentious monk, a simple lay person, and the poet himself. He compares the monk to a bird, the lay person to a mouse, and himself to a bat.

> I resolved to see the moon over the mountains of Kashima Shrine this autumn. I was accompanied by two men, a masterless sumurai [Iwanami Sora (1649-1710), a disciple who would later accompany him on his journey to the Northern Interior] and an itinerant monk. The monk was dressed in robes black as a crow, with a pouch for sacred objects hanging from his neck and an image of the Buddha descending the mountain [a common image of the enlightened Buddha returning to the world to save human beings] placed reverently in a portable shrine on his back. Off he strutted, thumping his staff, alone in the universe, no barriers between himself and the Gateless Gate [a Zen image for the entrance to enlightenment]. I, however, am neither a monk, nor a man of the world; I could be called a bat - in between a bird and a mouse.

Though he was no monk, Basho had studied Zen with Zen master Butcho, whom he visited on this trip. What is significant about this travel diary is Basho's choice of a syntax simpler than the Chinese *kanji*. He wrote in *kana*, the Japanese phonetic syllabary. This allowed him to achieve the contemporary quality of vernacular speech. Basho's search for a less formal style reverberates with that of other literary giants who broke with tradition to write in their own vernacular — among them, Chaucer who wrote the *Canterbury Tales* in the Midland dialect of English speech, rather than Latin, and Dante who wrote his *Commedia* in everyday Italian, rather than Latin.

The Knapsack Notebook

To accompany him on his third walking tour, Basho picked a disciple who was also a drinking companion. You might recall his haiku discussed on page 143. Etsujin had a great fondness for sake and a talent for singing ancient poetry to the accompaniment of the Japanese lute. This journey resulted in *The Knapsack Notebook*, which wasn't published until ten years after the Basho's death.

In the book, Basho expressed his fears that writing in a vernacular form would not be enough to elevate the commonplace travel diary to a work of art, resulting instead in "mere drunken chatter, the incoherent babbling of a dreamer."At the beginning of his book, he mentioned a few of the poets who inspired his journey.

> Saigyo in poetry, Sogi in linked verse, Sesshu in painting, Rikyu in the tea ceremony—the spirit that moves them is one spirit. Achieving artistic excellence, each holds one attribute in common: each remains attuned to nature throughout the four seasons. Whatever is seen by such a heart and mind is a flower, whatever is dreamed is a moon.

Before they left, there were a number of parties to celebrate their adventure. Many of his disciples gave gifts of clothing and food.

> It was the beginning of the Godless Month [classical name for the tenth month], with the sky unsettled and body like the aimless, windblown leaves. I will call myself "the wayfarer." Friends and disciples offered poems or prose, money for sandals, paper clothing and padded cloak, hat and socks. Some invited me onto their boats, others gave parties at their villas, still others brought food and drink to my hut, celebrating the journey ahead, regretting farewell. It almost seemed that someone important was departing – rather extravagant I thought.

These travel journeys were not merely material for Basho's writing. You can tell from the accounts that he was searching as much for a style and form as he was for adventure.

> Among the diaries of the road, those of Ki, Chomei, and the Nun Abutsu are consummate works, bringing to fulfillment the feelings of the journey, while later writers merely imitate their form, lapping their dregs, unable to create anything new. I too

> fall short, my pen shallow in wisdom and feeble in talent. "Today rain fell, it cleared at noon. There was a pine tree here, a certain river flowed over there": anyone can record this, but unless there is Huang's distinctiveness and the freshness of Su, it's really not worth writing. And yet the scenes of so many places linger in the heart, and the aching sorrow of a mountain shelter or a hut in a moor become seeds for words and a way to become intimate with wind and clouds. So I've thrown together jottings of places unforgotten. Think of them as the delirium of a drunk or ramblings of one asleep, and listen recklessly.

Once again, as with *A Visit to Kashima Shrine*, there is more humor in *The Knapsack Notebook* (except for the journal's final passage) than the dark intensity found in *Bleached Bones*.

> I rented a horse so I could ride up Walking-Stick hill, but my pack-saddle overturned and I was thrown from the horse.
>
> if only I had walked
> Walking-stick Hill:
> falling from my horse

Toward the end of the journey, Basho is filled again with melancholy, the feeling that nothing in this world is permanent, a recognition of Dukkha, the First Noble Truth, that this marvelous world is laden with sorrow. He ends this travel journal with a long prose account, both narrative and meditative:

> With each slow step, my knees ached and I grew increasingly depressed. After spending three days in Yoshino, enjoying the cherry blossoms from pre-dawn to dusk and past midnight when the moon was growing pale, my mind stirred and my heart overflowed, but I was too moved to write even one poem, especially when my melancholy heart remembered famous poems like Saigyo's broken-branch path and Teishitsu's "this! this!" [Basho is referring here to Teishitsu's haiku about Mt. Yoshino, p. 248] But words would not come, and I could only close my mouth. All my lofty pretenses and poetic ambitions aside, my journey produced no poetry.
>
> As my worn-out feet dragged me along, I was reminded of Saigyo and how much he suffered trying to cross the Tenyru

River. When I hired a horse, I remembered a famous priest who was humiliated when his horse threw him into a moat.

I was moved nonetheless by the beauty of the natural world, rarely seen mountain vistas and coastlines. I visited the temporary hermitages of ancient sages. Even better, I met people who had given over their whole lives to the search for truth in art. With no real home of my own, I wasn't interested in accumulating treasures. And since I traveled empty-handed, I didn't worry much about robbers.

I walked at a leisurely pace, preferring my walk even to riding a palanquin [also called palankeen – a covered litter supported by poles carried on the shoulders of four men, commonly called "shoulder carriages" or "sedan chairs"], eating my fill of coarse vegetables, which were more satisfying than meat. My way turned on a whim since I had no set route to follow. My only concerns were whether I'd find suitable shelter for the night or how well straw sandals fit my feet. Each twist in the road brought new sights, each dawn renewed my inspiration. Wherever I met another person with even the least appreciation for artistic excellence, I was overcome with joy. Even those I'd expected to be stubbornly old-fashioned often proved to be good companions. People often say that the greatest pleasures of traveling are finding a sage hidden behind weeds or treasures hidden in trash, gold among discarded pottery. Whenever I encountered someone of genius, I wrote about it in order to tell my friends.

An ancient writer suggested autumn as the best time to visit. I found a deep sense of solitary loneliness in the landscape. And yet I would be a fool to think that by coming here in autumn I might have written better poetry. Such a thought only illustrates my poverty of imagination.

The Narrow Road into the Interior

A few years later Basho would take his last great journey, this time to Japan's northern interior, that mountainous region that lies between Miyagino and Matsushima. This trip became the basis of his book, *Oku-no Hosomichi.*

He was in chronic poor health by then and had already traveled on foot through most of southern Honshu (the main island of Japan). He was living in a comfortable cottage built for him by his students along the banks of the Sumida River.

Considering his declining health, it seemed a good time to settle in and write the last of his haiku. But he had always wanted to travel north along the Ou Highway to visit the Tokugawa shrine at Nikko, which is both naturally and artificially so magnificent that a popular proverb says, "Don't say 'kekko ["splendid"] until you've seen Nikko." From Nikko he continued north to cross the famous Shirakawa Barrier, see Matsushima, go west to the other side of Japan to Sakata, then work his way south past the Ichiburi Barrier, and all the way down past Tsuruga Harbor, Lake Biwa, and finally Ogaki to see the shrine of Ise.

Crossing the Shirakawa Barrier would have been a feat in itself. The barrier lay between the uncivilized north and the southern regions. The winters were cold there, the summers warm, and between May and October, rain constantly fell.

> The months and days are the travelers of eternity. The years that come and go are also voyagers. Those who float away their lives on ships, a lifetime adrift in a boat, or who grow old leading horses are forever journeying, and their homes are wherever their travels take them. Many of the men of old died on the road [Basho is thinking here of the T'ang poet Tu Fu (712-770) and the wandering monk Saigyo (1118-1190)], and I too for years past have been stirred by the sight of a solitary cloud drifting with the wind to ceaseless thoughts of roaming.
>
> Last year I spent wandering along the seacoast. In autumn I returned to my cottage on the river and swept away the cobwebs. Gradually the year drew to its close. When spring mists began to rise from the fields, I thought of crossing the Shirakawa Barrier into Oku. I seemed to be possessed by the spirits of wanderlust, and they all but deprived me of my senses. The guardian spirits of the road beckoned, and I could not settle down to work.
>
> I patched my torn trousers and sewed a new strap on my bamboo hat. To strengthen my legs for the journey I had moxa [used in Eastern medicine as a counter-irritant] burned on my shins. By then I could think of nothing but the moon at Matsushima. So I placed my hut into another's hands and moved to Mr. Sampu's summer house to stay until I started on my journey. I hung this poem on a post in my hut:

A statue commemorating Matsuo Basho's arrival in Ogaki

kusa no to mo	even a thatched hut
sumikawaru yo zo	may change with a new owner
hina no ie	into a doll's house.

The Everlasting Self

The Japanese Zen scholar D. T. Suzuki has described Basho's philosophy in writing poetry as one requiring both "subject and object entirely annihilated" in meditative experience. Nobuyuki Yuasa likewise writes: "Basho had been casting away his earthly attachments, one by one, in the years preceding the journey, and now he had nothing else to cast away but his own self, which was in him as well as around him. He had to cast this self away, for otherwise he was not able to restore his true identity, what he calls the 'everlasting self, which is poetry.'" Yuasa further notes: "*The Narrow Road into the Interior* is Basho's study in eternity, and in so far as he has succeeded in this attempt, it is also a monument he has set up against the flow of time."

Crossing the Shirakawa Barrier

His traveling companion was his friend and fellow poet Sora (1649-1710), some of whose haiku Basho quotes in the book. Sora's given name was Kawai Sogoro, but Sora was his poet's name, which means sky. As a precaution against those on the road who might harm them, Sora shaved his head and donned the robes of a Zen monk, a tactic that often worked at dangerous crossroads.

The two poets shared the journey's pleasures and hardships, heading north and crossing the Shirakawa Barrier. The Shirakawa Barrier gate was formidable, built for protection, but over the centuries since Basho's journey, it has fallen into ruins. Today the original gate and monuments are lost. Only a few old huts remain, along with a nearby park and shrine visited daily by tourists who flock there inspired by Basho's famous work.

Many Barriers, Many Mountains, Many Rivers to Cross

During their six-month journey, Basho and Sora crossed the Shitomae Barrier, the Okido Barrier, the Koromo Barrier, the Nezu Barrier, the Ichiburi Barrier, the Muyamuya Barrier and the Uguisu Barrier at Yuno-o Pass.

They climbed or walked along Mt. Fuji, Mt. Hina, Mt. Shirane, Mt. Gassan, Mt. Yudono, Mt. Aizu, Mt. Kinka, Mt.

Unohana, Mt. Chokai, Mt. Itajiki, Mt. Asaka, Mt. Sueno-Matsu and Mt. Nikko, at the foot of which sat a small inn run by a fellow named Joe Buddha.

They were ferried by boats across the Bay of Nago, Surugo Harbor, Sakata Harbor, the Angry Ariso Sea, and around Cape Ogura. They crossed the Odae Bridge and the Asamuza Bridge.

They visited the places that poets before them had made famous: Kurozuka Cave, Azelea Hill, Yamanaka Hot Springs, the Weeping Gravemound, the Hall of Immortals, the Reeds of Tamai, Marugo Hot Springs, the Mirror Pond, Returning Hill, Shiraito Falls, Dog-Shooting Grounds, and the cave at View from Behind the Falls.

They crossed the Tama River, the Falcon Rapids, Mogami River, the Abukama River, and all forty-eight rapids of the Kurobe River. They passed through Straw Raincoat Village, the Abumizuri Pass, the Nambu Plain, Nasu Moor, Saba Moor, Obuchi Meadow, Mana Moor and Kurikara Valley.

They visited Iro Beach, Shiogama Beach, Ojima Beach, and Mizu Island, Magaki Island, Pine Island and Umbrella Island. They paid their respects and wrote haiku at the Yakushido Shrine, the Kehi Myojin Shrine, the Gongen Shrine, the Hachimen Shrine, the Ungen Temple, the Shrine of Two Wildernesses, and the Tada Shrine where they saw Sanemori's Helmet.

At the Shrine of Muro-no-Yashima they lit candles for Kono-hana Nasakuya-hime, the Goddess of Blossoming Trees and symbol of delicate earthly life as well as the goddess of Mount Fuji and all volcanoes. According to legend, she became pregnant the day of her marriage to the god Ninigi, who questioned her fidelity, fearing the child was not his. So to prove their child's divinity, she locked herself inside a hut and set it on fire, declaring that the child would not be harmed if it were truly his offspring. She was unharmed and had three sons by Ninigi.

Basho and Sora then climbed Feather-Back Mountain, Moon Mountain, and the Three Holy Mountains of Dewa. They visited the ruins of Hinchi Castle and entered the Shiroishi Castle and the Taga Castle. On one of the moors, they found the Tomb of Lady Tamamo, who was said to have turned herself into a stone.

They visited the ruins of Hiraisumi where the Fujiwara

generals had once achieved glories and Yoshitsune and his loyal retainers had died a most heroic death. It was here that Basho composed one of his most famous haiku:

natsugusa ya	ah, now only summer grasses
—tsuwamono domo ga	the warriors' brave deeds
yume no ato	have proved an empty dream

They met a farmer who agreed to lend them his horse so they could climb the mountain that sheltered the famous Murder Stone surrounded by a hot spring that spewed poisonous gas, which explained the pile of dead bees, butterflies, birds, and other insects lying on the ground. Before they left for the mountain, the farmer surprised Basho by asking him to compose a poem, which Basho said he would do. As they descended the other side of the mountain, the horse returned to its master by itself, carrying the haiku Basho had attached to its reins.

Turn your head little horse
Sideways across the field,
So I can hear the cry of the cuckoo.

The journey carried them to many beautiful places where Basho felt at peace or was overcome with emotion. On Mount Sueno-matsu, the two travelers found a temple called Masshozan.

> There were graves everywhere underscoring Po-Chu-i's famous lines quoted in the *Tale of the Genji*, "wing and wing, branch and branch," and I thought, "Yes, what we all must come to," my sadness heavy.

And there were times they struggled to persevere, to push through their fatigue and the frequent storms.

> Beyond Narugo Hot Springs, we crossed Shitomae Barrier and entered Dewa Province. Almost no one comes this way, and the barrier guards were suspicious, slow, and thorough. Delayed, we climbed a steep mountain in falling dark and took refuge in a guard shack. A heavy storm pounded the shack with wind and

rain for three miserable days.

Eaten alive by lice and fleas
now the horse
beside my pillow pees

Eventually we made our way through deep forest dark as night, reminding me of Tu Fu's poem about "clouds bringing darkness." We groped through thick bamboo, waded streams, climbed through rocks, sweaty, fearful, and tired.

After several days, clouds gathering over the North Road, we left Sakata reluctantly, aching at the thought of a hundred thirty miles to the provincial capital of Kaga. Through nine hellish days of heat and rain, all my old maladies tormenting me again, feverish and weak, I could not write. I climbed Mount Gassan on the eighth. I tied around my neck a sacred rope made of white paper and covered my head with a hood made of bleached cotton, and set off on a long march of eight miles to the top of the mountain.

I walked through mists and clouds, breathing the thin air of high altitudes and stepping on slippery ice and snow, till at last through a gateway of clouds, as it seemed, to the very paths of the sun and moon, I reached the summit, completely out of breath and nearly frozen to death.

Presently the sun went down and the moon rose glistening in the sky. I spread some leaves on the ground and went to sleep, resting my head on pliant bamboo branches. When, on the following morning, the sun rose again and dispersed the clouds, I went down towards Mount Yudono.

It is said that at Naoetsu in Echugi Province, they asked for a night's lodging at a Buddhist temple, but the priest, looking at their shabby attire, refused their request, so they slept under the eaves of the temple instead. At Yamanaka, Sora, suffering from persistent stomach ailments, was forced to leave and return to his relatives in Nagashima. Sora wrote a parting haiku:

Sick to the bone
if I should fall
I'll lie in fields of clover

Basho said their leave-taking was like "paired geese parting in the clouds." At Ogaki he briefly met up with a few of his other disciples before leaving again for Ise to witness the ceremony of the removal of the Great Shrine — the temples were built entirely of wood and reconstructed every twenty years as part of impressive and solemn ceremonies. Unfortunately, he arrived too late for the ceremony. The visit to the Ise Shrine marked the end of his travelogue.

The Travel Journal Versus the Literary Travelogue

Returning home, Basho spent the next five years working and reworking the poems and prose of *Oku-no Hosomichi* before publishing it. Based on differences between draft versions of the account — Sora's diary (finally published in 1943 as *Sora's Journey Diary*), and Basho's final version — it's clear that Basho took a number of artistic liberties in the writing. Sora's travelogue was extremely factual, a precise account of where the two men stayed, how far they traveled, the weather, and the names of people they met. Basho's was the more literary, and he spent five years revising and polishing his book. It became one of the highest achievements in the history of poetic diaries. Reading both accounts, it is hard to believe the two men made the same journey.

Scholars have written numerous accounts comparing the two versions and speculating why Basho chose to re-arrange the sequence of some events and embellish others. Book publishing and reading were at an all time-high, and the public was hungry for all kinds of books on every conceivable subject, from scholarly historical works and studies of geography, mathematics, and moral conduct to picture books and popular novels. Travel journals and diaries as well as sightseeing books became very popular, all due to the increased prosperity under the Tokugawa government, the growth of towns, the increase in literacy, the larger workforce and the improvement in production methods. Booksellers began to appear by 1650, and by 1886 there were over eight hundred in the Tokyo area alone. The time was ripe for a literary travelogue like Basho's.

You Say Memoir, I Say Auto-Fiction

Basho's final version of his travelogue may be an early example of "fictive memoir," or "auto-fiction," as it is sometimes called. For example, in the Senjushu ("Selection of Tales") attributed to Saigyo, the narrator passes through Eguchi when he is driven by a storm to seek shelter in the nearby cottage of a prostitute. This leads to an exchange of poems, after which he spends the night there. Basho includes in *Oku-no Hosomichi* a similar tale. He and Sora find a local inn for the night and have an exchange with two prostitutes staying at the same inn. But in Sora's account, there is no mention of this experience. I suspect that the literary travelogue has always blurred the line between memoir and fiction. As Basho tells it:

> Today, we came through some of the most fearsomely dangerous places in all the north country with names like Children-Desert-Parents, Lost Children, Send-Back-the-Dog, Turn-Back-the-Horse. And well named. Weakened and exhausted, I went to bed early, but was roused by the voices of two young women in the room next door. Then an old man's voice joined theirs. They were prostitutes from Niigata in Echigo Province and were on their way to Ise Shrine in the south, the old man seeing them off at this barrier, Ichiburi. He would turn back to Niigata in the morning, carrying their letters home. One girl quoted the Shinkokinshu poem, "On the beach where white waves fall, / we all wander like children into every circumstance, / carried forward every day." And as they bemoaned their fate in life, I fell asleep. In the morning, preparing to leave, they came to ask directions. "May we follow along behind?" they asked. "We're lost and not a little fearful. Your robes bring the spirit of the Buddha to our journey." They had mistaken us for priests. "Our way includes detours and retreats," I told them, "But follow anyone on this road and the gods will see you through." I hated to leave them in tears, and thought about them hard for a long time after we left. I told Sora, and he wrote down:
>
> Under one roof,
> courtesans and monks sleep—
> moon and bush clover

That Basho added fictional elements to his narrative has to do with the differences between the travel diary, which could be classified as merely a "recording" diary, in which basic facts are recorded, and the "narrative" diary, or "literary travelogue," which is often enhanced by fictional dialogue and characters, who could be either fabrications or composites of real people. One could say the same about the difference between the basic memoir and the "literary" memoir. In the hands of a writer, all memoirs are "literary" memoirs. Often as not, the lines separating all these genres becomes blurred by the perogative and imagination of the author.

Contemporary Travel Diaries

While this practice may have been particular to the genre as practiced in Japan, it's not unusual to see fictional elements in travel diaries throughout history, with narratives rooted in fact, but enlarged by the impulses of artistic expression. Henry James likened the effect to a balloon that moved about in the air while still attached to firm ground by a cable.

W. G. Sebald's novel *The Rings of Saturn* (2001) is written in the form of a memoir of historical reflection, an account of a walking holiday through Suffolk on the eastern coast of England in 1922. An aura of melancholy pervades Sebald's account. The narrator encounters lonely eccentrics, Sir Thomas Browne's skull, a matchstick model of the Temple of Jerusalem, seaside towns hit hard by the recession, beautiful hillsides, Rembrandt's painting "The Anatomy Lesson," and all while the narrator ruminates on topics such as the history of the herring, the bombing of World War II, the dowager Empress Tzu-hsi, and the silk industry of Norwich.

Another such novel/memoir/travelogue is Iain Sinclair's *London Orbital* (1996), an account of the author's trek along the asphalt loop of the M25 — the 120-mile freeway that encircles London like a giant artery, or as some have said, like a concrete noose. This epic journey on foot along one of the world's busiest highways is transformed by Sinclair's prose into a unique poetic vision. Sinclair's narrator encounters converted asylums, apartment complexes, industrial and retail parks monitored by surveillance cameras, golf courses, warehouses, shopping malls, and lost villages. This journey through "nowhereland" becomes a modern journey into the heart of darkness.

The Way of Elegance

Basho's significance as a poet is rooted in his aesthetics, which favored a style called "The Way of Elegance" (*fuga-no-michi*), noted for sincerity and authenticity of speech. An elegant sadness pervades Basho's work, a quality it shares with the classics he revered. His notion of the Way of Elegance involved the tension between the surface of the poem, which focused on ordinary things, and the core of the poem, with its emotional resonances.

Basho's loneliness is existential, an elemental aspect of being, an awareness of life's temporality. All things pass. The beautiful surfaces of the world — mountain views, stately pines, tranquil lakes, gorgeous sunsets! Such fading beauty moves us in part because it reminds us of life's transience.

> The sky cleared the morning of the sixteenth. I sailed to Iro Beach a dozen miles away and gathered several colorful shells with a Mr. Tenya, who provided a box lunch and sake and even invited his servants. We drank tea and hot sake, lost in a sweeping sense of isolation as dusk came on.
>
> Loneliness greater
> than Genji's Suma Beach:
> the shores of autumn.

Basho's sense of ephemerality in the "shores of autumn" brings us back to the sadness he so often elevated to a work of art. But there is also an unspoken assumption that, however temporal the world, the poem lives on. As Basho writes in another prose prologue:

> After a long, sleepless night, we packed our things and left, distracted, tired, but moving on. Sick and worried. I worried about my plans. With every pilgrimage one encounters the temporality of life. To die along the road is destiny. Or so I told myself.

The Way of Elegance also refers to the "aftertaste" of *sabi*. The poem, implies Basho, should leave that aftertaste of *sabi* (or essential loneliness) in the reader's mouth. The poet should strive for a perfect balance in which there is no tilting toward either elevated language or sincere emotion; both aspects must enhance and balance the other in order to create the most satisfying aftertaste.

Do the Magic, Not the Trick

Basho believed that the greatest art hides its artifice, the way a magician hides the mechanics of a trick to produce the illusion of magic. Around the same time I started writing haiku, I became fascinated with magic tricks, whether it was prestidigitation (fast fingers or sleight of hand) or the mechanical "gimmick" (a secret compartment, hidden button, hollow object or marked card). If the trick required prestidigitation, I spent hours in front of a mirror repeating the move until it came naturally. One summer, my father hired a local magician to give me lessons in the art of magic. The guy had a store that sold magic tricks, and he was often hired to entertain at parties and events.

Every Sunday afternoon I caught the Nashville bus, transferred to the St. Charles streetcar, and rode it to the edge of the French Quarter. I walked the six blocks down Royal Street, which was full of antique stores, art galleries, and bars, down to his magic store. We started off doing easy tricks with simple gimmicks, like a fake compartment or a hidden button, tricks that didn't involve sleight of hand. Eventually, he taught me to "palm" an object to hide it from the audience, then reach behind someone's ear and, presto, there it was. First he'd take a trick from the display case and do it for me. I loved that part. Seeing the trick for the first time was like watching someone invent fire. Then he'd say, "Now this is how it's done." Then he'd teach me how to do it.

One day I pointed to a shiny red ball the size of a golf ball on a black velvet pad. "Ah," he said, "that's a hard one. You're not ready for that one." I asked him to show it to me anyway.

"Okay," he said. Before doing a trick, he always explained its origin, who invented it, what it was called, and how it evolved. "This one is called Multiplying Balls," he said, "invented in 1875 by August Roterberg, who called it Excelsior Multiplying Balls. Some people say he stole it from a guy named Bautier de Kolta, who called it Chicago Balls. No one knows what Chicago had to do with it, maybe because he had the balls made at a machine shop in Chicago. It's very mysterious."

Then he took the ball out of the class case and held it between thumb and forefinger. He turned his hand front and back so I could see there was no other ball in the palm of his hand, and nothing up his sleeve. Then he reached up and appeared to grab another ball out of thin air – the first ball still between thumb and forefinger, the second between forefinger and middle finger. Once again he turned his hand both ways to demonstrate that there was nothing in his palm, nothing up his sleeve, then he reached up again, and now there were three balls, one between thumb and forefinger, one between forefinger and middle finger, and a new one between middle finger and ring finger. Then he reached up a final time and voila, four red balls between his fingers, the last one between ring finger and pinkie. Then he reversed the effect, reaching up and making a ball disappear each time until there was only one ball left, which he threw to me so I could catch it. I examined the ball. It was solid. No gimmick, no secret compartment.

"How did you do that?" I asked.

"Prestidigitation," he said.

"What's prestidigitation?"

"Fast fingers," he said. "Presto means fast. Digit is your finger. Prestidigitation means fast fingers. But you're not ready to do this one," he said.

"No, I'm ready," I said. "I swear, I'm ready. Show me."

So he showed me. The trick involved all three skills: a hidden gimmick, mis-direction, and fast fingers. His fingers were long and tapered, not like mine, which were small and pudgy. He was able to manipulate each ball one at a time. "Your fingers are too short," he said. But he showed me each move, how to roll one ball at a time between the fingers of the hand, how to place each new ball in my palm by misdirection. Then he told me to take the balls home and practice.

I went home and for weeks I practiced in front of a mirror. It was hard enough to hold the balls between my fingers, but sliding one after another into position was even harder. I dropped the balls hundreds of times. But I pressed on. I was able to slide one ball from my palm to my fingers, appearing to pluck the ball out of thin air. Weeks went by, and I was able to grab the third ball without the first two falling. Finally, I got all four. Didn't drop one. I practiced another few weeks, almost willing my fingers to grow longer and stronger. Then I worked on the reverse, which was actually more difficult. I dropped the balls so many times they had dozens of little dents. But the effort and repetition paid off. I marched into his store one Sunday and did the trick for him. I did it perfectly, didn't drop one. He clapped his hands and nodded his head.

"Very good," he said, "excellent. You've got the mechanics down pretty well," he said, "but you're still just doing the trick. Don't do the trick, do the magic." It took me a moment to realize what he meant: I had to believe that I was actually reaching up and pulling those balls out of nowhere, one at a time, between the fingers of my hand. Technical mastery and belief went hand in hand. He also corrected me when I used the word trick. "It's not a trick," he would say, "It's an illusion. And you must enter the illusion and believe in it."

Sunrise, Sunset, The Flash of Green

Studying magic at an early age schooled me in the creative process, as well as the work ethic associated with regular practice and the responsibility that comes with devotion to an art. It was a natural progression from practicing an illusion in front of a mirror countless times to practicing poetic devices and tropes in a notebook. When I was in fifth and sixth grades, I wrote hundreds of haiku, most of them pretty bad, but I learned something about the form and the work involved in writing any kind of poem. In high school I practiced writing metaphors and other devices found in poetry, such as alliteration, incremental repetition, transferred epithets, syllepsis, polyphonic prose, and objective correlatives, to name just a few.

When I was fifteen, I had a summer job downtown. At 7:30 in the morning, I walked the eight blocks down Fontaine Bleau to where I could catch the Broad Street bus, transferred to the Tulane Avenue bus, and began the day scooping out ground glass that had accumulated in machines used to grind lenses for eyeglasses. After work, I hopped on the Tulane Avenue bus, transferred to the Lakeview Avenue bus and rode all the way to the end of the line, a few blocks from the marina where the boats were docked by Lake Pontchartrain. There was a jetty at the end of the marina, and I found a spot where I watched the sun set into the lake. Each sunset was spectacular. I opened my poet's notebook and wrote lengthy descriptions, doing my best to capture the uniqueness of each one: sunsets on cloudy days, sunsets on clear days, sunsets through storm clouds and sunsets in which the sun exploded as it slid into the lake. I filled the entire notebook that summer with nothing but descriptions of sunsets. A couple of times, I got to see that "flash of green" caused by atmospheric scattering. At sunset, blue wavelengths scatter completely, and red comes straight at you, but green scatters just a little and takes a longer path. If atmospheric conditions are right, you'll see that green flash that lasts a second or two as the sun sinks into the water.

The funny thing is, today, whenever I write a poem which mentions the sun setting, I just say, "the sun set."

The Poetry of Magic and the Magic of Poetry

There's another thing about the art of magic. When performing an illusion for an audience, there's a moment in which you create wonder in someone's life. It's like that thunderclap of haiku. Red balls disappear or appear out of thin air. A handkerchief transforms into a metal walking stick. There's the escape, the restoration, the transportation, the levitation, the penetration of a pencil through a deck of cards. As the performer, you know the trick, but your audience experiences the magic, and if in your own mind you do the magic, even you are surprised when the six of diamonds escapes from the deck and lands in the back pocket of the man sitting in the back row.

A poem can have the same effect. I had an experience when I was 5 years old reading an anonymous poem about a purple cow. Four lines of poetry, the words and the sounds of those words had an effect upon me that I can still recall nearly 70 years later. Ever since, I've read poetry in search of that experience. Most poems I enjoy, but every so often a particular poem will effect me so deeply, I'm five years old again, experiencing wonder, that thunderclap that feels, if I may be so hyberbolic, like enlightenment. "I never saw a purple cow, I never hope to see one, but I can tell you anyhow, I'd rather see than be one." I have lived my life reading in order to experience that jolt again.

Crows Above a Cornfield

When I was six years old, our first grade class went on a field trip to see the Vincent Van Gogh exhibit of paintings and drawings that was touring the United States in 1948. I stood before his painting "Crows Above a Cornfield" and experienced that sense of wonder that cannot be explained or analyzed, but it was like seeing a magic trick, a sudden re-arrangement of the world. I wrote about that experience a few years ago in a piece titled "Sunday Morning." Here's a part of it:

> I am six. The class takes a bus with Miss Cook to the Delgado Museum on Elysian Fields Avenue. We're going to see Vincent Van Gogh. We are marched single-file from the bus in the parking lot to the front of the museum, then single-file from one room to another, walking past each painting that hangs just above our heads. I look up at the paintings. I can't believe what I am seeing. Everything mysterious and horrible about the world vanishes. He paints like I paint! Trees outlined in black. All those wavy lines, all those colors. And he piles the paint on. He's wasting all that paint, just like I did before they told me not to waste all that paint. He sees everything I see. The moon is where the sun is. The street that goes nowhere is in his bed. It's not just raining rain, it's raining crows and bats. He sees the blood, he see the faces. Everything so bright it's on fire. Everything so dark it swallows me up. The man cuts his ear off. The man leans against the table so sad. The man dies on the floor of the empty kitchen. I stop in front of the painting with crows above a cornfield. The world I see is real. I bring my hand up and touch the dried paint. It's real! Mounds of paint, swirls of paint, rivers of paint! But it's not paint. It's real. It's the world.
>
> "Don't touch the painting!" Miss Cook yells. She pulls my hand away. She yanks my arm into the center of the room. She wags her finger in front of my face. "Never ever touch a painting!" She drags me outside to the parking lot and shoves me into a seat in the back of the bus. But it doesn't matter. The world I see is real. I fold my hands in my lap. I know what I will do. I will write about the real world.

I had three epiphanic moments in childhood that seem to have set me on a course that has lasted my whole life: reading that purple cow poem, seeing that Van Gogh painting, and discovering magic. It doesn't matter that those tricks were trivial entertainments. What mattered was the sense of wonder I wanted to elicit in others, whether through the illusions of prestidigitation or the writing of poems.

The Bardic Tradition of Magic

Alan Moore – writer, ceremonial magician, and anarchist, best known for the classic *Watchman* and *The League of Ordinary Gentlemen*, whose recently published epic novel *Jerusalem*, described as Joycean because it's twice as long as *Ulysses* and

Infinite Jest (sometimes referred to as "doorstop novels") – says that magic is indistinguishable from art whether it be writing, music, sculpture, or any other form.

> "There is some confusion as to what magic actually is. I think this can be cleared up if you just look at the very earliest descriptions of magic. Magic in its earliest form is often referred to as "the art". I believe this is completely literal. I believe that magic is art and that art, whether it be writing, music, sculpture, or any other form is literally magic. Art is, like magic, the science of manipulating symbols, words, or images, to achieve changes in consciousness. The very language about magic seems to be talking as much about writing or art as it is about supernatural events. A *grimmoir* for example, the book of spells, is simply a fancy way of saying grammar. Indeed, to cast a spell, is simply to spell, to manipulate words, to change people's consciousness. And I believe that this is why an artist or writer is the closest thing in the contemporary world that you are likely to see to a Shaman. In all of magic there is an incredibly large linguistic component. The Bardic tradition of magic would place a bard as being much higher and more fearsome than a magician. Writers and people who had command of words were respected and feared as people who manipulated magic, transformative forces that can change a human being; that can change a society."

The Rabbit of Poetry

There's a deeper component to the analogy between the art of magic and the writing of poems. Poems are mechanical objects in which the poet manipulates language in such a way as to create a moment of wonder in the last line. That last line reconfigures the images, ideas, or emotions invoked in the previous lines into an unexpected insight, like a rabbit being pulled out of a hat. In haiku, the juxtaposition of images in a mere three lines is meant to evoke wonder in the reader. Like the magician, the poet has practiced this art of juxtaposition. The same skill required to write a three line haiku can be applied to a poem of ten or twenty lines. Admittedly, there is some trickery involved: metaphor, simile, analogy, and all the other devices associated with poetry. But there is also the magic that informs the art. The good poet doesn't just do the trick; she does the magic.

I've Wasted My Life

In a poem that mimics the wonder of magic, the realization or epiphany is not a *fait accompli*. There's a difference between the poet who presents a narrative or a series of feelings and ideas which have already been worked out consciously, and the poet who comes to a realization in the very act of writing the poem, so that both poet and reader experience the thunderclap of insight. A poem can be a dynamic construct, instead of a passive recitation of already realized ideas. It's one thing to know the rabbit is inside the hat and retrieve it, and another to hold the empty hat of the poem in your hands and discover there's a rabbit inside.

Let's say the poet is sitting in a café with an open notebook and contemplates her life as she sips a cup of coffee. She comes to the realization that she's wasted many opportunities. She then begins to write a poem with that in mind and begins the poem, "I have wasted my life," then proceeds to lay down a series of lines explaining it. Or perhaps a poet is sitting under the proverbial oak tree, contemplates his impact on others, on friends and loved ones, and comes to the conclusion that he's made no lasting connections with others. So he begins a poem, "I'm alone and have no one to give my love to." Many poems begin this way, as Wordworth said, "with the spontaneous overflow of powerful feelings, emotions recollected in tranquility," where the recollection or remembrance is presented as a *fait accompli*, not as a discovery made in the act of writing the poem. The poet begins with a perception and goes on to explain it in poetic terms. There's no discovery at the end, only the presentation of the idea or feeling.

I'm not criticizing this approach. I'm saying there's a difference between a poem that presents an idea or narrates an experience already known to the poet, and a poem that is – in and of itself – a dynamic process, a construct that includes the very realization that comes in that last line. This is what Robert Frost meant when he said writing poetry is "a feat of performance and association." One image leads to another image, and the images lead to a realization that leads to another image, like a chain reaction, and so on until the rabbit of the last line is pulled out of the hat of the poem. This is not "what" the poem means, this is how the poem "works." You could say the poet has a knack for this, but it's not a knack. It's a learned skill.

Like the magician, the poet practices the trick, not in front of a mirror, but on the blank page, again and again. Eventually, she learns to do the magic.

How Does a Poem Work?

John Ciardi, whose translation of Dante's *Commedia* is still my favorite of all subsequent translations, published *How Does a Poem Mean* in 1959, a book which has proven to be amongst the most-used book of its kind. The title of the book indicates that Ciardi was not going to explain how to figure out "what" a poem means (at a time when "explicating" the meaning of a poem was all the rage), but rather "how" the poet conveyed the meaning through various poetic devices. The book explored the "how" of it, not the "what" of it. I'd like to propose another idea: How does a poem *work*? To me, this question goes to the heart of the mechanics, the trick, the illusion. We don't ask the magician what the illusion *means*, we ask, "How did you do that?" There are countless poems that express a feeling or describe an event but fail to provide that thunderclap at the end, the way a last line or image rearranges the sequence of images that preceded it and makes it into something unexpected. This is what I practiced writing haiku (not that I always succeeded, but it's what I strove for). I've quoted many haiku in this essay, but I'd like to mention three poems that achieve that effect in less than twenty lines, the last line transforming the ideas in the poem into something larger, more profound.

Lying in a Hammock

James Wright's poem "Lying in a Hammock on William Duffy's Farm in Pine Island, Minnesota" is a good example. This poem has been variously interpreted for its meaning, and some critics have discussed "how" it means, but I've not come across any that discusses how the poem actually works. Ann Beattie wrote a story titled "Yancy," in which Wright's poem makes an appearance. The narrator of the story is an aging poet who relates an encounter she had with an IRS agent auditing her tax return. Toward the end of the ordeal, she recites the poem to him:

Over my head, I see the bronze butterfly,
Asleep on the black trunk,
Blowing like a leaf in green shadow.
Down the ravine behind the empty house,
The cowbells follow one another
Into the distances of the afternoon.
To my right,
In a field of sunlight between two pines,
The droppings of last year's horses
Blaze up into golden stones.
I lean back, as the evening darkens and comes on.
A chicken hawk floats over, looking for home.
I have wasted my life.

You Must Change Your Life

Literary critics have had a field day with that last line, prompting long analysis and debate. Is that last line a lamentation, a wry observation, a witty quip? Perhaps Wright had in mind Rilke's line, "You must change your life." In Beattie's story, the IRS agent is surprised to have a poem recited, and isn't quite sure what to make of it.

> "Is that really a poem?" he finally said.
> "What else would it be?"
> "I've never heard anything like that. The last line comes out of nowhere."
> "I don't think so. He could have said that from the beginning, but he gave us the scene so that we'd be seduced, the way he'd been, and then he changed the game on us—on himself—at the last moment."
> "That's the kind of guy who'd stick a pin in a balloon!" he said.

Wry Laugh, Witty Quip, Meaningless Truth, or Religious Statment

But David Mitchell has a different take on the poem, preferring to think that last line was uttered by the poet "with a wry laugh":

> I've wasted my life! He's kind of smiling. I've done it again, all this wasted time, he thinks—but at least I know it. Though he hasn't really wasted all of his life—he knows that, too. You

> have to enter the hammock, put the world on hold, to really see things clearly the way the poem does. He's been to this hammock before, and he's had moments like this before, and it's mostly positive. It's self-deflating, but not depressing. It's sad, and longing, and nostalgic, and wry—the ironic half-bark of a laugh.

Thom Gunn thinks the last line is "different from the rest of the poem," and it surprises us because the line is "meaningless." In his 1964 essay in *The Yale Review,* Gunn writes: "The more one searches for an explicit meaning in it, the vaguer it becomes. Other general statements of different import could well be substituted for it and the poem would neither gain nor lose strength." I think Gunn couldn't be more wrong, and two years later Robert Bly, a close friend of Wright's, took issue with this interpretation, saying that "it is clear Gunn does not understand the poem, or rather, it is not the poem he doesn't understand but the emotion." Gunn's ego, he thinks, has erected too many compartments:

> Other people, chaotic ones, may have wasted their lives, but not he. What prevents Gunn from understanding is his habit of discursive reasoning, his rationalism. . . . In poems the deepest thoughts are often the most painful thoughts, and they come to consciousness only despite the rationalist road-blocks, by slipping past the defenses of the ego. In most men, the inner thoughts are never able to slip by these defenses of the ego. The ordinary mind has pickets everywhere, who make an impregnable ring.

Wright himself, in an interview two years before his death, said, "I think the line is a religious statement." He then went on to say

> here I am and I'm not straining myself and yet I'm happy at this moment, and perhaps I've been wastefully unhappy in the past because through my arrogance or whatever, and in my blindness, I haven't allowed myself to pay true attention to what was around me. And a very strange thing happened. After I wrote the poem and after I published it, I was reading among the poems of the eleventh-century Persian poet, Ansari, and he used

exactly the same phrase at a moment when he was happy. He said, "I have wasted my life." Nobody gave him hell for giving up iambics. You can't win."

The Worry Bead of Truth

While I believe there are many possible ways to interpret the poem, to discuss how the poem means, I'm more interested in how the poem works. I hold firmly to the belief that the last line is a statement without irony, without humor, without anything other than the deep confessional insight that a man might make realizing that despite all he's accomplished materially and existentially speaking, his life was without significance. Most of us worry this bead of assessment at some time in our lives, but we either resolve it, get past it, or sink into debilitating depression. The narrator in Wright's poem seems to come to this conclusion at a moment of deep reflection. What prompts this startling conclusion? How does the poem work? It works because of the images Wright brings to mind, each one leading inexorably to that last line, a line that is, as poets like to say, earned.

We might imagine that the poet just remembered the experience that way, ignoring the possibility that he constructed the poem, one image at a time, with great craft, so that the realization at the end grows organically out of those images as if the poet and the reader both come to that realization at the same moment. It's very deftly done. Abracadabra. How did the poet do that?

And Miles To Go

Start with the title. He's lying in a hammock, an image of repose, of laziness, of retreat. But is it *his* hammock, a hammock on his *own* farm, a place for rest after a long day's work? No, he's lying in William Duffy's hammock on William Duffy's farm. Wright makes this fact explicit in the title. Is he visiting his friend? Probably. Is he homeless? Probably not. But, one can *feel* homeless nevertheless. Uprooted. Dislodged. Abandoned. Adrift at sea or amiss on land. He and the bronze butterfly, sleeping on the log, both in repose, but the butterfly, at least, after the hard work of transformation, has earned his rest. The narrator's gaze shifts to an empty house, peopleless as it were. Could it be the narrator's home, abandoned due to economic or emotional curcumstances? These images effect the narrator's awareness of his psychic condition, and the reader, not sure yet where this is heading, follows. Behind the house, the lowing of the cows and the sounds of their cowbells drift into oblivion. To his right, between two pines, horse droppings seem to flower into flames. Next, the narrator notices that evening darkens. We are lulled into an awareness of death, day's end if not life's. These images are not random, they work on the poet/narrator as well as on the reader. Wright then presents us with an image of a chicken hawk, who is looking for home. Like the narrator perhaps, who is homeless in an existential way. The image of the hawk brings us to the starkest of truths. We have no home, we have wasted our lives. The last line doesn't come out of nowhere. The poem is masterful, not so much for what it *means*, or *how* it means, but how it *works*. The last line could well be the last line of a haiku, its six syllables shocking us into the realization that – to quote the last line of Robert Frost's poem "Stopping by the Woods on a Snowy Evening" – we have miles to go before we sleep, and miles to go before we sleep.

We can never really know if the poet was aware beforehand where the narrator was headed. Perhaps both came to that sudden realization in that last line. But the meaning of the poem and how the poem acheives its meaning is not as compelling as how the poem works. It's a dynamic construct that finds its meaning in the act of writing, where poet, narrator, and reader experience the startling significance of that last line, as if the trick and the magic were one.

Perchance To Dream

A similar realization occurs at the end of a poem by James Schuyler written after his breakdown while in the Payne Whitney Psychiatric Clinic in Manhattan. In the poem, "Sleep," ("Aye, there's the rub!"), Schuyler presents a series of images that lead us to the awful realization of the last line. It's a well-oiled poem constructed with a series of sentence fragments and images, each one building on the image before it. Where Wright's narrator is conscious of a day coming to a close, Schuyler's narrator focuses on the coming of winter, the bleakness of death, and his own isolation.

The friends who come to see you
and the friends who don't.
The weather in the window.
A pierced ear.
The mounting tension and the spasm.
A paper lace doily on a small plate.
Tangerines.
A day in February: heart
shaped cookies on St Valentine's.
Like Christopher, a discarded saint.
A tough woman with black hair.
"I got to set my wig straight."
A gold and silver day begins to wane.
A crescent moon.
Ice on the window.
Give my love to, oh, anybody.

The Transformation

The last line is remarkable by the placement of one word: oh. Take "oh" out of that last line and the emotional truth is lost. The sequence of images in Wright's poem are not random, and neither are the images in Schuyler's poem. The first line is as revealing as the title of Wright's poem. "The friends who come to see you and the friends who don't." Schuyler is alone, both emotionally and existentially, facing the bleakness of his own mortality in the dead of winter, ice on the window. The last line reaches out to the world that has abandoned him, that "oh," a moment of hesitation. Who shall he give his love to, who are his loved ones, his friend? He can't think of one. Give my love, he says, to anybody. Each image in that poem is an indicator of his emotional state. His physical discomfort. A discarded saint. The bright day falling into night. Ice on the window. Give my love to . . . . oh . . . . anybody.

The Escape

Wright's poem is thirteen lines long, Schuyler's sixteen. Yet both work the same way a haiku works, the juxtaposition of images leading to the realization of the last line. The poems are not, as Wordsworth said, an experience or feeling remembered in tranquility. The poem is an act of remembrance, the realization coming from the act of writing the poem itself. The poem sets itself in motion and turns itself off. Like a magic trick, the realization appears out of thin air, the handkerchief is transformed into a walking stick, and sometimes, for Charles Bukowski, in his poem "Old Man Dead in a Room," the poem is the way out, the escape.

> ...this thing upon me,
> great god,
> this thing upon me
> crawling like a snake,
> terrifying my love of commonness,
> some call Art
> some call Poetry;
> it's not death
> but dying will solve its power
> and as my grey hands
> drop a last desperate pen
> in some cheap room
> they will find me there
> and never know
> my name
> my meaning
> nor the treasure
> of my escape.

The Circle of Emptiness

Likewise, Basho believed that something more than The Way of Elegance was required for the poet's creative process. When composing the poem, the poet must enter "The "Wheel of Emptiness" or "The Circle of Emptiness," as described two hundred years before Basho by Komparu Zenchiku (1405–1468), who was a skilled Japanese Noh actor, troupe leader, and playwright. Actors, counseled Zenchiku, should strive for "unconscious performance" in which they enter the "Circle of Emptiness." Such a state of being is the highest level of artistic or religious achievement. The effect should be one of *mushin*, "the art of artlessness."

Poets and actors sometimes talk of being in the "zone," an

experience comparable to the "Wheel of Emptiness." For a long time I thought there was a separation between the actor's technique and their emotional authenticity. But how often did I witness an actor or poet claim they were in a zone during the creative performance only to write poorly or act badly? And what about those actors and poets who were technically proficient, yet lacking in emotional truth? Surely the two approaches could be brought together, so that one could be in the zone of the creative process and still focus on the demands of technique. Then one day in acting class my teacher, Milton Katselas, made a statement that has remained with me to this day. "When you're really in the scene," he said, "when you're totally involved in the moment, you're not only aware of the other actors and the set and the objects in front of you, but your scope of awareness widens to include the guy in the wings pulling the ropes or the person behind the camera or microphone, and the people behind them, the entire sound stage or theater. You're there," he said, "totally aware of everything. Your technique and your emotional truth are one. The make-believe and the real are inextricably bound into one greater reality. Being in a zone doesn't mean you're isolated from what's outside the zone. The zone is all of it." So, I reasoned, one can be aware of the mechanics of the performance (just as I was aware of the mechanics of my fast fingers) while still being connected to the intended illusion. One's technique and emotional connection were one.

The same is true of writing poetry. One can be aware of the mechanics of craft while retaining a connection to the emotional truth of the poem. The zone, or Wheel of Emptiness, includes everything. from the mechanics of the technique to the emotional believability. Each one creates the other, each one flows out of the other.

The Circle or Wheel of Emptiness invoked by Zenchiku in 15th century Japan actually has its roots in the 3rd century Tibetan Buddhist concept of "emptiness" (Sanskrit: *sunyata*), a central teaching of Buddhist master Nagarjuna (150-250 AD), widely considered one of the most important Buddhist philosophers after Gautama Buddha. Nagarjuna founded the Madhyamaka school of Mahayana Buddhism. He warned his followers that the term "emptiness," wrongly grasped, was like "picking up a snake by the wrong end." Where the Japanese concept of the "Wheel" or "Circle of Emptiness" refers to a state of mind during the creative performance (Robert Frost called it "feats of performance"), the term "emptiness" from which it may have been partially derived through Confusion philosophy via Tibetan Buddhism, involves a larger sense of being and reality that is difficult to articulate in a few sentences. Often called the most misunderstood word in Buddhism, *sunyata* – literal translation from the sanskrit, emptiness – can be seen as the reality of all worldly existence; its realization is the skillful means both towards enlightenment as well as the fruit of enlightenment. But emptiness is not complete nothingness, nor does it mean that nothing exists at all. My own take would be to say that emptiness is not the same as the nothingness of being or the nothingness of essence or reality found in Western philosophy and science. The Buddhist nothingness that emptiness implies is filled with the possibility of everythingness, the awakened mind of wisdom, bliss, compassion, clarity, and courage.

Basho told his disciples to absorb everything in both nature and art, then throw out the rules and write from the calm center of one's being. Trust, he said, that all you have studied and experienced and suffered will remain as a residue that filters through the words you write. Without that residue, you have nothing but rules. But without the rules of one's craft, the possibilities of everythingness remain trapped within the nothingness of emptiness.

Being Is Agonizing

Along with Zen practice and philosophy, Basho cultivated such residue through an immersion in poetry, history, Buddhism, Taoism, Confucianism, and Shinto religious traditions. Most renowned poets of Basho's time were also teachers of poetry, with disciples who followed their teaching. Basho was influenced by some of the great poets of the T'ang Dynasty, the period considered the Golden Age of Chinese Poetry, which includes Li Po, Tu Fu, Po-Chu-I, Wang Wei, and Xue Tao. T'ang Dynasty poets not only had a great influence on Japanese poetry, but have continued to influence world literature.

Basho's life of study included the work of a poet who lived several centuries before him, Kamo-no-Chomei (1154-1216), author of a manual on writing, the *Mumyosho*, and of the *Hokoki*, poems based on tragic events in his life that led to his abandoning the world for a "ten-foot-square hut."

Chomei's poems are infused with compassion that arose from his understanding of Buddhism's First Noble Truth: "Being is agonizing." For Basho, the poems of Chomei were a model for the compassion that lies at the heart of his own work.

Withered Chestnuts

That sense of compassion, and the relationship between nature and human nature, could also be found in the work of those T'ang poets of the 8th century he so admired. In the afterword to the first full-length anthology of his students, *Withered Chestnuts*, which contained 424 haiku by 110 poets — 44 by Kikaku and 14 by Basho — Basho writes that his students' poems can be categorized by "four principal flavors." The first flavor was the lyrical quality found in the poems of Tu Fu and Li Po, "like drinking wine of the poetic heart." The second flavor was Han Sahn's "rice gruel"of Zen sensibility. Han Sahn was a legendary figure associated with a collection of three-hundred poems said to have been written on bamboo, wood, stones, cliffs, and even on the walls of peoples' houses. His poems were noted for their straightforwardness, which contrasted sharply with the cleverness that characterized some of T'ang Dynasty poetry. Basho must have loved the great heart and sense of humor emanating from a poem by Han Sahn, in which the poet broke all the rules his master was teaching him.

> Mister Wang the Graduate
> laughs at my poor prosody.
> I don't know a wasp's waist
> much less a crane's knee.
> I can't keep my flat tones straight,
> all my words come helter-skelter.
> I laugh at the poems he writes—
> a blind man's songs about the sun!

The third flavor Basho mentions is "the lovely poverty and elegance found in the mountain home of Saigyo and in the wormy chestnuts that people ignore."

The fourth flavor "plumbs the feelings of love in various circumstances," found in the love poems of Po Chu-i, one of the most prolific of the T'ang poets, who wrote over 2,800 poems known for their plain, direct style. It is said that Po Chu-i would rewrite a poem if one of his servants was unable to understand it. To ensure their survival, he copied and distributed the poems himself. Much of his work is political and satirical, but he also wrote intensely romantic poems.

Considered one of the greatest Chinese poets, Po Chu-i's detractors belittled his raw imagery and use of vernacular. Critics called his poems common and vulgar. One critic said that many men of mature strength and classical decorum "may have been ruined by his poems because of their lascivious phrases and overly familiar words which have entered people's flesh and bone and cannot be gotten out, and unfortunately, I have no position and cannot use the law to bring this under control." I imagine Basho rubbing his hands together with delight while reading the poems of Po-Chu-i.

Basho's Autumn Road

By the time *Narrow Road into the Interior* was published, the Basho style had attained its zenith. Basho was at the height of fame, having numerous disciples all over Japan. Collections of haiku written by his followers were published every year. On a visit to Osaka, the great center of commerce, several poetry gatherings were held in his honor. Ironically, the Danrin School flourished in Osaka, and though Basho had many pupils, very few of them realized the full significance of his style. The Danrin School was still influential. So many poets and their readers enjoyed poetry that was mere ornament, characterized by clever images and metaphors. What Basho was advocating penetrated to the emotional core of human conflict, life's essential sorrow, as well as joys.

It was at a poetry party held at a tea-house in the suburbs of the city that he composed the following haiku:

kono michi ya	none goes
yuku hito nashi ni	along this way but I,
aki no kure	this autumn eve.

How he felt about his fame and the dissemination of his style is hard to say, but it meant a great deal to him that haiku had become something more than a common parlor game or the clever witticisms of courtly poets.

The Mushrooms of Madame Shiba Sonome

A few days after that party, a gathering was held by one of his zealous pupils, Madame Shiba Sonome (1664-1726), who provided a sumptuouos feast in his honor. Sonome is not only a famous haiku poet, but a notorious figure in the history of haiku. In one of Basho's famous haiku, he compared her to a pure white chrysanthemum.

shiragiku no	white chrysanthemum
me ni tatete miru	without a speck of dust
chiri no nashi	the eyes can catch

Sonome was ambitious, independent, daring, and became one of the first women to teach haiku professionally. She wrote haiku as a young girl, and later married Shiba Ichiyu, an eye doctor who also wrote haiku. When her husband died, she continued her husband's work as an eye doctor, while publishing her haiku in many journals.

toshi yoreba	when you grow old
nezumi mo	even mice avoid you—
hikanu samusa kana	how cold it is!

yo ni hito no	some blossoms there are
shiranu hana ari	that nobody sees—
miyama shii	an oak deep in the woods

That last haiku was probably part of that web of allusion, inspired by Basho's famous haiku:

yo no hito no	few there are
mitsukenu hana ya	who notice those blossoms—
noki no kuri	a chestnut by the eaves

Her notoriety stemmed from the rumor that Basho's death was caused by the mushrooms she served him at that party. The dinner she served did not digest well for the poet, but it's unlikely that it caused his death. Basho had been in frail health and had been suffering from indigestion for quite awhile. After overeating the mushrooms, he had severe pain that night, and the illness, probably dysentery, became more and more severe over the next few days. He was eventually moved to the back parlor of the house of a florist, and dozens of his disciples hurried to the house, nursing him night and day.

News of his illness spread through the adjacent provinces, and pupils and friends flocked to the home to see him. One of his disciples suggested they send for a doctor, but Basho said, "No, I am quite satisfied with your treatments. I need no other assistance."

A day or so later, there was an unexpected call from Kikaku, who happened to be traveling about the neighborhood and had had no knowledge of the master's illness. The two wept both for joy and sorrow. Basho died the next morning at the age of fifty. Hundreds attended the funeral. Miyamori Asataro, who translated those poems in the blue book that Mrs. Aime had shown us back in fifth grade, the one with gold lettering on the cover and the colorful paintings, says this about Basho's life.

> Basho was a slender and small-statured man, with a thin, fair face, with thick eyebrows and a prominent nose. He had delicate health and suffered from indigestion all his life. It is to be inferred from his letters that he was quiet, modest, scrupulously careful, large-hearted, and faithful to his relatives and friends. He loved his immediate pupils as if they had been his own children, and they, on their part, served him with a sort of filial piety. Although he suffered from poverty all his life and lived half his life on his pupils' sustenance, he was quite indifferent to poverty and always maintained a calm and easy mood. Tradition says that his pupils all over Japan were more than two thousand, each exerting his influence in spreading the poet's teachings. This immense influence of Basho is due, it is true, to his wonderful poetic genius, but his excellent character undeniably contributed something toward it.

Oku-no Hosomichi
Narrow Road into the Interior

The title of Basho's final travel diary, written in the form of the *haibun* (prose and poetry combined), has been variously interpreted, partly because *michi* (road or way) may be either singular or plural, and partly because the word *oku* is an epithet applied to the northern provinces of Japan. *Oku* can also mean something like "interior" or "within" or "dead-end place." The interior can refer to a place such as a forest or region, as well as the interior of one's self.

Crossing the Shirakawa Barrier was a notable achievement for Basho. Beyond that point, the journey became more arduous as Basho entered the country's inmost part, the *oku*. In the Heian period, the Buddhist monk and *waka* poet Tachibane no Nagayasu, known simply as Noin (one of the "Thirty-six Medieval Poetry Immortals"), composed the following poems about the region:

Miyako wo ba kasumi to tomo
ni tachishikado akikaze zo fuku
Shirakawa no seki.

I left the capital with the spring haze,
but at the barrier of Shirakawa
the autumn wind blows.

Arashi fuku
mimuro no yama no
momiji-ba wa tatsuta no kawa no
nishiki narikeri

Blown by storm winds,
Mt. Mimuro's autumn leaves
have become Tatsuta river's
richly hued brocade!

In the Edo period the area prospered as a castle town (a settlement built adjacent to or surrounding a castle). After crossing the Shirakawa Barrier, Basho was too exhausted to compose a haiku, but later, when asked if he had done so, Basho made one up on the spot.

We spent the day with the poet Tokyu, who asked about the Shirakawa Barrier. The trouble of the long journey had tired me in body and mind, and moreover, I was carried away by the scenery and the old-time feeling that it evoked, so that I was not in any condition to compose a poem at the moment. But when Tokyu asked if I had composed a haiku, I thought it a pity to let the moment pass in silence, so I made this haiku:

> The beginning of all art:
> a song when planting a rice field
> in the country's inmost part.

I gave him this for an answer, and we added a second and a third haiku to it, and so made it into a renga [a linked verse].

Like his haiku "Old Pond," this short poem elicits numerous interpretations, but it's hard to ignore the basic metaphor — planting a rice field in the interior, in the heart of the country, is akin to delving into the psyche or soul. But the word delving is not strong enough. The poet is not delving, but planting, he is placing seeds in the earth. The word "planting" has a ring of permanence about it, to plant seeds is to produce roots from which a "self" grows. It's a powerful idea — to plant something deep within oneself that will nourish one's being.

The Otherness of the Self

The other day, I was having a conversation with someone about the implication of one of those cave paintings at Lascaux—not the one of the bison or horse, but the outline of the painter's palm made by spraying paint around the hand that had been placed against the wall of that cave. (Of course, at that time in human history, the only way to spray paint was with the mouth.) The outline of that hand was the artist saying, "Here I am, the one who painted that bison. I exist. I live. I am here." The bison may be seen as the "other," what exists outside of us, but the palm print is the self. Yet it is also the "otherness" of the self, as if the interior had been projected outward to become the exterior.

The implications are as profound as any I have encountered in the writings of Western philosophy. The image of that palm, outlined on the wall of that cave in France, makes me shudder with awe every time I think of it. The inner made outer, the "self" made into the "other."

Sekai-no Hate-made Hiroi Michi

Wide Road to the Edge of the World

But Basho didn't say in that haiku that the beginning of all art is planting a rice field in the country's inmost part, what he says is the beginning of all art is the song we sing. It's the song we sing when planting something within ourselves that feeds the spirit. Beyond planting, beyond the palm print, is the song we sing as we travel that *oku-no hosomichi*, that narrow road into the interior. What is to be found there is an individual matter, but the journey to reach it is the life we live. That life, if we're lucky, is full of encounters that enlarge us.

If our eyes are open, say the haiku masters, if we pay attention, such encounters are everywhere: in the stone, in the cup, in the petal, in the eyes of the beloved, in the crow, in the water the crow uses to wet his bread, in the leaf, in the broom, and in the sound the wind chimes make when the broom smacks them. From that narrow road into the interior, our lives become a wide road that takes us to the very edge of the world.

After all my efforts to define haiku in these pages, definition remains elusive, yet isn't haiku's elusiveness part of its charm? Still, scholarly debate goes on.

The Upshot in a Nutshell

There's something comical about a book of haiku with a 316-page introduction. There are those who have advised me to make *Wide Road* two separate books, the first being this essay, and the second comprised of my 301 haiku. "No one's going to read this essay anyway," many have chided me. Well, here you are, dear reader, reading this and I appreciate that you've trudged your way through to this point. This essay is my attempt to consider the history of haiku, its development over the course of the last four centuries, and how American haiku has slowly caught up with the changes in Japanese haiku, due to translations over the last four decades.

I also hoped to convey my personal relationship with haiku, having been taught to write it back in 5th and 6th grades by a teacher who was the greatest influence on my own writing, not counting, of course, my own father, who once suggested, after I showed him a fantastic tale with numerous plot twists, that I try writing about "a crumb of bread." Mrs. Aime was a stickler for structure and form, while my father stressed the hard-to-define essence of a story – the nature of character, and how great meaning can be found in the most ordinary of things.

Both Japanese and American haiku poets have wrestled with the tension between adherence to form, which is easy to define, and the amorphous essence, which is almost impossible to define. Remember how long it took (thousands of words) for the Haiku Society of America to come up with a concise definition of haiku, while the official Japanese dictionary provides dozens of examples and no definition at all?

What makes a haiku a haiku and not just a short poem? And does it really matter? Can one write a short poem that embraces the haiku essence without adhering to the strict, traditional form? And if one adheres to the strict, 3-line 17 syllable form, is it a haiku if it fails to contain the proper internal essence, the use of the *kigo* word, the juxtaposition of images? Not to mention the focus on Buson's and Shiki's idea of presenting only the image from nature and avoiding commentary on human nature, and of course, finally, all that *sabi, wabi, yugen, iki, mujo, karumi,* and *mano no aware*? If you really care about such nit-picking and hair-splitting, 'tis a puzzlement, *n'est pas*?

Perhaps I can sum up the differing points of view by quoting three poets: Takahama Kyoshi, writing in 1935; Harold Henderson, whose *Introduction to Haiku* published in 1958 influenced a generation of poets; and Nicholas Virgilio, a New Jersey poet whose distinctly American haiku has influenced so many contemporary haiku poets.

The Cramped Universe of Hiaku

For Takahama Kyoshi, Shiki's first disciple (see pages 187-188 and 197-198 for more on Kyoshi), haiku and life were intertwined, each informing the other. He eventually rejected Shiki's modernist stance and willingness to discard some of the traditional requirements such as the use of a *kigo* (season) word and the reliance on "imitative realism." As editor of *Cuckoo*, Kyoshi exerted almost dictatorial power on the course of haiku in his time. When asked about his stress on traditional haiku and what influence the Second World War had on his own haiku or his own ideas, he responded, "None whatsoever." He remained steadfast in his belief in traditional form. He wrote the following in 1935.

Those who burn with the hot blood of youth are always aflame with the ambition to do something new and original. Young people who have edged their way into the cramped universe of haiku are still anxious to try new experiments, breaking the 17-syllable form and throwing off the iron chains of kigo; however, this will only result in the destruction of haiku and will place the iconoclast outside the pale of the haiku world. Such poets often fall into the danger of creating poems that are not really haiku. I am more inclined to think that more new paths will be found by venturing deeper and deeper down already existing roads. Seeking deeper and deeper into the form is not a novelty of the moment but will live long and stay new. That is why I repeat over and over that *shin* (deep) is *shin* (new).

Haiku is a classical art form. As long as it is severly restricted by the limitations of 17 syllables and season words, we cannot expect such great departures to spring from its roots. It is an old vessel. But I am working now to explore as deeply as I can within these limits. I will continue to seek to brew rich new wine in the old vessel.

Hopeless Junk

When the magazine *American Haiku* first came out in 1963, Harold Henderson wrote a letter to its editors, James Bull and Donald Eulert, on the difficulty of defining haiku and weeding out those that followed the traditional form but lacked the proper essence.

> I have come up against some of your problems – and so far have been frustrated in trying to find the answers. In the past few years, literally thousands of (so-called) "haiku" have been sent to me. As you can well imagine, most of them have been hopeless junk. But every so often a gleam of pure light has come through. [But those haiku that follow the traditional form without grasping the essence] are not poems, whatever the form. Even worse, it seems to me, is the fetish that a haiku must be 5-7-5. It makes some sense in Japanese, where every syllable ends with a vowel (or a nasal "n" sound, which counts as a syllable in haiku), and all vowels are short, "long" vowels being counted as two syllables. But Basho, Buson, et. al. did not feel they had to stick to it. And in English! No! To me 5-7-5 is a good norm, but not a Procrustean bed on which a poem must be made to fit — and

tortured to death if necessary! I do think 5-7-5, "seasonal" reference, "internal comparison" [juxtasposition], etc., etc. — all Japanese conventions - can well help in putting across a genuine emotion (even — or perhaps especially — if it is a minor emotion). But I don't think they are absolutely necessary. The one standard that seems to me important is that haiku be starting points for trains of thoughts and emotions (That is too didactic, and cannot be taken literally).

To sum up. My point is that there was — and is — real validity in most of the Japanese criteria, BUT, that they do not necessarily apply to English haiku. If there is to be a "real" *American Haiku*, we must — by trial and error — work out our own standards.

Haiku Shmaiku

On December 22, 1988, New Jersey haiku poet Nick Virgilio gave a reading at the Painted Bride restaurant in Philadelphia. It was his last reading. He died a few weeks later of a heart attack. His comments were recorded and later transcribed.

See, my stuff is heavy. I'm not a great poet, I'm a good poet. Until I can add more comedy into my writing, if I can live long enough to write enough comedic things, then I might really achieve something. But what I'm saying is, I suck the dregs of tragedy to get to the bedrock absurdity of life. And then, you know, when you get that far down, you go bananas. Then you've gotta be funny or you go crazy. But I haven't reached that point yet, so I'm still crazy.

I don't care if you call what I do haiku, shmaiku, or whatever, but I know what I do is poetry and that's what I care about. And that's what's important. Poetry. Whether it's a haiku, whether I could ever discern a haiku, I don't think, speak, or live in Japan. It would probably take me ten years to do that. So maybe I don't know what a haiku is, because I only know it by translation. Some people think you have to wear a robe and slippers to write haiku. You know? Be true to your experience! I feel that since I did not study in a Zen monastery like Basho, I could not even attempt to write like Basho and I wouldn't. It would be a phony thing. So I'm a city slicker poet-artist-musician type poet. That's where I'm comin' from. And if I don't, I'm bullshit otherwise. I just don't . . . I don't want to be phony. I mean, what's the point of me living — I'm sixty years old — if I

> don't decrease my hypocrisy. There are no absolutes in a relative world. If I don't keep workin' on my own hypocrisy, what the hell good am I? Really! And that means to grow and become more aware. Poetry should not be an escape from reality. It's an "escape *into* reality." I think T. S. Eliot said that.
>
> I don't know if my poetry is great. Of course, when you're into art, the more you get into it the smaller you get, so you really can't think you're great. You get a tiny tight package of humanity. And maybe if you are that, you're great. If you do achieve that. I don't know. If you become that modicum, that mote of the universe, that facet of the universe, then you become it all.

I can't see Virgilio and Kyoshi hanging out together, but I can imagine Virgilio in his tee shirt and jeans joining Basho in his robe and slippers, along with Basho's ten disciples, sitting in a circle in Basho's Banana Hut, pouring the sake for each other, writing haiku, listening to the frogs outside splashing in the old pond.

The Net of Essence vs The Net of Form

As I immerse myself in haiku's multiplicity of voices and perspectives, I find myself less interested in formal rules and structural definitions. Yet, as I set out to write my own haiku, I felt the need to make a decision: Do I play with the imaginary net of essence, or the real net of traditional form? I chose, by default, to play with form — the traditional seventeen syllables in three lines of 5-7-5. Except for those five haiku whose legs I could not fit into the steamer trunk, they're all 5-7-5.

When I say I chose by default, I mean that the form had become so entwined with my love for haiku, that however much freedom I gave myself to play, to experiment, to explore haiku's essence, that classic form held sway. I've heard that we think about emotional experience in our first language, even if we are fluent in another. That's what it feels like for me, writing haiku in that classic form. My daily life is an immersion in other languages (other forms), yet I dream, I feel, in three lines of 5-7-5 syllables.

A boyhood spent in haiku clubs left me nostalgic for the classic form, and I admit, embarking on this haiku journey was partly driven by nostalgia. It's become more than that, but I no longer feel the urgent call to break free of traditional form. At this point in my life, I'm content to follow in Basho's footsteps. His embrace and elevation of homely images, of ordinary life and ordinary feelings, rings a bell within me. It rings a bell that reverberates with my yearning for a simplicity informed by love and compassion and observation of other people and the physical world around me. How could I not love things for their own sake? I'm still here to see them! What luck! And so I thought of Basho, and decided to follow in his footsteps, along with those of my son, whose love for writing and for the writing of haiku awakened in me a hunger for those distillations of experience in 5-7-5 syllables.

A Clearing in the Woods

Tennis *with* a net. I'm not a traditionalist by nature. I chose the traditional form because it brought me back to my childhood, counting syllables with Jerry, Max, Eugene, Oriole, Eddie, Donald, and Hope. Our world was smaller then, and simpler, and so full of Zen moments. Who knows, I may still have an epic poem in me, but for now, in this haiku moment, I feel as though I've come to a clearing in the woods.

This long, and long-winded, introduction attempts to mimic Basho's *haibun*, the form he chose for *Narrow Road into the Interior*: fifty-some odd haiku, each preceded by several prose paragraphs. The difference: I've lumped all my prose paragraphs into this introductory essay. Furthermore, I ask that you read the haiku sequentially, from start to finish, as you would read Basho's travel journal *Narrow Road into the Interior*. I know, we like to flip through a book of haiku, reading them at random, helter-skelter, hither and yon. They're like bon-bons. But like Basho's *Narrow Road*, my book of haiku is also a travelogue of sorts. It's for a critic to discern whatever unity and whatever meaning resides in these poems, but allow me this one suggestion: Read the first line of the first haiku, then read the last line of the last haiku. This might give you a hint of the arc of the journey, a hint of the unity, a hint of what lies within "The Wheel of Emptiness" that I chose to show on the cover of my book and on this page.

In the woodblock print by Hokusai Katsushika, the old workman attends to one slat at a time, an endless endeavor as the ring formed by the enormous wooden tub rolls beneath him.

This print is one of Katsushika's "36 Views of Mt. Fuji", the most famous of which is the giant ocean wave we've seen in many books and reproductions. The image of the barrel-maker is deservedly one of the most celebrated in the whole series. Mt. Fuji rises in the distance, covered with snow, beyond a stretch of dried-up paddy fields where the earth has cracked in almost geometrical patterns. Look closely at the old workman. There's a smile on his face. Like Sisyphus, who had to roll a rock ceaselessly up a mountain, the barrel-maker, to quote Albert Camus, has found his burden. "One always finds one's burdern," Camus writes as consolation. Camus claims that Sisyphus is happy when rolling the rock upward, because he is relieved of the existential burden of consciousness, the contemplation of life's meaning. Only when walking back down the mountain toward the rock below does Sisyphus face the ultimate question of his own existence. So the barrel-maker works on, working the slats of the tub one by one. Like Sisyphus, he is happy.

Look again at the picture.That fellow crouching in the "wheel of emptiness," writing his poems in that "circle of emptiness," is me, a smile on my face, humming as I work, humming as I write my haiku, humming that five-syllable refrain, "dum de dum de dum." I hummed it when I was ten, and I'm humming it now. It's part of that song we sing when planting our poems in the country's innermost part.

It feels odd to be writing haiku now. I can't tell whether I'm returning to the simple childhood pleasure of playing with words, or if my attempt to find some deeper truth within that classic form is a product of my age. In either case, here they are, my haiku, the stones and feathers of a windswept spirit, still listening for that thunderclap at the edge of the world.

俳

WIDE ROAD
to the Edge
of the World

世界の果てまで広い道

301 Haiku

俳

dum de dum de dum
the trees fly past from back seat
from world upside down

俳

down upside down up
window closed open window
daddy back door comes

俳

milky way star bright
the hazy moon hazy sun
little bird at door

俳

rain rain go away
come again another day
big bad wolf won't sleep

俳

jump over puddle
man on floor dying pillow
no one home no one

俳

my mother is big.
Father sleeps in the kitchen.
Be nimble, be quick.

俳

Circumcision day.
Little brother in the crib.
The bloody diaper.

俳

Hearing Mom and Dad
fighting in the bedroom room.
Outside, the red moon.

俳

go that way, they say.
I stand in line to get milk.
That way, no that way.

俳

Can't spell cat or dog.
I look outside the classroom.
A sunbathing snail.

俳

TV's test pattern,
but I watch it all day long:
Lonely popsicle.

俳

"Going to the moon,"
I tell my father's brother,
asleep on the floor.

俳

"Going to Pluto.
I can fly like Superman.
See my hand go up!"

俳

I am lost in school.
Where's the bathroom? No one says.
I pee in my pants.

俳

A BEE SEE A BEE.
SEE A BEE SEE A BEE SEE.
A BEE SEE A BEE.

俳

The billboard said Ritz.
The first word I learned to spell.
Everything's ritzy.

俳

Watching the asphalt,
I'm run over by a car.
I am five, moonstruck.

俳

I'm at the movies.
Frankenstein meets Dracula.
in the safe darkness.

俳

In the safe darkness
of the theatre I find truth:
Annie gets her gun.

俳

There's Charlie Chaplin
running but getting nowhere—
a plan for a life.

俳

It's Charlie Chaplin,
though not wearing his mustache—
old man in Limelight.

俳

Edgar Kennedy
eats a crab leg, shell and all—
crunch ha crunch ha crunch

俳

Edgar Kennedy
wipes his palm across his face.
Slow burn head to chin.

俳

I practice slow burn
in front of the hall mirror.
It's not so funny.

俳

Van Goo paints the sky,
cuts off his ear, paints those crows.
I am six, sunstruck.

俳

Mr. Kern's back yard.
The Garden of Paradise.
We climb the wood fence.

俳

White goats are on Mars,
plain as the nose on my face
under the covers.

俳

A slice of pickle
right there on the cement curb.
Another year gone.

俳

I'm eaten alive
by mosquitos on this boat.
Dad's pulling up fish.

俳

Teacher in fifth grade
tells us all about haiku,
Japan, and the bomb.

俳

Basho and Issa,
then Buson, then Shiki.
Oh, those syllables!

俳

Nose pressed to paper,
every syllable counted.
The world's so compact.

俳

Buson and Shiki:
Trivialities of sandbox,
grains of syllables.

俳

Why is it five seven five?
Seven five seven
works just fine, if you ask me.

俳

Why count syllables?
Haiku-like life, teacher says.
Each face in its place.

俳

Moon face, then sun face.
Even the years wander on.
My body grows up.

俳

Basho says heron
speechless in blazing sunlight.
Who tells the cuckoo?

俳

All those red flowers!
Shriveled chestnuts on the lawn.
Oh Basho! Don't go.

俳

The first girl I date
trades kisses for haiku.
Issa! Pucker up!

俳

Tight jeans, chewing gum.
I drive my Chevy Bel Air
into her driveway.

俳

Pacified English.
Verbs lie dead on the highway.
Those poor nouns wound tight.

俳

The rain comes down hard.
I'm writing longer poems.
The world breaks open.

俳

My boxing coach says:
Throw your body into space.
Take punch like a man.

俳

There's no more small world.
This is the world you wanted.
Quit your complaining.

俳

Just close the window.
Breaking up is hard to do.
Eternal return.

俳

Leave it in the past,
this day to day syllable.
Spelling's my forté.

俳

Consider violence:
Eliza Delacruz's
body in dumpster.

俳

The wide road's mouthful.
Impatiently, we swallow
one, then another.

俳

A bird in the hand.
Crush it. Rip each feather out.
Two in the bush next.

俳

In the pretty whore's house
I kept looking at her tits.
Oh, those sweet nipples.

俳

Rows and rows of lips.
London. Paris. Newfoundland.
Kiss the Earth goodbye.

俳

Some ride bikes uphill.
Bendable truth a rose bush.
Snows of yesteryear.

俳

Cluttered memory.
Too much for one man to save.
Blood. Bones. Father's hat.

俳

Before going home,
I stop for coffee and toast
long enough to sing.

俳

Yellow-eyed blackbird,
its neat, mud-lined, cup-shaped nest,
warning of danger.

俳

At Café DuMonde,
drinking chickory coffee,
I write my poems.

俳

Such grouchy poets
in midnight coffee houses
reciting rubbish.

俳

Picture this apple,
eaten to the bitter core
where Being resides.

俳

Oh, Heaven help us!
Naked like this, merciless.
Woe and woe and woe.

俳

All my life I have
counted syllables like this,
haikus of brief love.

俳

Sit still a minute.
Now, let your heart open wide
and see what falls in.

俳

Avenues of life:
People strolling back and forth
sing for their supper.

俳

Existential choice
cracks the mind / body problem.
No spirit between.

俳

The world continues.
Aristotle is Unmoved.
Ham & eggs for brunch.

俳

My Chevy Bel Air.
My Pontiac Bonneville.
Those backseat kisses.

俳

Eighty miles an hour
in the car on the highway
drinking tequila.

俳

I can stand all day
watching that bird sip water
from the dented brick.

俳

Inexplicable!
I cut a lemon in two.
Out squirts all the juice.

俳

Who is buried here,
next to my father's gravestone?
Hail fellow well-met.

俳

One quarter, a dime,
three pennies fill the ashtray
on my sweetheart's desk.

俳

Leaving New Orleans,
heading for Los Angeles.
Breakdown in Texas.

俳

Skittish frog in pond.
He's thinking of jumping out.
Basho says, "Not now."

俳

Nighttime wedded bliss.
My first wife cooks a chicken.
We both eat mouthfuls.

俳

On television
we land a man on the moon,
but moonlight's unchanged.

俳

Time for a roadtrip
under night skies filled with stars,
radar enforced.

俳

The mechanic says
"You need a new oil filter."
Sunny day in hell.

俳

Driving down I-5,
I love this sense of freedom.
Is one ever not lost?

俳

Chicago night club:
I face the firing squad—
Stand-up comedy.

俳

Rehearsing the scene:
When we act, we act the fool.
Play the part you want.

俳

Days I spend hiding
under the kitchen table.
No one's ever home.

俳

Here's where you battle
the world in all its splendor:
sheets of blank paper!

俳

When is the rent due?
Who took all my pretty poems?
Why am I so poor?

俳

Coal mines of my heart.
The canary dies.
It's time to get out.

俳

Empty apartment,
no furniture whatsoever.
Mind, heart, soul, afraid.

俳

I lost who I was.
Then I found who I would be.
Only who I was knew.

俳

After the divorce
my car died on the I-10.
Sold it for peanuts.

俳

Just what do you want?
Tears at the Comedy Store
or laughs in the dark?

俳

Sick of autumn moon,
and tired of winter sun
O night without stars.

俳

White lines on the glass.
A road trip to Las Vegas.
Reno at Sunrise.

俳

The jailer brings food.
Another poem to write
just for an apple.

俳

The days fall away!
I'm not sure about the past.
Can't I kill it yet?

俳

None of the logs burn.
The fireplace needs fixing.
But who tends the fire?

俳

See my second wife
washing dishes and those cups
we drank from last night.

俳

In the back garden
that ceramic bird perches
on our Buddha's head.

俳

Wilderness rush hour!
Desert rats scatter across
my red sleeping bag.

俳

A bear by the tree
came close to my sleeping bag,
then left for winter.

俳

Not far from Lost Lake,
the old buck smells our campfire,
asks what's for dinner.

俳

Cleo, my tabby,
sees me reading Cat's Cradle,
settles on my chest.

俳

"I'm pregnant," she says.
Big deep breath in the kitchen.
This phone in my hand.

俳

"Hey, Laughing Buddha,
what now?" "Yell Geronimo,"
he says, "all the way down."

俳

Too much to do now.
Time for my afternoon nap.
Dream of falling rocks.

俳

Josh came out peeing
on the day that he was born.
Lori laughs so hard.

俳

There's my son's toy train
in the middle of the floor
and a rubber sword.

俳

Drastic measures now:
I've canceled my subscription
to Time, Life, and Look.

俳

A fender bender
on the freeway coming home,
bubbles of red cheeks.

俳

Bad dreams, strange sounds,
just another sleepless night,
faucet's drip, drip, drip.

俳

Everyone loves prose.
For the most part, poetry's
a pain in the ass.

俳

A pie in the face,
that's what makes people laugh.
Now eat the meringue.

俳

We are swatting flies
in the belfry of our minds,
making room for bats.

俳

A new bed for Josh
instead of the nylon tent
from the year before.

俳

They open my chest
and then put my heart on ice
while my brain simmers.

俳

I dream I'm seven,
grabbing at those fireflies
just on their way home.

俳

Anonymous cups.
Five pillows for the trash man.
Gifts in paradise.

俳

Saying my prayers,
doubting the whole enterprise.
Then I eat a peach.

俳

All but the very old
break a few rules now and then.
Paltry permission.

俳

After a rainstorm,
the dark sky clears naked blue.
I see your face there.

俳

I am surrounded.
I laugh, stuck in the middle
between my own jokes.

俳

Okay pal, hands up.
Gimme all your money, punk,
And your heartache, too.

俳

Who knows me as I do?
The noise of all those faces.
I'm so lost in here.

俳

The dialectic's
undeniable power:
appropriation.

俳

At a loss for words?
Call Jack Grapes, home or office,
day or night, for help.

俳

Reading War and Peace—
that bird on the dented brick
as I turn a page.

俳

Shakespeare, bricklayer.
Dante, the wise carpenter.
Me? Corn to chickens.

俳

There's no place to hide.
The world out there calls to me.
I am still in bed.

俳

Life's big metaphor:
falling asleep in the rain.
Wake me when it's over.

俳

It's about panties'
ontological mystery –
whatness & howness.

俳

We talked about Kant
all night. Like a miracle,
the world is empty.

俳

Only mind exists.
Green apple on the table?
Prove me wrong. Eat it.

俳

Nothing but matter.
Just motions of particles.
Mind eats the apple.

俳

Transcendent ego.
But what about the table?
Who gets to eat that?

俳

Mind and nature blend.
A continuous table
in the apple's mouth.

俳

Which is the way out?
The fly in the flybottle
buzzing in the mind.

俳
Quicksand the spirit,
a blind groping turned inward,
an uncharted grave.

俳
An open window.
The dialectics of love:
Fidelity lost.

俳
Chairs in a garden.
The sinkhole in the middle
a frozen landslide.

俳
From Revelation,
the light's secret attraction
suffers involvement.

俳

Harmonious soul
produces happiness plus
rational knowledge.

俳

Just you, me, and God.
Nothing more you can go on.
Please leave a message.

俳

Handfuls of flowers
crying inside the church walls.
It's time to sing now.

俳

Thunder and lightning.
These are the years we grew up,
puddles everywhere.

俳

Poetry rears its head.
The dented brick on the lawn.
In the dent, a dime.

俳

I see my mother.
I see my mother see me.
This is how we die.

俳

I see my father.
I see my father see me.
This is how we live.

俳

I turn out the light.
All those years spent counting coins.
We try not to talk.

俳

Once I was a dog.
No one was afraid of me.
I licked people's hands.

俳

My son is my son,
a stranger in a strange land.
But I follow him.

俳

iPhones on subways.
Shy pickpockets rub elbows
with the Queen of Spain.

俳

So much poetry.
I love Dante and Shakespeare.
What will they write next?

俳

I would be with you
if I could not be alone.
But I can. I can.

俳

Poems not money
give such meaning to my life.
Sometimes meaning sucks.

俳

From the kitchen walls
Lori wipes my fingerprints—
smudged newpaper ink.

俳

I'll see her today
and wonder just who she is
all over again.

俳

We have it easy,
they say, lifting the white sheet
we lie on in sleep.

俳

We're fresh in the grave
when the grim minister speaks.
Blah blah blah blah blah.

俳

I'm out of clichés.
Where the hell did they all go?
I cry tears of joy.

俳

Hemingway is here.
Open shirt and hairy chest
and bottles of wine.

俳

Blanche Dubois is here.
A radish rose, open mouth
in her brief sweet world.

俳

So much is a blur,
the Kashmir of this long life,
a speeding bullet.

俳

Seventy-two years.
Time to clear out the clutter.
Toss the love letters.

俳

I'm still here, waving.
Where is everyone going?
So many goodbyes!

俳

My wonderful life.
When do I pay the piper?
Too much abundance.

俳

The end seems so near.
I should have kissed everyone,
house keys in my hand.

俳

Look how far we've come.
There's so much light in those eyes.
Are they mine or yours?

俳

Fortune cookie says,
"You will go on long journey."
Pay check. Leave at once.

俳

Living room of death.
I open all the windows.
West wind, wilt thou blow?

俳

I have always been
an inside-out outsider.
Everyone sees me.

俳

Sometimes, outside-in,
a stranger in a strange land,
but I see you, too.

俳

The broken-boned snow
cracks heart's fire with an axe,
melts the brain's tundra.

俳

So sick of cheap tears.
I'd pay a buck for laughter.
This empty wallet.

俳

Some things are too sad
to write about on paper.
My closed mouth writes too.

俳

Here. Gone. There. Gone. Here.
I'm never in the same spot.
Just this lost suitcase.

俳

Imagine pepper.
Hot little punches of spice.
Morning breakfast eggs.

俳

These little poems!
Nuclear deals gone awry.
Poems save no one.

俳

God sees everything,
that cricket in our bedroom,
the watch on my wrist.

俳

In the laundromat,
a fat man in a black suit
washing bars of gold.

俳

When I was a child
I wondered why the window
was called a window.

俳

I stop at the light.
The woman in the next car
almost married me.

俳

My childhood is gone.
I don't want to go back there.
Too much mystery.

俳

Stars fill the black sky.
Smooches come out of nowhere.
Prepare for the worst.

俳

All I have to give
now to everyone I've hurt:
my apology.

俳

Things that've been said.
Heart beats don't always tell time.
Now where's the bourbon?

俳

Crow on front fountain
cleans peanuts before eating.
Not a trace of rain.

俳

Out come all the weeds.
This California drought waves
goodbye to flowers.

俳

If my voice was clear
I would sing the lemon tree
that holds Carl's ashes.

俳

My afternoon nap
interrupted by spring rain.
Moon dreams swept away.

俳

These words on paper.
I cut them into pieces.
Memory holds on.

俳

Night walks with Jessie.
A quiet autumn evening.
Not a soul in sight.

俳

Today I am sick.
Head cold, fever, sore back.
Pale world in ruins.

俳

I love this sharp knife.
How it cuts the red pepper.
Salad filled with blood.

俳

I need a cricket
to bless this little haiku!
Oh cricket, come back.

俳

Basho talks of tears,
pilgrims' coins on the wet road.
Tragic wealthy souls.

俳

He's nearer to death
than to life but still finds time
to clean his hack saw.

俳

That crow has come back.
Our fountain filled with peanuts.
Piece of squirrel next.

俳

Basho to disciple:
Write ordinary poems,
adrift in a boat.

俳

Poetry kills me.
I can’t face its stern demands,
heart filled with cobwebs.

俳

My son grows each day.
I can’t figure this thing out.
He’ll know the answer.

俳

Poets write in smoke.
I write in flaming chicken.
Cluck, cluck, cluck, cluck, cluck.

俳

I'm speechless for now.
Like Hamlet, nothing to say.
Words, words, words, words, words.

俳

Love is nothing but
tears in the eyes of fishes.
Mwa, mwa, mwa, mwa, mwa.

俳

I'm sick of haiku.
Five seven five ties me down.
I need elbow room!

俳

Oh land, lotsa land,
lotsa poetry above,
haiku fence me in!

俳

Long slow walks at night,
summer is a comin'in.
Break words at breakfast.

俳

My neighbor's story:
She lost one breast to cancer,
asks about my wife.

俳

Weathered wood and gray
heart exposed to piercing wind,
my son driving home.

俳

I've squandered so much,
and given less than I could,
asleep in the rain.

俳

I'm a proud Virgo.
One day I'll be organized,
surrounded by worms.

俳

Write. Delete. Write.
Can't get my head into gear.
Delete. Write. Delete.

俳

Hey sun! I need rain.
What good's a haiku without rain—
a chill to my bones.

俳

Let the poets know
that I was a meat eater
who liked haiku raw.

俳

Oh, no! Frog and Crow
and *Cuckoo* and Cicada
want their own haiku.

俳

To write War and Peace:
In the stationary store
ask for more paper.

俳

From here I can't see
Mt. Baldy but I can see
that old homeless man.

俳

Tombstone beckons us.
Marie Laveau's voodoo call,
cemetery queen.

俳

I ate the apple.
Now I know nothing of love,
just this green apple.

俳

I'm a good patient.
Five white pills every morning.
Gulp, gulp, gulp, gulp, gulp.

俳

A sip of whiskey.
I wrote six haiku today.
This one's the seventh.

俳

Basho in moonlight.
Where the hell's the night heron?
Not here in L.A.

俳

Here comes the weekend.
Too tired to lift my glass.
Old bones, old heartbeat.

俳

I'm older than you.
Tomorrow I'll be younger.
Heart skips many beats.

俳

My hair keeps going
down the drain in the shower.
This head shuns sunshine.

俳

Salad on the plate.
I'm eating healthy today.
Tomorrow? We'll see.

俳

Killed a rattlesnake.
Cuckamonga wilderness.
Cooked it, ate it too.

俳

Flowers of the plum
says Yosa Buson sparkles.
Instead, I eat them.

俳

It's a dew-drop world,
says Kobayashi Issa.
No wonder my thirst.

俳

Frog leaps in old pond,
says old Matsuo Basho.
Me? I stay on shore.

俳

Sickbed diaries
of Masoaka Shiki
bleeding as he sings.

俳

Right after dinner,
I give her a tasty kiss.
What an appetite!

俳

Dogs follow me home.
I leave them on the sidewalk,
one pet for each head.

俳

Old man in full moon
mocking that teasing cricket.
Enough world for me.

俳

The world in tatters.
Crow! Try my neighbor's fountain
when I fly away.

俳

I get in my car,
drive to get a bag of chips,
live another day.

俳

He says, it might rain,
Wild geese sketched on parchment.
And now you, my friend.

俳

No one to talk to.
The sound of ocean nearby.
White sands, touch of frost.

俳

One day sweeps the porch.
One night, a thousand miles.
This year just a flash.

俳

Shadows everywhere.
I remember my first horse,
a Palimino.

俳

Some walk to stay home.
Some stay home, go everywhere.
One room still, one heart.

俳

Where are we going?
Body outside of body,
mind inside of mind.

俳

Raining on a raft,
water water everywhere,
just haiku for food.

俳

Paris! You've missed me?
I see you in the movies.
Not a word for me?

俳

Way of Elegance.
Wind, moon, sun, water, earth, love,
and forget the rules.

俳

Work in work. Rest in rest.
No love in work, no work in love.
Kiss the girls goodbye.

俳

Long journey these words
filled with many syllables.
Dance without music.

俳

I'm so happy now,
all alone writing haiku.
What could be better!

俳

wolves and dogs and flies
had their moment in the sun:
small cloud shelters crow.

俳

Twenty-four hours
in this gorgeous sunny day.
There goes a Chevy.

俳

How angry the birds!
All that chattering nonsense
makes me President.

俳

Pumping up the jam,
understandable enough:
vocabulary.

俳

Sitting in the dark,
palette of suppressed desire—
"Strangers on a Train."

俳

Moon shot or sun spot
with each click of the keyboard
the universe shrinks

俳

Two bums in springtime.
Nobody comes. Nobody goes.
Waiting for the G train.

俳

How to eat this life?
Break the past into pieces,
eat one piece at a time.

俳

Old man at bus stop.
I step on a bottle cap.
There goes Mt. Rushmore.

俳

Who grieves this lost pen?
So much ink wasted on verbs.
Stand still — cherished nouns.

俳

Please don't answer it.
The world is too much with us.
Call back when I'm home.

俳

A tennis court oath —
hardly a hors-de-combat.
Dull-spirited wrench.

俳

Antique mud wrestlers
scuttle their accomplishments,
dead, but unbidden.

俳

I dreamed my father
wanted to meet my son, Josh.
Then I woke, asleep.

俳

Orange harvest moon,
so low and bright in the sky
about to catch fire.

俳

Too few syllables
in Tu Fu's darkness-bringing clouds.
I settle for Li-Po.

俳

Because we were lost.
Because we dared to sell out.
Look, Chevy gets towed!

俳

Poets write of smoke.
They make burning timbers speak.
Rich soil. Thick forest.

俳

Trapped in heaven's skies:
from here, imperfect stones bloom.
There's no turning back.

俳

The breach once caused bait.
Cancelled tables ingrate ropes.
Try the fried chicken.

俳

Penny on cement.
Should I pick it up or not.
Miles promise hot food.

俳

My car resumes speech,
like life over waterfalls,
absurdist doorknobs.

俳

Grieve unsure footsteps—
national security
flounders on respect.

俳

My guilty pleasure—
melted vanilla ice-cream:
slurp, slurp, slurp, slurp, slurp.

俳

Even when I'm still,
this wide road to the edge
takes me there and back.

俳

Oh crow, go away.
I'm in no mood for your games.
Caw caw caw yourself!

俳

On it or in it,
my feet love this earth so much—
while hands touch the sky.

俳

When I'm gone, I'll sure
miss that dove whose song wakes me,
but will she miss me?

俳

Boarding pass in hand,
this plane for San Francisco,
chattering sparrows.

俳

Alone in the house.
Rain coming down in buckets.
I ask for nothing.

俳

My neighbor walks by.
I wave to her, she waves back.
Life's sweet afternoon.

俳

Small change in a cup.
I fish a few quarters out,
enough to feel rich.

俳

Found my walking stick
down in Devil's Canyon.
Now, it's in the attic.

俳

in line to buy stamps—
a green mint in my pocket
next to a nickel

俳

Say there's no traffic
and here comes the traffic jam.
Watch the road and shut up.

俳

Would that I was wise,
not this enlightened monkey
wearing monkey mask

俳

From my car window
harvest moon in autumn night,
big hole in the sky

俳

autumn leaves crunch sound
as I walk the brick path home,
street lamps all on fire.

俳

I keep writing poems.
My doctor says time to fast—
I'm overnourished.

俳

falling in rhythm
to the buzzing of the bees
over something dead

俳

driving the wet streets
in the bubble of my car—
I am ten again

俳

we walk on gravestones
in Hollywood Forever,
choosing our own plots

俳

Death is not final:
it's just a breath before sleep —
waiting for Godot.

俳

Seven crows! Count them!
What the hell is going on?
Where's the dead body?

俳

so getting tired,
so getting old but pressing
on and on and on

俳

it's day after day
after day after day, this
one day after day

俳

Lying here in bed,
in childhood's phantom dwelling—
all those vanished dreams.

俳

A jacaranda,
and a bouganvealia,
not to mention rose.

俳

Mexican workers
pull up in our front garden
all the damaged roots

俳

haiku dilemma:
no morning snow in L.A.
no cherry blossoms.

俳

I'm watching T. V.
Hey cricket! You're here again.
Aren't we a pair.

俳

God is everywhere.
I'm at the drive-in window.
Extra ketchup, please.

俳

Cash in my pocket
held by a small paperclip.
This line remains blank.

俳

Same moon, same night sky.
So much traffic on this earth.
How I love this life.

俳

There is no one way.
Empty hands and open heart.
Pick up the penny.

俳

Okay, done with haiku.
A thousand empty pages.
Might as well shut up.

俳

I embrace these words.
Last haiku. Quick drops of ink.
These heartfelt scribbles.

俳

Okay, here's the deal:
waiting for the next haiku —
dum de dum de dum.

Matsuo Basho
"The Hut of the Phanthom Dwelling," 1690

One need not be a haiku poet, but if someone doesn't live inside ordinary life and understand ordinary feelings, they're not likely to be a poet at all. In this mortal frame of mine, there is something, and this something can be called, for lack of a better name, the poetic spirit (*furabo*), a windswept spirit. This something in me took to writing poetry years ago, merely to amuse myself at first, but finally making it a lifelong business. But when all is said, I am not really the kind who is so completely enamored of solitude that he must hide every trace of himself. Again and again I think of the mistakes I've made in my clumsiness over the course of the years. It must be admitted, however, that there were times when I sank into such dejection that I was almost ready to drop this pursuit of poetry, or again, times when I was so puffed up with pride that I exulted in vain victories over others. Indeed, ever since I began to write poetry, I have never found peace with myself, always wavering between doubts of one kind or another. There was a time when I envied those who had government offices or impressive domains, and on another occasion I considered entering the precincts of the Buddha and teaching rooms of the patriarchs, wishing to measure the depth of my ignorance by trying to be a scholar, but, unskilled and talentless as I am, I gave myself wholly to this one concern: my unquenchable love of poetry. Po Chu-I worked so hard at it that he almost ruined his five vital organs, and Tu Fu grew lean and emaciated because of it. As far as intelligence or the quality of my writings go, I can never compare to such men. Yet, knowing no other art than the art of writing poetry, I hang onto it more or less blindly. But we all, in the end, do we not, live in a phantom dwelling? But enough of that – I'm off to bed.

"A Circle of Poetic Will"

An Afterword by Lisa Segal

Jack Grapes's new book of poetry, *Wide Road to the Edge of the World* – 301 haiku plus a 324-page essay titled "A Windswept Spirit" in 201 chapters and 601 paragraphs – is part memoir, part academic treatise, part literary criticism, and part poetry. The last of his many poetry books, *All the Sad Angels*, was a slim volume, "smaller than a dime novel," he would say, "something you can slip into your back pocket and take anywhere." Grapes then decided to make his next book even smaller. But what kind of poems would fit such a small book? Haiku, that's what! At first he thought he'd write just a few. Maybe 50 of them. He figured he could model his book on the great Japanese poet Matsuo Basho's masterpiece *Narrow Road into the Interior*, a slim volume of 50 poems published 1690, written in the late spring of 1689 during his journey through the villages and mountain temples of the northern interior of Japan. Each poem was preceded by a prose set-up. The 324-page introductory preface to *Wide Road* began as the story of his introduction to, and infatuation with, haiku as a school boy in New Orleans.

But Grapes, among other attributes, is expansive. The telling of that childhood memory merged with two other intrinsic parts of his personality – his love of scholarship and his inability not to teach. What he tackles in this book is what poetry always comes at, one way or the other – the humanness of living, and dying, knowing, not knowing, growing up, being grown up, love, solitude, loneliness, companionship, humor, artistic exploration, re-assessment of what has been and the anticipation of what's yet to come – all done within the restrictions of traditional haiku form.

The collection of 301 haiku in *Wide Road* makes a chronological arc through the poet's life – it would be a mistake to flip this book open and read the haiku at random. Read it from beginning to end, like a dime novel. The book makes a scholarly contribution to the understanding of haiku. Its poems add to the discourse of contemporary haiku. There is also the metaphoric journey of reaching an end and beginning again as the crow, a haiku symbol of death and rebirth, accompanies the reader throughout, from ancient times to the present, where over and over again, it becomes apparent that this literary form, which has more than once been seen as finished and done with, undergoes a rebirth in an ongoing dynamic of re-invention. The same must be said for the poetic rebirth Grapes experienced revisiting the source of his earliest poetic wranglings. He found that the deep well of haiku had not diminished, dried up, or died in the recesses of his childhood, but instead was as viable and enriching to him now as it was when he began to write poetry. He made this poetic discovery over the course of writing these 301 haiku. We make it with him as we read them. In this way, *Wide Road to the Edge of the World* adds to the metaphysical circularity which underlies Jack's output over the course of his writing life.

In 1986 (and staged again in 2010), Grapes wrote and starred in *Circle of Will*, a bizarre metaphysical comedy about the lost years of William Shakespeare, but the play came off more like a version of the Deep Thought computer from *A Hitchhiker's Guide to the Galaxy*. Both stagings of the play received rave reviews and theater-goers came back multiple times, never sure which play they were going to see. The play, like his poetry, is a mechanism to suss out the answers to Life, the Universe, and Everything. *Wide Road* is a continuation of Grapes' own circle of poetic will. He writes poetry as assiduously as Hokusai Katsushika's barrel-maker on the cover of the book tends to his barrel of wooden planks, each man to the circle of his life's work. The 301 haiku, like the barrel, have a structural circularity made of multiples of the same basic form. The beginning and the end of Grapes' haiku circle – the first poem and the last – are like a serpent biting its own tail, or its own tale, as it were.

It's a circle as well that Grapes' earliest poems were haiku and that as a mature poet he has returned to that form. Grapes' literary life has been defined by his continual engagement in the writing of poetry. Even though he has given much to many as a writing teacher and mentor for over five decades, not to mention the publication of several non-fiction books and prose essays, Jack Grapes is, first and foremost, a poet."

Jack Grapes is the author of *Method Writing* and *Advanced Method Writing*, and 15 books of poetry, including *The Naked Eye: New & Selected Poems*, 1987-2012; *Poems So Far So Far So Good So Far To Go*; and *All the Sad Angels*. David Ulin, *Los Angeles Times* book review editor, characterized his poetry as "operating somewhere in the middle ground between pop culture and philosophy." Through Bombshelter Press, Grapes has published over 100 books of poetry by Los Angeles poets and edited the acclaimed literary journal *ONTHEBUS*. Jack also co-wrote (with Bill Cakmis) and starred in *Circle of Will*, a metaphysical comedy about the lost years of William Shakespeare. He is currently working on four new books: a book of literary criticism on the history of modern poetries, *Etherized Upon a Table*; a series of critical and personal essays, *The Tendor Agonies of Charles Bukowski*; a non-fiction work, *How to Read Like a Writer*, and a new book of poems, *Any Style*, all due for publication next year. Jack lives in Los Angeles with his wife Lori and their cat Charles Aznavour, affectionately called Chuckie.

74563901R00228

Made in the USA
Middletown, DE
26 May 2018